Fifth Edition

Life
Centered
Career
Education

A Competency Based Approach

Donn E. Brolin

D1059828

Published by
The Council for Exceptional Children

Library of Congress Cataloging-in-Publication Data

Brolin, Donn E.
    Life centered career education : a competency based approach /
Donn E. Brolin. — 5th ed.
        p. cm.
    Includes bibliographical references.
    ISBN 0–86586–292–3
    1. Career education—United States—Curricula. 2. Special
education—United States—Activity programs. 3. Special education—
United States—Curricula. 4. Competency based education—United
States—Curricula. I. Council for Exceptional Children.
    II. Title.
    LC1037.5.B75   1997
    371.9—dc21
                                                    97–3894
                                                       CIP

ISBN 0–86586–292–3

Stock No. P180G

Printed in the United States of America.
10 9 8 7 6 5 4 3 2 1

Contents

List of Figures

Foreword

The Council for Exceptional Children is pleased to offer this fifth edition of *Life Centered Career Education: A Competency Based Approach*. Dr. Brolin's work supports CEC's policy on career education, which states that career education is the totality of experiences through which one learns to live a meaningful, satisfying work life. Within the career education framework, work is conceptualized as conscious effort aimed at producing benefits for oneself and/or others. Career education provides the opportunity for children to learn, in the least restrictive environment possible, the academic, daily living, personal-social, and occupational knowledge and the specific vocational skills necessary for attaining their highest levels of economic, personal, and social fulfillment.

CEC supports the belief that career education should permeate the entire school program and even extend beyond it. It should be infused throughout the curriculum by knowledgeable teachers who are able to modify the curriculum to integrate career development goals with current subject matter goals and content. It is the position of The Council that individualized, appropriate education must include the opportunity for every student to attain his or her highest level of career potential through career education experiences. Children with exceptionalities require career education experiences that will develop their wide range of abilities, needs, and interests to the fullest extent possible.

In order to assist students with exceptionalities to become productive workers and independent adults, special education professionals need to work in collaboration with parents, other educators, community service personnel, and the business community. The LCCE approach serves as a model for making this happen.

The author of the LCCE program, Donn E. Brolin, who died in 1996, dedicated his professional life to the development of materials in support of the career education concept. The LCCE curriculum is the foundation for life skills and transition education for thousands of young people each year. Drawing upon the experience and expertise of LCCE practitioners and professional colleagues of Dr. Brolin, CEC will continue to expand the LCCE line of products.

1. Career Education

The concept of career education was officially introduced to U.S. educators in 1971 by the U.S. Commissioner of Education at a national conference of secondary school principals (Marland, 1971). Education officials were vitally concerned with the high drop-out rate of students who failed to see the relevance of what they were being taught to their future life goals. A more practical and meaningful approach to education was being voiced in many quarters, and in response to this critical need, career education was born. A betting person would have given 100-to-1 odds against the newest educational reform lasting more than a few years. But career education has endured and weathered the usual rejection and resistance to innovations and is gathering greater momentum with the passage of time, although much is now embedded in newer terms such as *transitional programming, functional curriculum, supported work,* and the like. LCCE has been developed on the principles of the career education approach.

EARLY HISTORICAL PERSPECTIVE

Some special educators profess to have practiced a type of career education long before its introduction by Dr. Marland. They are partially correct. The work-study model (Kolstoe & Frey, 1965) of the 1950s and 1960s was to some degree a forerunner of the career education concept at the high school level. The "Persisting Life Situations" curriculum of the Wisconsin State Department of Instruction and several other curriculum models of the 1960s were also precursors of career education. It is not important, however, to give credit to anyone in particular for its invention. What is important is that in 1971 the U.S. Office of Education (USOE) gave top priority to career education as a critical educational need. The exact nature and definition of career

education were left to evolve from the field as it responded to the basic tenets of and need for this educational reform.

Special education and vocational education, in particular, responded favorably to the federal dictate of the early 1970s. Some noteworthy events that followed were: (a) the federal special education agency declared career education a top priority and gave it financial backing (1972); (b) The Council for Exceptional Children (CEC) and the American Vocational Association (AVA) cosponsored an extensive national conference on the topic; (c) a U.S. Office of Career Education was established (1974) and existed under the direction of Dr. Kenneth B. Hoyt until 1982; (d) the Division on Career Development (DCD), now the Division on Career Development and Transition (DCDT), was formed and became CEC's 12th Division (1976); (e) the Career Education Implementation Incentive Act (P.L. 95-207) was passed to help states infuse career education into school curricula for all students so it could become an integral part of the nation's educational process (1977); and (f) CEC issued a position paper describing its conceptualization of career education and its importance for special education students (1978). CEC also published the first edition of *Life Centered Career Education: A Competency Based Approach* (Brolin, 1978).

In 1982, the Career Education Incentive Act was repealed and the federal Division on Career Education (formerly the U.S. Office of Career Education) began phasing out. It is important to know, however, that this law was never intended to be renewed but was designed to provide federal incentive funds so that state and local districts could initiate career education and make it an integral part of their educational effort for all students. Many school districts did just that, and career education concepts, processes, and materials became imbedded in their curricula.

1

The flurry of curriculum and materials development that occurred in the 1970s and early 1980s was unprecedented, both for regular and special education students. But when the federal and state monies subsided, so, proportionately, did the efforts by most school districts, and the term *career education* was used less frequently than before. However, as indicated previously, in many districts career education became a part of the educational program to different degrees. The career education movement has had a significant impact across the country and is now known in some places by different terms and in different forms, although in many other areas of the country the term *career education* still prevails. A review of more recent career education and transition literature for students with mild disabilities (e.g., Clark & Kolstoe, 1990; Polloway, Patton, Payne, & Payne, 1989; Rusch, DeStefano, Chadsey-Rusch, Phelps, & Szymanski, 1992; Schloss, Smith, & Schloss, 1990; West et al., 1992) attests to the importance of career education in our present-day educational literature.

NEW AND RELATED EDUCATION CONCEPTS AND THRUSTS

In recent years, several new terms and movements have emerged that relate closely to the career education concepts and efforts of the past. These are the transition, functional skills, outcome(s)-based education (OBE), and self-determination movements. The LCCE approach contains substantial elements that relate to each of these movements as explained below.

Transition Services

The final rules for the Individuals with Disabilities Education Act (1990) defined transition services as

a coordinated set of activities for a student designed within an outcome oriented process that promotes movement from school to post-school activities including post-secondary education, vocational training, integrated employment (including supported employment), continuing and adult education, adult services, independent living, or community participation. The coordinated set of services must be (1) based on the individual student's needs, taking into account the student's preferences and interests, (2) include *needed activities* in the areas of instruction, community experiences, the development of employment and other post-school adult living objectives, and, if appropriate, acquisition of daily living skills and functional vocational evaluation. NOTE: Transition services for students with disabilities *may be special education* if they are provided as specialized designed instruction or related services, if they

are required to assist a student with a disability to benefit from special education. (300.18 Transition Services)

The IEP for each student should contain the transition services component, beginning no later than age 16 or at a younger age, if determined appropriate, and must include a statement of the needed transition services including, if appropriate, a statement of each public agency and each participating agency's responsibilities or linkages, or both, before the student leaves the school setting. If the IEP team determines that services are not needed in one or more areas, the IEP must include a statement to that effect and the basis upon which the determination was made. It is important to note that the U.S. House of Representatives committee reporting on the law stated, "Although this language leaves the final determination of when to initiate transition services for students under age 16 to the IEP process, it nevertheless makes it clear that Congress expects much consideration to be given to the need for transition services for students by age 14 or younger." The Committee encouraged that approach because of their concern that

age 16 may be too late for many students, particularly those at risk of dropping out of school and those with the most severe disabilities. Even for those students who stay in school until age 18, many will need more than two years of transitional services. Students with disabilities are now dropping out of school before age 16, feeling that the education system has little to offer them. Initiating services at a younger age will be critical. (House Report No. 101-544, 10, 1990)

The LCCE approach integrates classroom instruction with community-based experiences and the active involvement of family members, employers, and human service agencies in cooperatively preparing students with the skills needed for adult functioning. The curriculum is intended to begin during the elementary years so that students have sufficient time to learn and develop the critical skills they will need to be productive and successful upon making the transition from school to community life and work.

Functional Skills

There is more recognition now that students will need an appropriate blend of academic and functional skills instruction in school, home, and community settings if they are to be successful during their school years and after they leave the educational system. Functional skills are not just academic ones, they are also those needed for adult living, including independent living, social, communication, and vocational skills, which should be taught in part in integrated natural settings. Clark (1991) has defined functional curriculum as "instructional content that focuses on the concepts and skills needed by students in the areas of personal-social, daily living, and occupational adjustment."

The LCCE approach is designed to focus on 22 major functional skills or competencies that research has found critical for adult adjustment. In the process of learning these 22 competencies, students learn functional academic skills (e.g., reading, writing, math) as well. Thus, the LCCE Curriculum provides a comprehensive framework for delivering all or most of the functional, practical, everyday skills instruction that students will need to function as productive workers and citizens of their communities.

Outcome(s)-Based Education

Presently, many states and local educational agencies are adopting the basic tenets of the outcome(s)-based education (OBE) approach. Basically, OBE is

a philosophy which "drives" the way in which instruction is organized, delivered and evaluated in our schools. Its purposes are: (1) equipping all students with the knowledge, skills and competencies needed for future success in school, in the workplace and in advanced studies; and (2) establishing conditions in schools which maximize achievement and success for all students. (Missouri Department of Elementary and Secondary Education, 1992)

In the OBE system, student outcomes define the curriculum, and the learning time depends on the needs of each student. Grades are based on the mastery of specified outcomes, and expectations are high for all students. There is a close connection between academic and vocational goals. For students with disabilities, needed adaptations and modifications can be addressed through the IEP process.

The LCCE Curriculum is an outcome(s)-based education system. The 22 competencies that the approach advocates comprise the critical knowledge and skills an individual needs to be a successful and productive citizen and worker in today's society. Many schools implementing LCCE have recognized this fact and have designated LCCE as their outcome(s)-based response to their state's and/or school district's mandate to implement the OBE approach.

Self-Determination

There is a growing recognition in education that a critical factor in a successful transition from school to work is the degree to which a student learns to become self-determined. Although there is no one definition of self-determination that receives universal support, there is general consensus as to the characteristics that are typically exemplified by self-determined people. There common themes are evident in the most frequently cited definitions of self-determination. Ward (1988) defined self-determination as referring to

"both the attitudes which lead people to define goals for themselves and to their ability to take the initiative to achieve these goals" (p. 2). Ward identified self-actualization, assertiveness, creativity, pride, and self-advocacy as a set of characteristics of self-determination. Within this set of characteristics, a person must (a) be self-actualizing to achieve his or her full potential, (b) be assertive to act in a self-confident manner and to express his or her needs clearly and directly, (c) be creative to expand beyond stereotyped roles and expectations, (d) have pride to recognize his or her abilities and contributions to society, and (e) be self-advocating to ensure access to the services and benefits needed to facilitate the achievement of one's full potential.

Field and Hoffman (1994) defined self-determination as "one's ability to define and achieve goals based on a foundation of knowing and valuing oneself" (p. 136). Their model addresses cognitive, affective, and behavioral components that promote self-determination, and it has five major components: (1) know yourself, (2) value yourself, (3) plan, (4) act, and (5) experience outcomes and learn. Wehmeyer (1996) defined self-determination as "acting as the primary causal agent in one's life and making choices and decisions regarding one's quality of life free from undue external influence or interference" (p. 22). Individuals are self-determined if their actions reflect four essential characteristics: (1) the individual acted autonomously, (2) the behaviors were self-regulated, (3) the person initiated and responded to events in a psychologically empowered manner, and (4) the person acted in a self-realizing manner. These essential characteristics emerge based on the student's development or acquisition of a set of component elements of self-determined behavior, including choice- and decision-making skills; problem-solving skills; goal-setting and attainment skills; self-observation, self-evaluation, and self-reinforcement skills; positive perceptions of control; positive attributions of efficacy and outcome expectancy; and a positive, realistic self-awareness and self-knowledge.

The LCCE is uniquely suited to enable teachers to promote self-determination for students with disabilities. For example, Wehmeyer (1995) used lessons from 4 competency areas (10. Achieving Self-Awareness; 11. Acquiring Self-Confidence; 14. Achieving Independence; and 15. Making Adequate Decisions) and 17 subcompetency areas of the LCCE to promote self-determination for youth with mental retardation or learning disabilities. With the 350 lesson plans contained within these competency and subcompetency areas, instruction can begin with students as early as age 12 or 14 and continue through the senior high years. Using the LCCE, instruction in self-determination begins with instruction on issues of self-awareness. When students acquire a broader sense of themselves, they learn to apply that knowledge to building a positive self-image and gaining self-confidence. Only then do they begin to learn skills related to choice and decision making, goal setting, and self-organization. Instruction in self-awareness begins with the identification of basic physical and psychological needs, interests, and abilities.

Given the IDEA's emphasis on basing transition services on individual student interests and preferences, these lessons are particularly important. Students learn to distinguish between their physical and psychological needs and then learn ways to meet these needs. They use role-playing and brainstorming procedures to explore interests and abilities, including those common to most people as well as those unique to themselves. Students then discuss common emotions such as fear, love, hate, and sadness; how these affect their behavior and the behavior of others; and how to cope with such emotions.

Students then move from the emotional domain to basic physical awareness. The lesson plans involve demonstrating a knowledge of one's physical self, and they help students learn how their physical health has an impact on the ways they act. Students need to learn that there are physical causes for the way they feel and that how they feel affects the way they behave. This is an opportune time to import additional materials involving health and body systems. The final subcompetency teaching self-awareness involves demonstrating how one's behavior affect others. The students explore appropriate ways to act in a variety of situations and how to use cues to regulate one's behavior.

The next set of lessons applies self-awareness to acquiring self-confidence and self-acceptance. Students first learn to express feelings of self-worth. They identify their own positive physical and psychological attributes, how these make them feel, and how other people's actions affect their feelings of self-worth. Students move on to explore others' perceptions of them, listing potential reactions of others, constructing a view of how others see them, and describing how their behaviors affect others' reactions. As one component of this process, students discuss differences among people, including interests and abilities. Students then learn to give and accept praise and criticism. They learn appropriate and inappropriate ways to respond to each of these, list the effects and purposes of praise and criticism, and practice strategies to give and receive both. Finally, students identify their own positive characteristics, ways to express confidence in themselves, how to react to others' expressions of confidence, and how to appropriately make positive statements about themselves.

As illustrated by this sequence of instruction used by Wehmeyer (1995), the LCCE provides a comprehensive foundation upon which student instruction in self-determination can be accomplished and through which students can become more self-determined and involved in their educational process.

FEATURES AND BARRIERS

Through the years some people have had trouble differentiating career education from vocational education. Career education can be distinguished from vocational education and other related curricular concepts such as life skills education, transitional programming, functional curriculum, and supported work in the following manner.

1. *It interfaces education with work.* Work becomes a primary need for the vast majority of individuals when they grow up. Productive work activity, paid or unpaid, is something that makes a person an acceptable adult. People perform productive work in the home or community, on the job, and in enjoyable leisure-time and recreational pursuits. Adults spend much of their productive work time on the job; others spend most of it at home or on volunteer projects that benefit the community. Thus, students should be prepared to engage in the different roles and settings in which meaningful, productive work is done. The school curriculum offers the opportunity to teach many of the cognitive, affective, and psychomotor skills needed to perform various work roles.

2. *It is a K–12+ effort that involves all possible school personnel.* Children begin developing a work personality, as well as a general personality, in early childhood. Work attitudes, values, interests, motivation, needs, habits, and behaviors develop early and are susceptible to the influence of parents, teachers, peers, and experiences. Teachers are important in helping students learn about and clarify their values and potential for the world of work.

3. *It is an infusion concept.* Career education is not a course; rather, it is the process of integrating concepts, materials, and experiences into traditional subject matter. For example, when teaching mathematics concepts, the teacher can use practical examples of how to relate the instruction to productive work activities in the home, community, job, and avocational situations. Role playing, simulated businesses, occupational notebooks, job analysis assignments, and many other stimulating activities can be used to enhance academic learning.

4. *It does not replace traditional education or subject matter.* Career education requires a focusing of why and how subject matter is taught. Much of what is already being done in the classroom may be career education. Generally, however, the effort is too limited and unfocused. Educators can be taught to expand their career education efforts without discarding most of what they have done in the past.

5. *It conceptualizes career development occurring in stages.* The elementary school years, or the *career*

awareness stage, are when students need more instruction and experiences that will make them more aware of themselves, of the world of work and its requirements, and of how they might fit into it someday. The junior high or middle school years, or the *career exploration* stage, provide further career awareness opportunities but also offer students the opportunity to explore areas of interest and aptitude. This period is important because it is then that students can begin to determine their future roles as citizens, family members, employees, and participants in productive avocational activities. The high school period, or the *career preparation* stage, should focus on career planning and preparation for the world of work after high school or with future training. It is important to provide for these three stages of career development in the curriculum so that students can develop a satisfactory work personality and career maturity. The fourth stage, the *career assimilation stage* (placement, follow-up, and continuing education) occurs after the student leaves the secondary or postsecondary school and embarks upon the world of work, paid and unpaid.

6. *It requires a substantial experiential component.* Most people learn best with hands-on activity. Many special education students learn best if this method is a major focus of their instructional program. A major concern of many teachers is the behavior of their students. If students are busily engaged in something they like, and if it has a meaningful goal related to their future lives, motivation will increase and behavior problems will diminish. A basic principle is that the school must meet the needs of students; students should not have to fit into the exact needs and structure of the school and its personnel.

7. *It focuses on the development of life skills, affective skills, and general employability skills.* Life skills are important for productive work activity in the home and community. However, they are also directly related to job functioning. An individual must be able to dress and groom properly, have good table manners, make decisions about money, and use transportation to get to work. Interest and aptitude in certain life skill areas (e.g., cooking, cleaning, mending clothes, taking care of children, or athletics) provide valuable clues to possible job interests, instruction, and employment. Affective skills are important for acceptance by others in the home, community, and job site. General employability skills such as work motivation, dependability, promptness, safety, consideration for others, sticking to a task, and handling criticism are skills that all educators can help students acquire.

8. *It requires the school to work more closely with the family and community resources.* The majority of learning occurs outside school. Career education promotes a partnership with parents and community resources whereby what is deemed important to learn about the world of work is taught beyond the confines of the school environment. In the process, parents and community members can become more aware and supportive of the school's program and objectives.

As noted in the preceding discussion about the career education concept, career education proponents view an individual's career as more than his or her occupation. It includes all the productive work activities engaged in during a day and throughout life. From this perspective, career education is a total educational concept that considers the whole person, not just one part. Although it is not all the education a student should receive, it should be a pervasive part. Vocational educators can expand their role by providing more career awareness and exploration experience related to a variety of occupations and to home and community experiences. General educators should not view vocational teachers and counselors as the only ones who provide career education. They, too, can provide many important career activities.

Why, then, is career education not implemented more widely in American schools? This question is constantly before those who profess its virtues and promote its implementation. Although most school systems would report that they have implemented career education, few have done so systematically and comprehensively. Some possible reasons include the following:

1. *It is only one of many pressures being applied to school districts.* Financial pressures have cut into the heart of many school districts. Administrators have been forced to lay off faculty, deal with strikes and unions, cut back salaries and supplies, and face many other devastating problems. The mandate to implement Public Law 94-142 has posed serious problems in orienting, preparing, and convincing regular educators to accept students with special needs in their classrooms. Career education is just one more pressure that must be dealt with even though it offers an appropriate but sometimes unrecognized method for mainstreaming or inclusion.

2. *It is difficult to get people to change their approaches, even though most will agree openly to the importance of and need for change.* Educators tend to teach as they were trained and in the manner that meets their styles and needs. Once people establish a satisfying pattern it is difficult to change, even though what is being introduced makes sense. (There are, however, a great many educators who are exceptions and who are always seeking new and better methods.)

3. *There is often no reward for changing.* Many educators

find that there are no rewards for making changes. They get no time off to make the changes, no recognition, no inservice training, no extra pay, and often no additional funds or space. They have little incentive to change, especially if their colleagues are not changing. Change requires extra study and preparation. Who knows what the next innovation is going to be? How do we know whether there will be a job next year and what the pay will be?

4. *Many educators aren't convinced that this approach is better than what they are doing now.* What evidence is there that career education makes any difference? Many believe they are doing most of it now and much more. They think "career" means job. To many, the use of the term *career education* is confusing and is synonymous with vocational education.

5. *It requires educators to reveal what they are doing to their colleagues, parents, and community representatives.* Career education requires a cooperative spirit and a willingness to be open and flexible while listening to others' opinions. This attitude is not easy for those who believe they are hired and paid to teach specific subject matter and nothing else.

There are no doubt many other reasons for resistance to implementing the career education, transition, and functional skills concept. In many instances, the barriers are not a rejection of the concept and the need for it, but instead are an inability of the state or district to implement it, whatever the reason(s). It is difficult to reject the basic tenets on which the career education concept is built.

FUTURE DIRECTIONS

The need for career education and its conceptual framework continues to be strong in U.S. schools. The "Transition from School to Work" movement and other related concepts introduced in the 1980s reflect the recognition by curriculum developers that the career education approach provided the foundation upon which the current and contemporary models of the 1980s have been built. Unfortunately, it is the nature of the field to use new terms and discard the old every few years. But, whatever we are calling the need for life skills, interpersonal skills, and occupational skills preparation, we must continue to build upon proven methods from the past by recognizing and using their contributions.

Many of the problems noted in years past continue to pose barriers to implementing the concepts of career education in the 1990s. Some of the needs that must be addressed are the following:

1. *Career education must be provided more substantially at the elementary level.* The preponderance of career

education efforts for students with exceptionalities still seems to exist at the secondary school level, although earlier efforts are being implemented in some schools. Career education is probably even more important at the elementary school level. It is during this period that children form a work personality and develop critical prevocational and affective skills. Teachers can make academic subjects more interesting and effective by integrating substantive career education concepts, materials, and experience.

2. *A cooperative learning and teaching environment should be provided in the school.* The very nature of career education requires teachers and students to be intimately involved as active participants in the learning/teaching environment. Both career education and cooperative learning offer powerful mechanisms for effective mainstreaming and career development. Their merits must be given considerably more promotion. Several recent efforts at coteaching by special and regular class teachers are yielding improved results.

3. *A continuous system of career and vocational assessment must be implemented in later elementary years and be provided periodically and systematically thereafter.* The movement toward curriculum-based assessment (CBA) is long overdue and will provide educators and their students with more meaningful assessment data for individual educational planning. Curriculums such as the Life Centered Career Education program, which provide assessment instruments, should be reviewed for possible use.

4. *Schools need to develop more active and meaningful partnerships with parents, employers, and community agencies.* The transition movement has promoted this area as one of critical importance if students are to be successful after leaving school. Interactions with these groups will give educators a greater insight into the real world and its requirements. Many employers are receptive to partnership arrangements with schools if educators approach them first.

5. *Educators must make greater use of the community as a learning environment.* It is rapidly becoming recognized that most students with special needs can learn more and behave much better in a realistic work and community setting. Career awareness, exploration, and preparation activities will be greatly enhanced by community experiences. This will require more flexible staff assignments so educators can spend time in the community and then make curriculum changes based on their observations of need.

6. *More staff development opportunities need to be instituted in the schools so that regular teachers are better prepared to adopt career education and to mainstream students.* The lack of sufficient inservice time is a con-

stant problem that needs to be rectified. Unless adequate time for inservice training is allocated, any innovation will continue to be misunderstood, resisted, and neglected. The new LCCE staff development materials should be considered if interest in the LCCE approach is strong.

7. *More attention should be focused on the educational system and how it can better incorporate career education into its operation.* Educators have emphasized providing the student with general employability skills but have neglected a major goal of career education—changing the education system. Much attention needs to be directed toward school administrators and state education department officials who set the policies. The fact that the Council of Chief State School Officers still endorses career education should help to promote greater implementation. Special educators must convey to their state special education divisions the importance and need for increasing career education for exceptional individuals.

8. *The impact of career education must be demonstrated more clearly.* Little evidence is available to demonstrate the efficacy of career education, although most who profess it staunchly profess that it has great impact. A nationally organized program of research should be implemented to discern effective models and practices. Studies of the adjustment of adults should be part of this effort. The Transition Institute at the University of Illinois is the major current resource addressing this area, although it does not focus specifically on career education.

9. *State departments of special education must specify the inclusion of career education as an important component in the school district plan.* Unless there is a directive from the state funding agency, many school districts will not be responsive to the needs because of the many other requirements that they must fulfill. The transition legislation is now prompting some state agencies to be more directive to local districts than previously. Alabama is one example of a state agency that has endorsed the LCCE Curriculum and is promoting it throughout the state with substantial resources.

10. *Universities and colleges must increase their inclusion of career education in their curriculums.* There has been a considerable increase in this area in the past several years as the transition movement has made its impact. However, much remains to be done. We cannot expect those in the field to be responsive to this need if it was not even mentioned during their teacher preparation program.

These 10 areas include several mentioned in the previous edition of this curriculum. Unfortunately, the needs still exist,

because change in the field is slow. The movement that has occurred is encouraging; however, much more must happen if the needs of children and youth are to be realized.

CONCLUDING REMARKS

The time has never been better for the career education concept to become an important component of more appropriate educational programming for students with special needs. Whether it is called career education, transition, or something else, its tenets can be used to build better programs and interagency and parent collaborations, so that students can be better prepared to become productive workers and citizens in family, community, and employment settings. Much remains to be done, however, if the needs of these students are to be met. Special education and other programs for students with special needs must resist the constant push for an academic curriculum emphasis rather than the more important career/life skills approach that their students will need for successful community living and working. Administrators and boards of education must understand that these are the most important priorities for individuals with special learning needs.

The Division of Career Development and Transition (DCDT) of The Council for Exceptional Children continues to spearhead the career education and transition concepts for the special education field. It is dedicated to work closely with other CEC divisions and related organizations to get career education and transition integrated into instructional programs throughout the country so that every student has the opportunity to become a productive, working adult. This group of dedicated and hardworking individuals continues to provide conferences and publications that are enhancing the knowledge base and further development of the career education approach.

Chapter 2 will present an introduction to the Life Centered Career Education Curriculum that has been developed and refined over the past 20 years by the author and his associates. The curriculum continues to grow in its acceptance as a viable approach to providing a logical K–12 scope and sequence of career development experiences that will eventually lead students from school to a successful transition into work and community living.

REFERENCES

Brolin, D. E. (1978). *Life centered career education: A competency based approach.* Reston, VA: The Council for Exceptional Children.

Clark, G. W. (1991). *Functional curriculum and its place in the regular education initiative.* Paper presented at 7th International Conference of the Division on Career Development, Kansas City, MO.

Clark, G. W., & Kolstoe, O. P. (1990). *Career development and transition education for adolescents with disabilities*. Boston: Allyn and Bacon.

Field, S., & Hoffman, A. (1994). Development of a model for self-determination. *Career Development for Exceptional Individuals, 17*, 159–169.

Kolstoe, O. P., & Frey, R. M. (1965). *A high school work-study program for mentally sub-normal students*. Carbondale: Southern Illinois University Press.

Marland, S. P., Jr. (1971). *Career education now*. Speech presented before the annual convention of the National Association of Secondary School Principals, Houston.

Missouri Department of Elementary and Secondary Education (1992). *Questions and answers about outcome-based education*. Jefferson City, MO: Author.

Polloway, E. A., Patton, J. R., Payne, J. S., & Payne, R. A. (1989). *Strategies for teaching learners with special needs* (4th ed.). Columbus, OH: Merrill.

Rusch, F. R., DeStefano, L., Chadsey-Rusch, J., Phelps, L. A., & Szymanski, E. (1992). *Transition from school to adult life*. Sycamore, IL: Sycamore Publishing.

Schloss, P. J., Smith, M. A., & Schloss, C. N. (1990). *Instructional methods for adolescents with learning and behavior problems*. Boston: Allyn and Bacon.

Ward, M. J. (1988). The many facets of self-determination. *National Information Center for Children and Youth with Handicaps Transition Summary, 5*, 2–3.

Wehmeyer, M. L. (1995). A career education approach; Self-determination for youth with mild cognitive disabilities. *Intervention in School and Clinic, 30*, 157–163.

Wehmeyer, M. L. (1996). Self-determination as an educational outcome: Why is it important to children, youth and adults with disabilities? In D. J. Sands & M. L. Wehmeyer (Eds.), *Self-determination across the life span: Independence and choice for people with disabilities* (pp. 15–34). Baltimore: Paul H. Brookes.

West, L., Corbey, S., Boyer-Stephens, A., Jones, B., Miller, R. J., & Sarkees-Wircenski, M. (1992). *Integrating transition planning into the IEP process*. Reston, VA: The Council for Exceptional Children.

2. The Life Centered Career Education Curriculum

The curriculum is based on the position that career education is more than just a part of the educational program—it is a major focus of the program. The Life Centered Career Education Curriculum underscores this point with its emphasis on daily living skills, personal-social skills, and occupational skills, all supported by academic skills. This is not to imply that career education is the only education students should receive, but it should be a significant and pervasive part of what is taught. Career education is not simply another name for occupational education. Instead, it is education that focuses on facilitating growth and development for *all* life roles, settings, and events.

This broad life view of career education is readily apparent in the Life Centered Career Education Curriculum, which organizes 22 student competencies into three primary categories—daily living skills, personal-social skills, and occupational guidance and preparation. Instruction to develop academic competencies is seen as supportive to skills in these three categories. This is illustrated in Figure 2–1.

FIGURE 2–1
Curriculum Areas for the Life Centered Career Education Curriculum Model

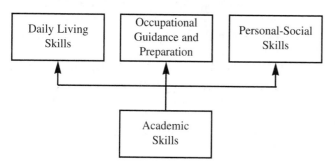

Based on previous research (Brolin & Thomas, 1971, 1972; Brolin, 1973; Bucher, 1985) and input from several other studies and professional opinions, 22 career education competencies were identified as priority areas. Each can be classified under one of the three primary curriculum areas and should constitute the basic objectives of programs at this level. A discussion of each curriculum area and its competencies is presented in the following section.

CURRICULUM AREAS AND COMPETENCIES

Daily Living Skills

Most students receiving special education services have the potential to become independent or semi-independent citizens. Most can become home managers or homemakers; they will marry and raise families. A large percentage will not make large salaries; thus, it is crucial that they learn how to manage a home, family, and finances as effectively as possible. The competencies contained in this curriculum area include the following:

1. *Managing Personal Finances.* It is particularly important for individuals to learn how to manage their money. This knowledge includes using and realizing the value of simple financial records, knowing how to obtain and use bank and credit facilities, and planning for wise expenditures. Computational skills in maintaining a checkbook and budget are also necessary.
2. *Selecting and Managing a Household.* Students must learn how to care properly for a home, its furnishings, and its equipment, particularly since such equipment is

9

expensive to purchase and repair. Repair of appliances, broken furniture, electrical plugs, plumbing, and so forth should be emphasized in the curriculum.

3. *Caring for Personal Needs.* Knowledge of grooming and hygiene methods, sexual matters, and physical fitness are examples of information an individual must have to take care of personal bodily needs. Lack of competency in these areas creates problems of acceptance and adjustment.

4. *Raising Children and Meeting Marriage Responsibilities.* Students need to understand the components of effective family living: setting goals and making decisions, choosing lifestyles, managing available resources, expanding and controlling family size, providing for needs of children and adults, and ensuring the safety and health of all family members. (Also of importance is the understanding of childhood, adolescent, and adult sexual experiences.)

5. *Buying, Preparing, and Consuming Food.* A great majority of children in low-income families grow up with significant nutritional deficiencies. Instruction in planning meals; purchasing, caring for, and storing food; and preparing proper meals is extremely valuable. Learning how to work safely in the kitchen should be stressed, including the proper use and care of knives, stoves, and other equipment.

6. *Buying and Caring for Clothing.* Learning how to purchase appropriate clothing and how to clean, press, and repair clothing should be included in the student's instruction. Another area of importance is constructing garments and other textile projects, such as drapes, wall hangings, and weavings.

7. *Exhibiting Responsible Citizenship.* To become contributing members of the community, students must learn about the laws of the United States, what rights they have, how to register and vote, citizen responsibilities, state and local laws, customs, and other pertinent citizenship matters.

8. *Using Recreational Facilities and Leisure Time.* Presently in the United States we are moving toward shorter work weeks while employment is becoming more difficult to obtain. Therefore, it is crucial that knowledge of possible leisure activities and resources be made available to all students. Such activities can also be valuable in building friendships, self-confidence, and other skills.

9. *Getting Around the Community (Mobility).* Students need to be able to use intercity and intracity travel resources. They should learn to drive a car, obey the traffic laws, and know the agencies that can aid in mobility needs. In this mobile society, it is paramount that an individual be able to get around efficiently for work, leisure, and civic pursuits.

Personal-Social Skills

Developing independence, self-confidence, and socially acceptable behaviors and maintaining friendships are critical skills for students to learn if they are to adjust satisfactorily in the community. Continuing the previous list, the primary competencies that should be learned in this curriculum area are:

10. *Achieving Self-Awareness.* Students must learn to understand, accept, and respect their uniqueness as individuals. They must gain an understanding of their abilities, values, aspirations, and interests and how they can be incorporated into a lifestyle that will be meaningful and fruitful. Learning who they are and what they can do with their lives is an important precursor to each of the subsequent competencies needed for societal assimilation.

11. *Acquiring Self-Confidence.* People from minority groups, including those with handicaps, are often the subject of ridicule and rejection. They are frequently made to feel different, incompetent, and unwanted, which causes them to have degrading feelings and attitudes about themselves. Students need to be in an environment that gives them positive reinforcement, motivation, and appropriate conditions for learning and behaving. Unless negative feelings are overcome, and students can experience success related to community experiences, many students will fail at community living. This is a time of great change and personal confusion for youth, and they need to explore extensively their roles as individuals in this society.

12. *Achieving Socially Responsible Behavior.* There are many children in our schools who fail to understand modes of social etiquette and appropriate social behaviors. Understanding the characteristics of others, how to react in various situations, how to form and maintain social relationships, dating, and eating out are examples of coping behaviors dealt with in this unit.

13. *Maintaining Good Interpersonal Skills.* Learning to get along with people is one of the greatest problems all of us face. In too many instances, research has demonstrated this to be a prime reason for loss of jobs, especially for workers with disabilities. Having an appropriate circle of friends with whom to associate during recreational and leisure time is another area of focus. Many people apparently lack knowledge of how to develop meaningful friendships.

14. *Achieving Independence.* Concentrated efforts to develop independence must be made; students must learn to do things by themselves. They must learn to accept responsibility for their own actions—for example, getting around in the community, choosing friends, getting to school on time, and deciding what to wear.

15. *Achieving Problem-Solving Skills.* Throughout the developmental years, many children, especially children with disabilities, have decisions made for them. All children must learn what constitutes a good decision, the steps involved, and the many factors entailed in decision making.

16. *Communicating with Others.* Students must have the necessary communication skills to express themselves and understand others so that they can interact effectively, both verbally and nonverbally. The ability to make one's thoughts understood is extremely important, but it may be difficult, especially for slower learners.

Occupational Guidance and Preparation

Many people do not attain their true potential in the labor market. They are relegated to unskilled, low-paying jobs and become marginal workers. If people are to approach their true potential, they need to become more aware of diverse job possibilities, develop the necessary skills, be provided with varied work experiences, and learn to make logical and viable job choices as they move through the educational system. Thus, early educational efforts must be initiated in the areas of occupational awareness and counseling, work evaluation, work adjustment, vocational education and instruction, job tryouts, job placement, and follow-up. The competencies deemed important in this curriculum area are:

17. *Knowing and Exploring Occupational Possibilities.* Many children and youth have an extremely limited perspective of the world of work. They lack both relevant information and experience. Field trips, community speakers, summer work experience, the state employment service, films, and literature must be made available in a concentrated fashion.

18. *Selecting and Planning Occupational Choice(s).* Students must become aware of their specific abilities, interests, and needs, and how these relate to their future life work. Concentrated and periodic vocational evaluation and guidance are needed so that students will have sufficient information about themselves and their occupational options.

19. *Exhibiting Appropriate Work Habits and Behaviors.* It is important for educational programs to simulate working environments in the school setting besides those available in the community, so that appropriate work behaviors can be learned. Too many students possess a false concept of the characteristics of a good worker and do not develop the type of skills needed to enter the job market.

20. *Seeking, Securing, and Maintaining Employment.* One of the greatest problems students face is not knowing how to find, apply for, and maintain employment. Students must learn the strategies to secure employment and know about resources available to help them when they need assistance (e.g., state employment service, vocational rehabilitation, social services, rehabilitation facilities, classified ads).

21. *Exhibiting Sufficient Physical-Manual Skills.* Schools must begin developing students' physical and manual abilities in the elementary program. Many jobs available for people entering the job market require considerable fine or gross finger dexterity and standing, pulling, pushing, lifting, and carrying abilities.

22. *Obtaining a Specific Occupational Skill.* Learning a specific job skill will not pigeonhole students for life and will not disqualify them later for work or instruction in another occupation. Vocational education and on-the-job training while attending the secondary program are crucial to a student's ultimate level of vocational attainment.

Each of these competencies has been divided further into subcompetencies, which are presented in Chapter 3, "Competency Units." Previously there were 102 subcompetencies comprising the 22 primary competencies. A recent study by project staff to validate the competencies in today's society (Bucher, 1985) found the 22 competencies (with some rewording) to be of major importance. There was some change in the subcompetency structure, however. Several subcompetencies were deleted, some were added, and a few were combined, resulting in a total of 97 rather than the original 102. The revised competency matrix appears in Figure 2–2.

THE LCCE TRANSITIONAL MODEL

The Life Centered Career Education Curriculum presents educators with a framework for organizing an effective functional curriculum that will lead to the successful transition of special education students from school to work. Figure 2–3 illustrates how the LCCE competencies and the four stages of career development can be integrated into the scope and sequence of an academically based curriculum. The model promotes the concept of infusion—that is, that LCCE competencies and career development should be taught in regular subjects when possible and that the involvement of parents and community resources is critically important. Inspection of the lower part of Figure 2–3 reveals who should be involved with school personnel in the delivery of career education. It is recommended that special educators assume the primary responsibility until approximately age 21, with vocational rehabilitation counselors becoming primarily responsible afterwards.

The LCCE Transition Model is based on 12 important propositions that are the result of previous research on and experience with the process of career development, education, and preparation of persons with special needs for successful adult functioning. These are as follows:

FIGURE 2–2
Life Centered Career Education Competencies (Revised 1/87)

Curriculum Area	Competency	Subcompetency: The student will be able to:	
DAILY LIVING SKILLS	1. Managing Personal Finances	1. Count money & make correct change	2. Make responsible expenditures
	2. Selecting & Managing a Household	7. Maintain home exterior/interior	8. Use basic appliances and tools
	3. Caring for Personal Needs	12. Demonstrate knowledge of physical fitness, nutrition, & weight	13. Exhibit proper grooming & hygiene
	4. Raising Children & Meeting Marriage Responsibilities	17. Demonstrate physical care for raising children	18. Know psychological aspects of raising children
	5. Buying, Preparing, & Consuming Food	20. Purchase food	21. Clean food preparation areas
	6. Buying & Caring for Clothing	26. Wash/clean clothing	27. Purchase clothing
	7. Exhibiting Responsible Citizenship	29. Demonstrate knowledge of civil rights & responsibilities	30. Know nature of local, state, & federal governments
	8. Utilizing Recreational Facilities & Engaging in Leisure	33. Demonstrate knowledge of available community resources	34. Choose & plan activities
	9. Getting Around the Community	38. Demonstrate knowledge of traffic rules & safety	39. Demonstrate knowledge & use of various means of transportation
PERSONAL-SOCIAL SKILLS	10. Achieving Self-Awareness	42. Identify physical & psychological needs	43. Identify interests & abilities
	11. Acquiring Self-Confidence	46. Express feelings of self-worth	47. Describe others' perception of self
	12. Achieving Socially Responsible Behavior	51. Develop respect for the rights & properties of others	52. Recognize authority & follow instructions
	13. Maintaining Good Interpersonal Skills	56. Demonstrate listening & responding skills	57. Establish & maintain close relationships
	14. Achieving Independence	59. Strive toward self-actualization	60. Demonstrate self-organization
	15. Making Adequate Decisions	62. Locate & utilize sources of assistance	63. Anticipate consequences
	16. Communicating with Others	67. Recognize & respond to emergency situations	68. Communicate with understanding
OCCUPATIONAL GUIDANCE AND PREPARATION	17. Knowing & Exploring Occupational Possibilities	70. Identify remunerative aspects of work	71. Locate sources of occupational & training information
	18. Selecting & Planning Occupational Choices	76. Make realistic occupational choices	77. Identify requirements of appropriate & available jobs
	19. Exhibiting Appropriate Work Habits & Behavior	81. Follow directions & observe regulations	82. Recognize importance of attendance & punctuality
	20. Seeking, Securing, & Maintaining Employment	88. Search for a job	89. Apply for a job
	21. Exhibiting Sufficient Physical-Manual Skills	94. Demonstrate stamina & endurance	95. Demonstrate satisfactory balance & coordination
	22. Obtaining Specific Occupational Skills		

3. Keep basic financial records	4. Calculate & pay taxes	5. Use credit responsibly	6. Use banking services	
9. Select adequate housing	10. Set up household	11. Maintain home grounds		
14. Dress appropriately	15. Demonstrate knowledge of common illness, prevention & treatment	16. Practice personal safety		
19. Demonstrate marriage responsibilities				
22. Store food	23. Prepare meals	24. Demonstrate appropriate eating habits	25. Plan/eat balanced meals	
28. Iron, mend, & store clothing				
31. Demonstrate knowledge of the law & ability to follow the law	32. Demonstrate knowledge of citizen rights & responsibilities			
35. Demonstrate knowledge of the value of recreation	36. Engage in group & individual activities	37. Plan vacation time		
40. Find way around the community	41. Drive a car			
44. Identify emotions	45. Demonstrate knowledge of physical self			
48. Accept & give praise	49. Accept & give criticism	50. Develop confidence in oneself		
53. Demonstrate appropriate behavior in public areas	54. Know important character traits	55. Recognize personal roles		
58. Make & maintain friendships				
61. Demonstrate awareness of how one's behavior affects others				
64. Develop & evaluate alternatives	65. Recognize nature of a problem	66. Develop goal-seeking behavior		
69. Know subtleties of communication				
72. Identify personal values met through work	73. Identify societal values met through work	74. Classify jobs into occupational categories	75. Investigate local occupational & training opportunities	
78. Identify occupational aptitudes	79. Identify major occupational interests	80. Identify major occupational needs		
83. Recognize importance of supervision	84. Demonstrate knowledge of occupational safety	85. Work with others	86. Meet demands for quality work	87. Work at a satisfactory rate
90. Interview for a job	91. Know how to maintain postschool occupational adjustment	92. Demonstrate knowledge of competitive standards	93. Know how to adjust to changes in employment	
96. Demonstrate manual dexterity	97. Demonstrate sensory discrimination			
There are no specific subcompetencies, as they depend on skill being taught.				

FIGURE 2–3
LCCE Transition Model

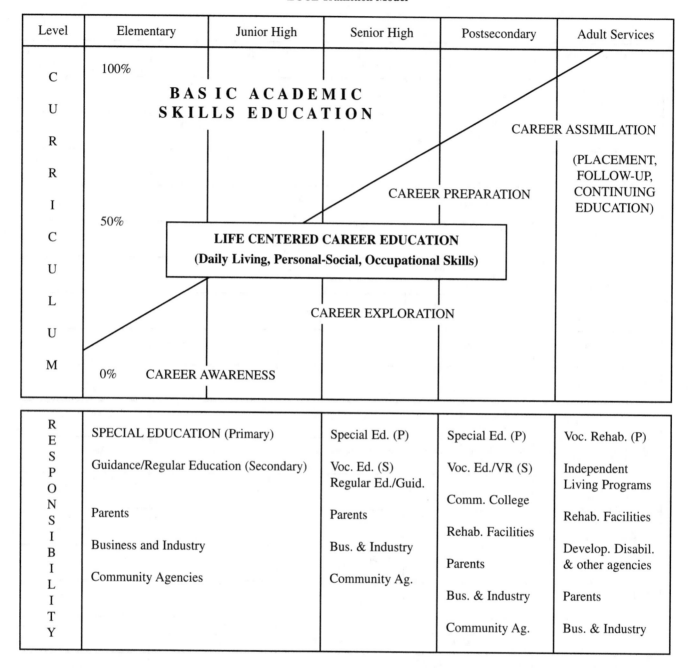

Level	Elementary	Junior High	Senior High	Postsecondary	Adult Services

C U R R I C U L U M

100%

BASIC ACADEMIC SKILLS EDUCATION

CAREER ASSIMILATION

(PLACEMENT, FOLLOW-UP, CONTINUING EDUCATION)

CAREER PREPARATION

50%

LIFE CENTERED CAREER EDUCATION
(Daily Living, Personal-Social, Occupational Skills)

CAREER EXPLORATION

0%   CAREER AWARENESS

R E S P O N S I B I L I T Y				
SPECIAL EDUCATION (Primary)	Special Ed. (P)	Special Ed. (P)	Voc. Rehab. (P)
Guidance/Regular Education (Secondary)	Voc. Ed. (S) Regular Ed./Guid.	Voc. Ed./VR (S)	Independent Living Programs
		Comm. College	
Parents	Parents	Rehab. Facilities	Rehab. Facilities
Business and Industry	Bus. & Industry	Parents	Develop. Disabil. & other agencies
Community Agencies	Community Ag.	Bus. & Industry	Parents
		Community Ag.	Bus. & Industry

1. The development of a *work personality* (i.e., an individual's own unique set of abilities and needs) *begins shortly after birth* and matures sufficiently only if provided with early and adequate reinforcers in the environment. Thus, it is critical that schools and parents provide early on the experiences and reinforcements that are necessary for appropriate career skills and maturity to develop.

2. One's *career is more than an occupation.* A career also includes the important unpaid work that one engages in at home and in various community functions. Thus, one's career is multifaceted, consisting of the productive work activity that one does in the home, in avocational pursuits, and as a volunteer for the benefit of the community, as well as any paid employment. For many individuals with disabilities this concept is particularly important because at least half will be unemployed at times, yet their need to work can still be realized.

3. There are *four sequential stages of career development* that must be provided for if the individual is to acquire

the necessary skills to meet his or her potential and needs, resulting in career satisfaction. Career awareness (including self-awareness) begins almost immediately in the elementary school and continues into adult life. The three other stages of career development begin later, as depicted in Figure 2–3, the extent of need depending on the individual. Sufficient career awareness and career exploration are essential for later success in vocational education courses.

4. *There are four major domains of instruction* that are necessary for successful career development and living skills to be achieved: *academic skills*; *daily living skills*; *personal-social skills*; and *occupational skills*. *Academic skills* are the fundamental skills a person needs to read, write, compute, appreciate art and music, and so forth. *Daily living skills* relate to both independent living and occupational functioning—for example, being able to manage finances, maintain a home, care for personal needs, and prepare food. *Personal-social skills* relate not only to knowing oneself and establishing and maintaining satisfactory interpersonal relationships, but also to problem-solving, independent functioning, and other qualities necessary for living and working. The final important domain, *occupational skills*, should be given earlier and greater attention by school personnel so that students can develop vocational interests, needs, aptitudes, and abilities and achieve future job success.

5. Career education/competency instruction can be *infused into most subject areas.* As indicated earlier, the four domains are inextricably interrelated and often can be taught simultaneously (e.g., important math skills can be taught in relation to an LCCE competency and stage of career development). Thus, career education is not a separate course as some still believe.

6. Successful career development and transition require an *active partnership between the school, parents, business and industry, and community agencies* that are organized to provide various health, social, psychological, and vocational services for disabled individuals. Although this relationship is generally agreed upon as necessary, in practice it has been difficult to achieve. This is a major tenet of the "Transition from School to Work" concept. In the LCCE model, this relationship is inherent throughout the school years and beyond, not at just the high school level. Education occurs in more places than within the four walls of the school building.

7. *Hands-on experiential learning* is an important need of learners who have disabilities. Many are more able to respond to motivating, relevant, and familiar learning activities that relate to the real world and its vocational, social, and daily living requirements. Educators must incorporate as many of these experiences into their lesson plans as they can.

8. *Normalization* through the *principle of inclusion* is critical to successful career development and transitional efforts. Persons with disabilities must learn to live and work with all types of people if they are to survive as adults. Administrators and special educators are key to this. Regular class teachers must be taught better methods of mainstreaming, and they must be given the time and consideration they need to carry it out.

9. *Cooperative learning environments* (Johnson & Johnson, 1983) are more successful than competitive and individualistic environments in helping disabled learners acquire a higher self-esteem, interact more, feel accepted by teachers and nondisabled students, achieve more, and behave more appropriately in the classroom. Cooperative learning environments can build positive relationships among all students.

10. *Informal and formal career/vocational assessment* is an important component of successful career development and transitional planning. This assessment should begin in the late elementary years with a "Worker Profile" and by late junior high or early senior high years be a more highly organized, formal assessment by a trained certified vocational evaluator (CVE) using a broad armamentarium of reliable and valid measures including specialized/standardized interest and aptitude tests, work samples, job analysis, and job-site evaluations.

11. A *Career Education/Transitional Resource Coordinator* is necessary to assume responsibility for monitoring and carrying out the program. The coordinator should have a local team to carry out the program, as noted by the Harold Russell Associates study. The most logical disciplines to assess are the special educator (to age 21) and the vocational rehabilitation counselor (thereafter).

12. Appropriate *interagency agreements* and *cross-agency inservice training* are important to secure so that everyone involved agrees upon and understands the transitional program's goals, roles, and responsibilities and the commitment of resources, facilities, and money. Written guidelines should be developed after inservice discussions and agreements.

The LCCE model views transitional programming as needing to begin at the elementary level with purposeful and organized instruction directed at the development of a work personality and important career/life skills needed for successful adult functioning. Employment success depends on the acquisition of a mixture of academic, daily living, personal-social, and occupational skills. The majority of former special education students lose their jobs because of poor self-concepts and limited confidence in themselves, inability to relate to others and use their leisure time appropriately, lack of knowledge of how to function independently in the community, and the like. A whole-person approach such as LCCE can prepare these students for life after school by giving them the opportunity to learn all that is necessary to become productive adults.

IMPLEMENTING THE LCCE MODEL

How can a comprehensive program such as LCCE become a reality? Implementing career education means selling change; this is not always easy to do.

If career education is to be implemented there must be active cooperation and involvement of both school and non-school personnel (i.e., parents, business and industry workers, and community agency representatives). The total curriculum needs to be sequenced definitively and logically, from the elementary to postsecondary levels. Elementary and secondary personnel must coordinate their efforts to provide sequentially for the learning of each competency.

Career education requires a shift from the traditional content-based curriculum to one that is more process based. Moore and Gysbers (1972) cautioned against viewing students as having to be brought up to a grade level by the end of the school year at all costs. This creates passive-dependent students who may be apathetic, irresponsible, or rebellious. A process-oriented approach, relating curriculum directly to the outside world and focusing on each student's unique ways of learning and becoming motivated, is more appropriate. In process education, primary emphasis is on developing skills; acquiring knowledge and information (content) is secondary. In curriculum development and lesson planning, the key question is: What skills (competencies) are essential to the individual in order to make him or her a more effective person? In process education, the content of the curriculum is selected for its utility in facilitating and exercising those skills. The skills are the goals within the curriculum, the vehicle by which the goal of skill development may be realized (Cole, 1972). Thus, a competency-based curriculum should be designed to ensure that each student acquires competencies deemed essential to function adequately as a productive worker and citizen. Students who learn more slowly may require more time to acquire the competencies deemed essential for community living. Extended secondary programs or appropriately designated postsecondary programs may have to be considered.

The proposed competency-based curriculum approach does not necessarily mean the abolishment of courses and structure currently operating in school programs. It does require, however, that instructional content be selected according to its appropriateness for facilitating student acquisition of the competencies. It is recommended that academic studies be taught primarily in conjunction with the student's need for such instruction in acquiring each competency. Students should be placed in classes that offer the best method of competency attainment. It is important to remember that the role of the curriculum is to guide instruction, not to prescribe the means. Therefore, each school system must decide how it can infuse the teaching of the Life Centered Career Education competencies into its curriculum.

It is apparent that LCCE transition will succeed only if one agency is clearly responsible for individuals with disabilities throughout their lifespan and if a truly cooperative, collaborative spirit exists among the school, parents, and community. The professionals who are best prepared for coordinating and monitoring the transitional process and its necessary services for each individual are the special educator and the vocational rehabilitation counselor. No other professionals are better trained to understand and meet the needs of disabled children and youth (5–21) than the special educator or the needs of disabled adults (age 21 up) than the vocational rehabilitation counselor. This is why they are designated in Figure 2–3 as having primary responsibility. The LCCE coordinator (special educator or vocational rehabilitation counselor) must know and be able to make use of the numerous community agencies, businesses, and industries, as well as family resources.

The key to program change is to involve school and community personnel who will plan, implement, and evaluate the new program. Whenever possible, citizens who have disabilities and parents should be involved in the effort. The first step is for a group of interested educators to gain the endorsement of the school district's leadership personnel (e.g., superintendent, principals, and directors of special education, vocational education, guidance, and curriculum and instruction). With this endorsement, the team can then organize an LCCE committee consisting of other significant school personnel, parents, employers, disabled persons, and representatives from such agencies as Vocational Rehabilitation, Job Service, Developmental Disabilities, and JTPA. This committee should come to an agreement on the basic purpose, goals, and objectives of the program. The next step is to prepare and conduct an inservice training program for selected school personnel, parents, and agencies so that cooperation, responsibilities, and involvement are established. Written guidelines and cooperative agreements with agencies can be formalized afterwards. A more detailed account of the organization and planning for LCCE curriculum implementation is contained in the *Life Centered Career Education Trainer's Manual* (Brolin, 1993).

INSTRUCTIONAL RESPONSIBILITIES

Implementing an effective career education program is predicated on the appropriate redirecting of traditional teacher/counselor roles and a heavier involvement and investment in educational programing from parents, community agencies, and business and industry personnel. In the development of each school's career education plan, these roles should be clearly explicated by the LCCE committee, which includes parents and community representatives.

THE LIFE CENTERED CAREER EDUCATION PROGRAM AND INCLUSIVE PRACTICES

Role of Special Educators

The LCCE approach advocates a change in role for the special education teacher. The teacher would become more of a consultant/advisor to other school personnel, parents, community agencies, and industries by coordinating services and integrating the contributions that school, community, and home can make in meeting students' life career development needs.

Special education teachers will still be needed to provide specific classroom instruction when it cannot be provided appropriately to certain students in regular classes or community services. In addition, special tutoring will be necessary for many exceptional students to enable them to keep up in regular classes.

Special education teachers will need to advise school and nonschool personnel on how they can best work with each student. The following support will be needed from special education teachers: (a) inservice assistance; (b) methods and materials consultation; (c) modification/development of materials; and (d) sharing of relevant information on the student's basic academic skills, values, and attitudes.

Integration of students with special needs into regular classes is highly recommended, but only when there are assurances that it will be beneficial to these students in competency attainment. A major responsibility of special educators should be to monitor each student's progress and to assume the responsibility of determining where, how, and when each competency is to be acquired. Coteaching and integrated classes with a regular class teacher are becoming more prevalent in providing LCCE competency instruction.

Role of General Educators

Needs assessment studies have revealed that most teachers and counselors believe that students with special needs can learn at least some of the LCCE competencies as part of their regular subject matter curriculum if teachers are shown how to infuse the material appropriately into their lessons. The investigations also revealed that there are different patterns of competencies appropriate for the same discipline at different grade levels.

With program goals and objectives more clearly delineated and assistance from special education teachers readily available, most students with special needs should be able to be assimilated into many regular classes and programs.

Role of the Family

Family members are crucial to the success of a career education program for students with special needs. No matter how good the curriculum and its instructional services, a student can fail if the family is not supportive. Families must believe that the school is genuinely interested in their children and that it has designed a meaningful curriculum. Parent involvement in the Life Centered Career Education inservice workshops and the development of local curriculum plans is absolutely necessary so that roles and responsibilities may be clearly delineated.

With guidance and assistance from school personnel, the family can contribute to the learning of every competency. The home is a fertile ground for teaching personal-social, daily living, and occupational skills. Parents can assist their children by structuring responsibilities, developing career awareness, teaching specific skills, and providing a secure psychological environment where self-confidence and independence can be developed adequately. Family members should also be encouraged to participate in class activities.

Role of Community Personnel

Community Agencies and Organizations. Professional workers from such agencies as the state vocational rehabilitation agency, employment service, social service agency, public health agency, rehabilitation centers and workshops, and mental health agencies are examples of major governmental services that should be involved in the career development of students with disabilities. In addition, there are several community service organizations, civic clubs, and other resources in most communities that can be major contributors to the career education program. Some examples of service organizations are the YMCA, YWCA, Red Cross, League of Women Voters, and American Legion. Examples of civic clubs are the Jaycees, Rotary Club, Kiwanis, Elks, and Lions Club, all of which generally involve themselves in projects for community improvement. Some other community resources that might be used are local associations such as the Arc, churches, hospitals, nursing homes, libraries, and Big Brothers, to name a few.

Business and Industry. Community workers are particularly significant in the Occupational Guidance and Preparation curriculum area. Field trips and on-the-job tryouts in business and industry inject the realistic components needed in a career education curriculum. Representatives from business and industry should be requested to speak to classes, serve as resource persons, serve on career education advisory committees, sponsor cooperative work-study programs, provide appropriate media for classes, and assist in course development. Clergymen, bankers, politicians, firemen, policemen, medical personnel, and other community workers can assist in the Daily Living Skills curriculum area. In recent years many partnerships have evolved between school districts and the business community.

An effective and comprehensive school-community relationship will greatly enhance the implementation of a meaningful career education curriculum for all students. Life Centered Career Education requires the effective use of community resources so that students may adequately explore and be prepared for the real world.

REFERENCES

Brolin, D. (1973). Career education needs of secondary educable students. *Exceptional Children, 39,* 619–624.

Brolin, D. (1993). *Life centered career education trainer's manual.* Reston, VA: The Council for Exceptional Children.

Brolin, D., & Thomas, B. (1971). *Preparing teachers of secondary level educable mentally retarded: A new model* (final report). Menomonie: University of Wisconsin–Stout.

Brolin, D., & Thomas, B. (1972). *Preparing teachers of secondary level educable mentally retarded: Proposal for a new model.* project report). Menomonie: University of Wisconsin–Stout.

Bucher, D. (1985). *Validation study of The LCCE curriculum competencies for special education students.* Research Report No. 2. Columbia: University of Missouri.

Cole, H. P. (1972). *Process education: The new direction for elementary-secondary schools.* Englewood Cliffs, NJ: Educational Technology Publications.

Johnson, R. T., & Johnson, D. W. (1983). Effects of cooperative, competitive, and individualistic learning experiences on social development. *Exceptional Children, 49,* 323–329.

Moore, E. J., & Gysbers, N. C. (1972). Career development: A new focus. *Educational Leadership, 30*(3), 257–260.

3. Competency Units

This chapter presents the competency units that have been developed to assist school personnel in teaching the 22 career education competencies.[1] The competency unit is a systematized unit approach to teaching each of the 97 subcompetencies contained in the revised version of the LCCE Curriculum.

COMPETENCY UNIT STRUCTURE AND CONTENT

Each competency unit contains three sections, in addition to its identification: objectives, activities/strategies, and adult/peer roles, designed to assist teachers and counselors in providing students with experiences to develop and demonstrate each competency. No specific grade or developmental level is suggested for the teaching of each competency unit (subcompetency)—this is left to the discretion of the individual school and its LCCE plan. Obviously, some competency units could be taught during the elementary years, whereas others are more appropriate at the junior high and senior high levels. A Competency Rating Scale (CRS) can be used to determine what competencies and subcompetencies have been acquired so that appropriate educational programming can be done for each student. A description of the CRS is presented in Chapter 4, and the CRS manual is presented in Appendix A. An LCCE Inventory, consisting of a Knowledge Battery and a Performance Battery, is also available to provide more objective assessment of the student's competency level. It is described in Chapter 4. Each section of the competency unit is discussed below.

Objectives

Each competency unit contains suggestions for the sequencing of performance objectives for a specific subcompetency. An attempt has been made to arrange the objectives in a logical order, although they can be arranged according to the instructor's evaluation of student needs, to fit a class, or to correspond to the availability of resources. Objectives may be expanded and/or developed into smaller components to meet the specific learning abilities of the students. Additional performance objectives can be added to meet the individual needs of the learner.

Activities/Strategies

Activities are the vehicle by which teachers and counselors shape the competencies. The suggested activities and strategies have not been arranged in a rigid hierarchy, although some consideration has been given to difficulty levels. More appropriate activities may be inserted, depending on the characteristics of the students and the available resources. The suggested activities/strategies make use of a wide assortment of resources and plans for instructions to prompt the teacher to approach the teaching task with variety. Utilization of community personnel to provide instructional activities and support is highly encouraged.

Adult/Peer Roles

School personnel must continually attempt to bring their students into contact with community representatives—particularly role models for the demonstration of the competencies. In addition to owners of businesses and industries, individuals who have jobs similar to those which special education students might later obtain should speak to the class about their work.

---

[1] Appreciation is extended to Harry Drier, Jr., Ohio State University and Charles Kokaska, California State University at Long Beach, for their valuable contributions in preparing the first edition of this chapter.

The adult/peer section includes adult models, sources of information from a career perspective, former students who are closer in experience, parents, and peers (e.g., siblings, fellow students from regular classes, and fellow students from the same class). In some cases, parents have been identified as the most appropriate agent. In other cases, parents and peers could participate with the student. The instructor should select the most appropriate agent, based on agent availability, student's level or ability, and the sequence of activities. Numerous activities require the same community source or person.

INFUSION

To achieve the goals of the Life Centered Career Education Curriculum, educators must examine other ways to realistically provide career-relevant experiences and content within a *career education* context. The career educational construct (or vehicle) brings new life role meanings to the existing curriculum. Therefore, a change process referred to as *infusion* is suggested.

Infusion refers to the process of integrating career development goals based on student career development competency needs with current subject matter, goals, and content. This curriculum development concept is used to ensure the delivery of an integrated career education program.

Two important tasks must be considered in both the development and use of the competency units. Relationships among the units must be established, and the points at which they are infused most effectively into the total curriculum must be determined. The relationship of some units to a single discipline or subject will be obvious, while others will not be as easily identifiable. The *progression of skill development*, concept difficulty, and application of knowledge may also need refinement as the units are used in a given sequence.

GUIDELINES FOR EFFECTIVE USE OF COMPETENCY UNITS

Effective instructional use of these units is contingent on certain conditions or factors. As in any instructional program, teachers and counselors are obligated to make decisions and adjustments regarding the use of each unit activity in the light of (a) the needs and motivations of their students; (b) varying teaching/learning styles; (c) factors of the physical and psychological environment; and (d) standards of excellence and the instructional policies of the school administration. Thus, most specific questions that teachers and counselors may ask about the use of these units should be answered with reference to (a) what is more facilitative and growth producing for individual students; (b) the given or appropriate mode of interaction among faculty and students, considering for example, their individual teaching/learning styles; and (c) the requirements or expectations of the local school district.

Faculty members may pose questions and express concern regarding issues such as scope and sequencing, grade level specifications, modification of learning activities, use of alternate activities and resource time restrictions, coteaching arrangements, and so forth. An appropriate but general response to these matters would be to encourage the faculty to exercise their personal and professional judgment in dealing with problems. The best choices a teacher or counselor can make are those that are most advantageous to the individual student in the quest to achieve career development growth. Thus, concern for the welfare of the student, given all of the implications of the teaching/learning environment (community, school classroom), should guide the users of this curriculum.

The Life Centered Career Education Curriculum advances the belief that curriculum development should take place in the local school system. The success of curriculum alteration depends on the degree to which affiliated teachers are involved in determining curriculum changes. Grass roots participation of teachers in determining curriculum goals, objectives, and teaching strategies should provide a higher quality career education program than adopting a commercially developed program. A curriculum framework for teaching competencies is suggested; however, this framework has been designed to be easily modified to meet special needs in local settings.

The competency units presented on the following pages are intended to serve as a guide for teaching the 22 life-centered competencies. We believe that these suggestions will result in a more meaningful education and ultimate success for all citizens. Persons interested in the more extensively developed set of lesson plans, an eight-volume set of 1,128 detailed lesson plans, should contact The Council for Exceptional Children. Information on the nature of these competency units and how they can be purchased is provided in Appendix C. Sample lesson plans from the Complete Package have been included to demonstrate how they expand the activities in this text. (See pages 22, 83, and 106.)

DAILY LIVING SKILLS

Domain: Daily Living Skills
Competency: 1. Managing Personal Finances
Subcompetency: 1. Identify Money and Make Correct Change

Objectives	Activities/Strategies	Adult/Peer Roles
1. Identify coins and bills less than or equal to $100.00 in value.	• Students practice with authentic money as much as possible. • Students quiz each other with money flash cards of coins and bills in values up to $100. • Students construct posters of different money values up to $100 using magazine cutouts and pictures.	• Parents and/or peers practice currency identification with student. • Parents and/or peers devise questions or games that allow the student to identify the varieties of currency from memory.
2. Count money in coin and bill denominations with sums less than or equal to $20.00.	• Students practice with authentic money as much as possible. • Students practice selecting different coin and bill denominations valuing $.01 to $20 from a box, and then count the money amounts aloud to each other. • Students devise buying/selling games using play money amounts up to $20. • Students play structured money games. • Students construct class bulletin board demonstrating money values up to $20.	• Parents and/or peers give the student different denominations of coins and bills up to $20 and ask the student to count out the combinations. Parents and/or peers allow the student, while shopping, to count out the necessary amounts for purchases equalling $20 or less. • Parents and/or peers allow the student, while shopping and making purchases equalling $20 or less, to receive the change and to count the change.
3. Make correct change from both bills and coins for amounts less than or equal to $50.00.	• Students practice making change with large denomination bills ($10, $20, and $50), using department store items and their prices on flash cards. • Students operate a "store" and "bank" to practice making correct change for amounts equalling $50.00 or less. • Class role plays situations in which students must make change for purchases of amounts equalling $50.00 or less. • Class identifies all possible situations where knowledge of making change would be important.	• Parents and/or peers allow the student while shopping to select the correct monetary denominations to give to the salesperson for a purchase amount equalling $50 or less, to receive the change, and to count the change and determine if the amount received is correct. • Parents and/or peers role play "customer" while the student role plays "clerk" using monetary denominations equalling $50.00 or less. • Parents and/or peers allow the student to make change from large denomination bills ($10, $20, and $50) for items listed in department store advertisement brochures or catalogs priced to $50.00.

LESSON PLAN 9

1.1.2P:9

LCCE Objective 1.1.3. Make correct change from both bills and coins for amounts less than or equal to $50.00.

Lesson Objective: Student will make the correct change for items purchased with $10.00, $20.00, and $50.00 bills.

Instructional Resources: Real or play money ($50.00, $20.00, $10.00, $5.00, and $1.00 bills, half dollars, quarters, dimes, nickels, and pennies), Store items with prices marked on them.

Lesson Introduction: Today each of you will role-play being a store clerk for the items that are displayed on this table. One person will be the salesclerk and another person will buy an item that has been marked with the sales tax included. The salesclerk will take the bill handed to him or her and count out loud the correct change to the customer.

School Activity: **Time: 1 session**

Task:

1. Display many differently priced items on a table. Place money in cash register or storage container.

2. Explain directions for role-play to students.
   - Students will take turns role-playing salesclerk.
   - Another student will select one of the items and purchase it with a $10.00 bill, then will buy an item with $20.00 and $50.00.
   - Salesclerk gives the correct change for each item.
   - Students who are observing should compute on a sheet of paper what they think the correct change should be.

Lesson Plan Evaluation:

Activity: Students will role-play customer and clerk in purchasing items.

Criteria: Student will make correct change for three priced items when role-playing the salesclerk.

Career Role: Family Member/Homemaker, Employee, Citizen/Volunteer, Avocational
Career Stage: Preparation

Sample Lesson Plan from *Life Centered Career Education Daily Living Skills*, p. 27

Domain: Daily Living Skills
Competency: 1. Managing Personal Finances
Subcompetency: 2. Make Responsible Expenditures

Objectives	Activities/Strategies	Adult/Peer Roles
1. Identify prices on labels and tags of merchandise.	• Students bring in containers that have tags and labels on items and identify their prices. • Students collect tags and labels from purchases and bring them to school for the bulletin board. Class constructs "Items Board" (from old cans, boxes, etc.) and marks approximate price with real labels and tags. Students then practice making wise expenditures in the classrooms. • Students take a field trip to the market to practice reading labels and unit pricing indicators.	• Parents and/or peers explain how to best utilize information labels and tags. • Parents and/or peers ask questions of students concerning purchasing prices of merchandise when shopping. • Representative of Consumer Protection discusses "problems" in reading labels.
2. Choose most economical buy among like items of a similar quality.	• Class discusses the difference between quality and quantity • Students collect magazine and newspaper ads, can labels, and tags, and with each other make comparisons in price, quantity, and quality. • Students go on a field trip to different stores to compare the price, quantity, and quality of different items. • Students practice computation in figuring single unit purchases when prices are shown in multiples (e.g., 3 cans for $.59). • Students operate a simulated grocery store to make comparisons of food products using empty food cans. • Students go on a field trip to different stores and locate sale items in the stores from their tags.	• Parents and/or peers discuss how they choose the most economical items to be purchased. • Parents and/or peers ask questions of students in making comparisons of the most economical items to be purchased when shopping. • Consumer Protection Representative discusses levels of quality.

DAILY LIVING SKILLS

Objectives	Activities/Strategies	Adult/Peer Roles
3. Identify purchases as necessities or luxuries in the areas of food, clothing, housing, and transportation.	• Class makes posters comparing necessary and luxury items that relate to food, clothing, housing, and transportation. • Class discusses luxuries and necessities in relation to individual life styles and economics. • Students collect newspaper ads that illustrate appeal to buy "luxury" items. • Students take field trips to several supermarkets for comparison of prices of luxury and necessary items. • Students collect newspaper/magazine advertising for various food, clothing, housing, and transportation necessity and luxury products for bulletin board. • Students watch television ads and discuss comparative advertising as it relates to predominance of either necessity or luxury items. • Students identify television/radio commercials and newspaper/magazine ads that are misleading. • Students quiz each other with flash cards that picture luxury and necessary items regarding the necessity of having the item.	• Parents and/or peers discuss which items are necessities and which are luxuries. • Parents and/or peers take the student shopping and ask the student to indicate several items that are luxury and necessary items.
4. Determine amount of money saved by buying sale items.	• Present to class various sale advertisements from newspapers. • Students distinguish between regular and sale prices of advertised items in newspaper ads. • Students plan a shopping trip based on selection of sale items. • Class discusses the fact that although money is generally saved when buying sale items, often these items are not returnable (e.g., final sale). • Students compute cost of two identical shopping lists, one using regular prices and one using sale prices, to illustrate savings obtained through wise use of "sales." • Students with each other will identify items on sale in the newspaper, the items' regular prices, and the amount of money saved as a result of being on sale.	• Parents review sale advertisements with the student. • Parents plan grocery shopping with the student, incorporating sale items. • Consumer education expert gives presentation.
5. Compare prices of an item in three stores.	• Students develop a list of five different grocery items and compare items' prices from three different grocery store newspaper advertisements. • Students take a field trip to three different grocery stores, indicate the items' prices from lists developed in the preceding activity, and discuss with each other the store that had the lowest price per item. • Class discusses cost comparison buying practices.	• Parents and/or peers and student discuss selection of the lowest price from three newspaper grocery store advertisements for several identical items. • Parents and/or peers take the student shopping in three different grocery stores and point out any price differences for identical items. • Parents and/or peers and student discuss family cost comparison buying practices.

Domain: Daily Living Skills
Competency: 1. Managing Personal Finances
Subcompetency: 3. Keep Basic Financial Records

Objectives	Activities/Strategies	Adult/Peer Roles
1. Construct a monthly personal budget for your present income.	• Students develop a list of budget expenditures (housing expenses, rent, food, bills, loans, etc.). • Students develop a list of income sources. • Class discusses sources of income and expenditures that should be included in a monthly budget. • Students develop a tentative monthly budget that includes all sources of income and expenditures (housing expenses, rent, food, bills, loans, etc.) • Students are given hypothetical financial information and must devise a budget that fits the information. • Students keep receipts of expenses such as medical, electric, gas, and entertainment. • Students keep a record of their income and major expenses for one week. • Students visit a store where they "purchase" particular items within a hypothetical budget. • In class activities, students list purchases to fit within a budget using ads and catalogs as bases for planning.	• Students participate with parents in constructing the family's budget. • Parents require the student to maintain a budget for a given period. • Budget counselor from a local community agency demonstrates budgeting techniques. • Parents and/or peers review with student the previous month's budget and its outcomes.
2. Identify financial information and financial records that should be retained.	• Students construct posters with examples of information that should be retained (warranties, sales slips, bills, contracts, leases, wage information, etc.). • Teacher states a situation in which the collection of forms is necessary, and the students develop a list of the necessary forms to provide. • Class discusses appropriate retention and storage procedures for financial information.	• Parents show the student what financial information they retain. • Financial counselor provides information for future planning, tax purposes, receipts of purchase, etc.
3. Record personal major income and expenses for 1 month.	• Students record all major income and expenditures for a month. • Class discusses advantages of maintaining records of income and expenses. • Students discuss business bookkeeping and how businesses use such information in their planning.	• Parents demonstrate how records help them plan for major purchases.
4. Calculate balances of major debts.	• Students use established debts or mock purchases to calculate balances after regular payments. • Class discusses time payment plans and procedures.	• Students participate with parents while paying bills to see calculation of balances of major debts. • Credit representative demonstrates how time payments operate.

Objectives	Activities/Strategies	Adult/Peer Roles
5. List basic terms used in keeping financial records	• Class discusses basic financial record-keeping terms. • Students develop a list of the basic financial record-keeping terms from a devised monthly personal budget.	• Parents discuss basic financial record-keeping concepts with student. • Parents review financial record statements with student.

Domain: Daily Living Skills
Competency: 1. Managing Personal Finances
Subcompetency: 4. Calculate and Pay Taxes

Objectives	Activities/Strategies	Adult/Peer Roles
1. Know types of taxes normally assessed in the geographic area.	• Class develops a display board showing the different types of taxes, using magazine pictures, drawings, and actual items. • Class members develop a quiz game by pasting pictures on flash cards representing the different types of taxes. • Class members play the quiz game they developed by displaying the cards, one at a time, to the student, and asking the student to guess which type of tax is appropriate for the picture.	• Parents identify occasions in which they pay taxes on particular items. • Local Internal Revenue Service Representative or County Tax Collector gives class lecture using a 1040 Short Tax Form as a reference.
2. Know penalties and deadlines for the payment of taxes.	• Class assembles literature relating to common taxes and their deadlines. • Class discusses the rationale for paying taxes, tax exceptions, late payments, failure to pay taxes, and the penalties established for late payments or failure to pay taxes. • Students take a field trip to IRS office.	• Parents notify the student when tax notices are received and discuss deadlines and exceptions. • Parents discuss their attitudes about paying taxes with students and the assumed consequences for not paying taxes or for the misrepresentation of income. • Guest speaker from the IRS or from a local income tax preparation office gives a presentation.
3. Know sources of assistance for the filing of taxes.	• Class discusses the advantages of soliciting assistance in filing income taxes. • Students are to locate sources of assistance for filing taxes (e.g. telephone book, yellow pages). • Students take a field trip to tax assistance services. • Class discusses how to find assistance, such as agencies, lawyers, and accountants.	• Parents identify their sources of tax assistance. • Representatives of tax agencies give demonstration.
4. Complete a 1040 tax form.	• Students establish a mock taxation system: file taxes, audit returns, penalize noncompliance, compute refunds, etc. • Students practice on tax forms (W2, 1040EZ, 1040, 1040A, state tax form). • Class discusses advantages of completing tax forms.	• Students should observe parents filling out family's tax forms. • Parents show the student their previously completed tax forms. • Local Internal Revenue Service Representative gives working demonstration of completion of tax forms.

Domain: Daily Living Skills
Competency: 1. Managing Personal Finances
Subcompetency: 5. Use Credit Responsibly

Objectives	Activities/Strategies	Adult/Peer Roles
1. Identify resources for obtaining a loan.	• Class lists possible reasons for applying for loans. • Class discusses difference between necessities and luxuries as they apply to filing for a loan. • Class identifies all sources of loans. • Class discusses the disadvantages of dealing with a "loan shark." • Students clip newspaper ads advertising sources of loans and then develop a poster of these sources of loans. • Students take field trip to the bank and receive information on loans and loan applications.	• Parents and students locate loan advertisements in the newspaper. • Parents and/or peers accompany students to banks or credit institutions and obtain loan information and applications. • Representatives from lending institutions discuss criteria for obtaining a loan, collateral, interest, etc.
2. Name advantages and disadvantages of using credit cards.	• Students obtain credit card applications from banks and lending institutions. • Students identify and discuss terms and conditions listed on credit card applications. • Class discusses the advantages, disadvantages, and responsibilities of using credit cards.	• Parents assist students in identifying key words or terms listed on credit card application forms (e.g., interest charges) • Parents discuss the responsibilities of credit card usage (e.g., payments, consequences of lost or stolen cards). • Representatives from banks discuss procedures for obtaining credit cards and the responsibilities of using them.
3. Complete a loan application.	• Students obtain loan applications from banks and other lending institutions and discuss loan terms with loan officer. • Students identify terms found on loan applications (e.g., rate of interest). • Students create a poster listing and defining loan application terms. • Students review and contrast terms identified on loan applications. • Students role-play the interaction between a loan officer and customer. • Students complete a loan application.	• Parents and student discuss procedures for obtaining a loan. • Parents accompany students to lending institutions to pick up loan applications. • Parents review loan applications with students to identify terms and conditions of loan applications (e.g., interest charges). • Representatives from lending institutions discuss the procedures for obtaining loans.

DAILY LIVING SKILLS

Domain: Daily Living Skills
Competency: 1. Managing Personal Finances
Subcompetency: 6. Use Banking Services

Objectives	Activities/Strategies	Adult/Peer Roles
1. Open a checking account.	• Students make a poster listing the process of opening a checking account (e.g., know social security number). • Students establish a "bank" and role-play the step-by-step procedures of opening a checking account. • Students take a field trip to a local bank and go through all the mechanics of opening a checking account.	• Parents inform student of needed information and procedures for opening a checking account. • Students observe parents paying bills by check and recording them in the checkbook log. • Bank personnel discuss the procedures for opening a checking account and the advantages of paying by check. • Parent assists student in opening a checking account (if financially feasible). • Parents allow student to make supervised transactions with their private banks.
2. Open a savings account.	• Students take a field trip to a local bank and go through all the mechanics of opening a savings account. • Students list on a poster the procedures of opening a savings account (e.g., know social security card number). • Students establish a "bank" and role play the step-by-step procedures of opening a savings account.	• Parents inform student of needed information and procedures for opening a savings account. • Parents help the student practice saving at home by establishing a home "savings account." • Bank personnel discuss the procedures for opening a savings account and the concept of interest. • Parent assists student in opening a bank savings account (if financially feasible). • Parents allow the student to make supervised transactions with their private banks.
3. Write checks, make deposits, and record checking transactions.	• Students take a field trip to a bank to discuss procedures to follow when writing checks, making deposits, and recording checking account transactions. • Students list on a poster the process of writing checks, making deposits, and recording transactions. • Class practices with mock checks, deposit slips, check registers, and monthly bank statements. • Class discusses the importance of accurate checking account record keeping. • Class devises mock checking system and students use checks to purchase classroom items.	• Parents inform the student of the procedures for writing checks, making deposits, and recording transactions. • Parents discuss with the student the family's checking account transactions and recording. • Bank personnel discuss the procedures for writing checks, making deposits, and recording transactions. • Parents assist student in making an actual transaction and in record keeping. • Parents involve the student in balancing the family's checking account.
4. Make deposits and withdrawals, and record savings transactions.	• Class establishes a mock bank and students practice transacting and recording with simulated money. • Class discusses interest rates and penalties.	• Parents review savings records and record transactions with the student. • Parents and students simulate or make actual bank deposits and withdrawals, and record savings transactions. • Guest speaker from a local bank talks to class.

Domain: Daily Living Skills
Competency: 2. Selecting and Managing a Household
Subcompetency: 7. Maintain Home Exterior/Interior

Objectives	Activities/Strategies	Adult/Peer Roles
1. Identify basic appliances and tools used in exterior maintenance.	• Students list common tools used in outside home maintenance. • Students construct a scrapbook or bulletin board with pictures of these tools. • Students take turns identifying flash card pictures of exterior appliances and tools.	• Parents and/or peers identify tools they commonly use for outside home maintenance. • Parents and/or peers ask student to identify these tools. • Member of home maintenance business demonstrates routine materials, tools, and types of jobs.
2. List routine cleaning and maintenance activities.	• Students work in pairs devising a list of basic interior and exterior housekeeping activities (e.g., wash/dry dishes, wash windows, take out the garbage, use a vacuum cleaner, operate garbage disposal, sweep floor, dust furniture, mow lawn). • Students take a field trip to a "mini-maid" type business or to hotel/motel to discuss routine housekeeping activities.	• Parents assist the student in making a list of housecleaning and maintenance activities in their home. • Parents supervise the student in performing household tasks. • Personnel from housecleaning business discuss the routine activities required in cleaning houses.
3. Outline a weekly housekeeping routine.	• Class discusses the procedures involved in housekeeping and the proper sequence in which they should be done. • Class discusses what housekeeping jobs need to be completed daily, weekly, and less frequently. • Students work in pairs to discuss and plan a routine which allows a scheduling of regular household tasks (e.g., floors washed and waxed every other Saturday, television dusted every other day, etc.)	• Parents explain to the student their own housekeeping routine and encourage the student to devise his or her own routine. • Maintenance persons (from business, motels, schools) explain their tools and their routine to the class.
4. Identify the uses of common household cleaning products and equipment.	• Students look through magazines and identify cleaning accessories. • Students construct a bulletin board which shows different cleaners and their specific uses.	• Parents have the student choose the proper cleaners for various cleaning jobs, and then demonstrate their use. • Member of a home cleaning business provides a demonstration of routine, materials, tools, and types of jobs.

DAILY LIVING SKILLS

Domain: Daily Living Skills
Competency: 2. Selecting and Managing a Household
Subcompetency: 8. Use Basic Appliances and Tools

Objectives	Activities/Strategies	Adult/Peer Roles
1. Name common appliances and tools found in the home and tell how each is used.	• Students look through magazines and cut out what they think are essential appliances. • Students construct a bulletin board representing the major appliances and tools found in the home. • Students take a field trip to an appliance store and observe demonstrations of appliance and tool usage. • Students construct a mock room or store of appliances.	• Parents introduce and demonstrate to the student all the appliances in the home. • Parents discuss what basic appliances and tools may be lacking in the home.
2. Demonstrate appropriate use of basic appliances and tools.	• Class lists on a chalkboard the appliances and tools found in the home and in the appliance store. • Students construct a mock room or store of appliances and tools and demonstrate their use to the class. • Students role-play using various appliances and tools not demonstrated in class.	• Parents and/or peers demonstrate how to use various appliances. • Parents let the student use as many different tools as possible within the home. • Maintenance personnel demonstrate various tools appropriate to their jobs and their use in the home.
3. Name safety procedures to follow when using appliances and tools.	• Class lists safety procedures on chalkboard or that are necessary when using appliances and tools. • Students construct a bulletin board which illustrates the do's and don't's of several tools and appliances. • Class is shown the proper way to handle appliances and tools.	• Parents demonstrate proper maintenance of tools. • Parents discuss the question of safety in relation to using appliances and tools.
4. Perform basic home care tasks.	• Class lists on chalkboard the minor repairs a person should be able to make at home (e.g., lights, locks, painting, leaky and clogged pipes, etc.). • Students take field trip to several repair shops and local hardware stores for repair demonstrations. • Students work in teams on a repair problem. • Students role-play actual performance of maintenance or repair jobs (e.g., grass cutting, painting).	• Parents and/or peers work through a repair job. • Small-appliance repair person demonstrates basic home repairs. • Parents involve students in home maintenance or repair jobs.

Domain: Daily Living Skills
Competency: 2. Selecting and Managing a Household
Subcompetency: 9. Select Adequate Housing

Objectives	Activities/Strategies	Adult/Peer Roles
1. List personal or family housing requirements, including space, location, and yard.	• In a group activity students identify and list basic requirements of adequate housing (i.e., shelter, living space, cooking and toilet facilities, location, neighborhood, house and yard size, etc.). • Class discusses what needs are important for the student and his or her family (e.g., number of bedrooms). • Class discusses housing needs for hypothetical situations (role-playing, simulation).	• Parents discuss reasons for buying or renting their dwelling. • Parents discuss with students what they might consider in renting or buying a house.
2. Identify different types of housing available in the community.	• Class discusses the different types of habitation (i.e., house, duplex, apartment, trailer). • Students construct a bulletin board displaying different kinds of habitations. • Students identify representative habitation in the community through newspaper ads and other media listings. • Students, using the housing/rental advertisements section of the newspaper, select several appropriate personal housing options.	• Parents show the student different types of dwellings. • Parents/peers supervise a student phoning for information about habitation. • Realtor discusses basic housing options offered in the community.
3. Identify advantages and disadvantages of different types of housing.	• Class discusses advantages and disadvantages of owning and renting (i.e., upkeep, cost, taxes, etc.). • Students develop a personal list of specifications for adequate housing, and make a comparison with advantages and disadvantages of various housing options. • Class takes field trip to local real estate companies to learn about advantages, disadvantages, and differences between various types of housing.	• Parents discuss with the student the various types of habitation available in the community. • Panel of peers or young adults discusses their choices of renting or buying. • Realtor presents information concerning the selection of different housing options.
4. Identify procedures for renting a house or apartment.	• Students are given a presentation of procedures for renting a house, signing a lease, paying rent, etc. • Students role-play the rental of an apartment or house. • Students take field trips to various types of homes and apartments for rent. • Students take field trips to real estate offices' rental departments.	• Parents obtain a copy of a rental agreement and discuss it with the student. • Real estate rental agent discusses procedures for renting and locating appropriate rental units. • Landlords explain their expectations and procedures.

DAILY LIVING SKILLS

Objectives	Activities/Strategies	Adult/Peer Roles
5. Identify procedures for buying a house.	• Students are given a presentation on procedures of securing a mortgage, making mortgage payments, making down payments, and paying taxes. • Students role-play the procedures involved in buying a home. • Students visit various homes for sale. • Students take field trips to real estate offices or home mortgage offices of local banks or lending agencies.	• Parents discuss with the student their reasons for buying a home. • Parents explain to the student the financial responsibilities involved in owning a home. • Real estate agent explains the procedures involved in purchasing a home. • Panel of peers or young adults presents their experiences in buying a home.

Domain: Daily Living Skills
Competency: 2. Selecting and Managing a Household
Subcompetency: 10. Set Up Household

Objectives	Activities/Strategies	Adult/Peer Roles
1. Describe procedures for connecting utility services.	• Class lists on chalkboard the types of utility services they utilize in their homes. • Students copy from the telephone directories the names and phone numbers of local companies that provide utility services. • Students take field trip to local utility companies to acquire information regarding utility service agreement contracts (e.g., installment deposits, delinquent fees, rates per month). • Class lists on chalkboard the procedures for connecting utilities. • Students role-play connecting/installation service agreement, telephone conversation, or in-person visit between utility service representatives and themselves. • Students complete the sample utility agreement contracts.	• Parents discuss with student the utilities used in the home. • Parents discuss and show student their records of utility installation agreements. • Utility service representative explains the procedures for utility service installation.
2. Acquire or ensure presence of basic household items.	• Class lists on chalkboard the general household items found in their homes. • Students construct a bulletin board of basic household items. • Class lists on chalkboard the stores where one can purchase the basic household items.	• Parents and student identify basic household items in the house. • Parents and student visit stores that sell basic household items.
3. Acquire or ensure presence of furniture and major appliances.	• Class lists on chalkboard the furniture and major appliances in the home. • Students construct a bulletin board displaying furniture and major appliances required to set up a home. • Class lists on chalkboard the stores in which one can purchase furniture and appliances.	• Parents and student identify furniture and major appliances in the house. • Parents and student visit stores that sell furniture and major appliances.

Domain: Daily Living Skills
Competency: 2. Selecting and Managing a Household
Subcompetency: 11. Maintain Home Grounds

Objectives	Activities/Strategies	Adult/Peer Roles
1. Perform common home mainte-nance and repairs (e.g., grass cutting, painting, bush trim-ming, etc.	• Students are shown films and demonstra-tions of common home maintenance or repair jobs. • Class discusses why and how often each of these jobs should be performed. • Students construct a bulletin board with pictures of various types of home mainte-nance and repair. • Students role-play actual performance of maintenance or repair jobs. • Class discusses the occasions when expert assistance is necessary or preferable.	• Parents identify the most common types of home maintenance. • School maintenance personnel demonstrate tools and procedures. • Parents involve the student in home mainte-nance or repair jobs. • Members of home maintenance businesses speak to class.

Domain: Daily Living Skills
Competency: 3. Caring for Personal Needs
Subcompetency: 12. Demonstrate Knowledge of Physical Fitness, Nutrition, and Weight

Objectives	Activities/Strategies	Adult/Peer Roles
1. Know ways nutrition relates to health.	• Students identify what foods build a partic-ular part of the body (e.g., milk builds teeth). • Class discusses the components of a bal-anced meal and indicates how the meal will make a body healthier (e.g., the beans in the meal contain vitamin B which is good for the nervous system). • Class discusses the relationship of height and weight to nutrition. • Class discusses the basic principles of food metabolism. • Each student keeps a personal log of height, weight, and measurements.	• Dietician discusses eating from the four basic food groups and how they relate to good health. • Member of Weight Watchers or Community Health Department representative discusses nutrition and obesity problems.
2. Know a meal balanced for nutritional and caloric content.	• Teacher displays foods from major food groups, and explains what each food does for the body. • Class constructs a chart of a balanced diet for all three meals, using magazine pictures or drawings. • Teachers lists the best foods to eat when attempting to lose weight. • Class discusses the body's need for proper nutrition.	• Dietician presents community resource information regarding the basic food groups. • Dietician explains procedure for determin-ing appropriate daily caloric intake per food groups. • Parents explain to the student how the fam-ily's nutritional needs are met.

DAILY LIVING SKILLS

Objectives	Activities/Strategies	Adult/Peer Roles
3. Know ways in which exercise relates to health.	• Class examines pictures of physically fit and unfit persons and discusses appearances, energy level, longevity, etc. • Class tours a physical fitness club. • Class discusses the emotional rewards of physical fitness. • Class discusses an appropriate regimen of physical exercise. • Class discusses the need for rest in a physical fitness program. • Class lists on chalkboard the ways exercise relates to healthy living.	• Community recreation personnel or coach or nurse discusses personal and family fitness. • Student and parents conduct family physical fitness program.
4. Identify and demonstrate correct ways of performing common physical exercises.	• Class lists on chalkboard the common physical exercises. • Students are shown the proper execution of push-ups, sit-ups, toe touches, chinning, leg lifts, etc., with an explanation of what body parts are affected by the exercises. • Students construct performance charts that record progress on particular exercises. • Students demonstrate correct ways of performing physical exercises. • Class tours a physical fitness club.	• Local athlete demonstrates exercises he or she uses in preparation for his or her own sport. • Parents encourage student to develop a home exercise routine.

Domain: Daily Living Skills
Competency: 3. Caring for Personal Needs
Subcompetency: 13. Exhibit Proper Grooming and Hygiene

Objectives	Activities/Strategies	Adult/Peer Roles
1. Demonstrate basic aspects of proper hygiene.	• Class discusses the areas of the body to be cleaned when bathing and showering. • Class lists on chalkboard the daily hygienic activities. • Class identifies and discusses the areas of the body that need to be specially groomed, and the grooming products. • Class discusses the necessity of proper hygiene for various parts of the body. • Class discusses the need for oral hygiene. • Students demonstrate the appropriatte hygiene techniques.	• Visiting nurse emphasizes the importance in caring for all body parts, including personal body parts. • Parents assist students in mastering hygiene techniques. • Dentist or dental hygienist emphasizes the importance of proper oral hygiene.

DAILY LIVING SKILLS

Objectives	Activities/Strategies	Adult/Peer Roles
2. Identify proper grooming.	• Class is given demonstration of grooming with grooming products (e.g., nail clippers and nail file, hairbrush, etc.). • Males are shown the proper use of shaving cream, razor, electric razor, etc. • Females are shown the proper use of shaving cream, razor, electric razor, hair curlers, perfume, make-up, etc. • Class is given demonstration of cleaning ears with cotton tipped swabs (i.e., Q-Tips), removing particles from eyes, etc. • Class is given demonstration of proper use of toothbrush, dental floss, gum massage, and water pick. • Class lists on chalkboard the procedures for shampooing and drying hair.	• Parents and/or peers model appropriate grooming. • Beautician or hair stylist demonstrates appropriate grooming. • Parents allow students to purchase grooming aids (i.e., shampoo, deodorant, cologne, etc.). • Parents observe and record whether student is brushing teeth properly.
3. Identify proper products for hygiene and where to obtain them.	• Students clip advertisements from magazines regarding products used to maintain proper hygiene. • Class lists on chalkboard the products used to maintain proper hygiene (i.e., toothbrush, shampoo, cotton tipped swabs, dental floss, etc.). • Class lists on chalkboard the names of stores where hygiene products can be found. • Class constructs bulletin board showing pictures of products related to proper hygiene.	• Parents and student discuss hygiene products found in the home. • Parents and student purchase hygiene products. • Health care professional discusses hygiene products and where to obtain them.
4. Identify proper products for grooming and where to obtain them.	• Students clip advertisements from magazines regarding products used to maintain proper grooming. • Class lists on chalkboard the products used to maintain proper grooming (i.e., hairbrush, nail clipper, etc.). • Class lists on chalkboard the names of stores where grooming products can be found. • Class constructs bulletin board showing pictures of products related to proper grooming.	• Parents and student discuss grooming products found in the home. • Parents and student look for grooming products carried in stores. • Beautician or cosmetologist and health care professional discuss grooming products and where to obtain them.

Domain: Daily Living Skills
Competency: 3. Caring for Personal Needs
Subcompetency: 14. Dress Appropriately

Objectives	Activities/Strategies	Adult/Peer Roles
1. List clothing appropriate for different weather conditions.	• Students clip pictures of clothing articles and paste them on flash cards. • Class constructs a bulletin board illustrating the major types of seasonal clothing. • Students identify various workers in the community who dress according to weather conditions (i.e., mail carriers, highway repair workers, construction workers, etc.). • Class lists on chalkboard the clothing appropriate for different weather conditions.	• Parents quiz student on appropriate clothing for weather conditions. • Parents take the student on shopping trips, pointing out the variety of seasonal clothing. • Clothes salesperson explains appropriate clothes for different weather conditions.
2. List clothing appropriate for different activities.	• Class lists on chalkboard the variety of occasions that require specific forms of dress. • Class collects pictures from magazines and newspapers depicting people dressed for particular occasions. • Teacher makes lists of clothing and events, and the students match clothing with event. • Students choose appropriate clothes for hypothetical situations. • Class has a fashion show to demonstrate appropriate clothing.	• Salespersons (males and females) from clothing stores address the class on the variety of clothing for particular occasions. • Student observes how parents dress for particular occasions.
3. Given an occasion, choose the appropriate clothing to be worn.	• Students select from magazines and catalogs the appropriate clothing for a simulated occasion. • Students make a collage of inappropriate clothing for specific occasions. • Class discusses clothing articles that "go together" appropriately.	• Parents discuss appropriate clothing selection. • Parents demonstrate to students their clothing selection for certain occasions.

Domain: Daily Living Skills
Competency: 3. Caring for Personal Needs
Subcompetency: 15. Demonstrate Knowledge of Common Illness, Prevention, and Treatment

Objectives	Activities/Strategies	Adult/Peer Roles
1. Identify major symptoms of common illnesses.	• Students construct a chart depicting symptoms of particular illnesses. • Students discuss how they feel when they have different illnesses. • Students role-play doctor and patient discussing symptoms of common illnesses.	• Parents or peers assist students in recording symptoms. • Local paramedics discuss their roles in dealing with illnesses. • Member of Health Department discusses community measures to combat disease.

DAILY LIVING SKILLS

Objectives	Activities/Strategies	Adult/Peer Roles
2. State how cleanliness is related to health.	• Class discusses the relationship between cleanliness and illness. • Students are shown the techniques of dish-washing as a preventative measure. • Class discusses the necessity of bathing regularly. • Class discusses the need for cleaning a cut or wound.	• Nurse or paramedic discusses cleanliness. • Speaker from Public Health Service discusses sanitation and personal cleanliness. • Parents instruct student of the need for cleanliness.
3. Locate sources of assistance with medical problems.	• Students go on a field trip to a local hospital. • Students learn the location of medical facilities in the area. • Students are asked to demonstrate how to obtain emergency assistance by telephone. • Class discusses the availability of medical specialists. • Students play a matching game in which they identify the doctor to use for particular kinds of problems. • Students identify community clinics, hospitals, and agencies that assist citizens.	• Doctor or nurse discusses functions of hospital and office services. • Parent instructs student on how to obtain emergency medical assistance by telephone. • Parents place emergency numbers near the telephone.
4. Identify dosage information from a medicine bottle label.	• Students take a field trip to a drug store. • Class discusses the information written on prescription labels. • Class discusses the differences between prescription and nonprescription medications. • Class discusses common terms used on prescription labels (i.e., tablespoon-tbls., teaspoon-tsp, daily, etc.). • Class brings several empty medicine containers to school and discusses the meanings of the labels. • Class makes up their own prescription labels and places them on the empty medicine containers. • Class discusses the precautions listed on medicine bottle and the importance of taking the prescribed dosages.	• Doctor or nurse discusses medications available for home use and the importance of taking prescribed dosages of medication. • Local druggist discusses the functions of home medications. • Parents show students what medications are kept in the home. • Parents discuss with student the labels found on medicine bottles in the home.
5. List common medicines found in the home and their uses.	• Class lists on chalkboard the common medicines their families keep in the home and identify one use for each medication. • Students construct a bulletin board of over-the-counter medicines that should be kept in their homes for minor illnesses and accidents. • Class role-plays contracting minor illnesses and accidents and the prescription of the appropriate medication.	• Parents discuss with the student the common medicines found in their home and their appropriate uses. • Pharmacist discusses the use of various medicines for minor illnesses and accidents.

DAILY LIVING SKILLS

Objectives	Activities/Strategies	Adult/Peer Roles
6. Demonstrate basic first aid techniques.	• Class discusses first aid techniques. • Techniques for specific emergencies are demonstrated. • Students role-play administering first aid to each other. • Students list situations that may require immediate assistance (camping, at home, at the beach, etc.). • Students identify vital information for emergency situations.	• Nurse or paramedic demonstrates first aid. • Members of emergency squad present their equipment and methods and discuss their training. • Red Cross training course is delivered by certified instructor. • Parents practice first aid techniques with the student at home.

Domain: Daily Living Skills
Competency: 3. Caring for Personal Needs
Subcompetency: 16. Practice Personal Safety

Objectives	Activities/Strategies	Adult/Peer Roles
1. Identify ways to secure home from intruders.	• Students discuss the purpose of securing one's home from intruders. • Students discuss methods of securing their home from intruders. • Students discuss other ways to deter intruders (pets, burglar alarms). • Class lists on chalkboard the ways to secure home from intruders.	• Parents discuss with student the risks involved in not securing one's home. • Parents and student discuss methods used in the home to secure home from intruders. • Neighborhood watch groups discuss the purpose and methods of home security. • Police officer explains techniques to secure home from intruders.
2. Identify things to do to avoid personal assault.	• Students define personal assault. • Class lists on chalkboard the activities which increase the chances of personal assault (hitchhiking, walking alone late at night, etc.). • Class lists on the chalkboard activities that reduce the possibility of assault (walking with a friend, carrying pocket change for telephone calls in case of emergency, parking your car in lighted areas at night, etc.). • Students role-play an assault situation and discuss what could have been done to avoid the situation.	• Parents discuss with student ways that people can be assaulted in the neighborhood. • Parents discuss precautionary measures they take to prevent assault. • Parents and student visit with law enforcement agency concerning techniques to avoid assault. • Parents and student visit a self-defense school. • Self-defense representative demonstrates self-defense to students. • Law officer discusses ways to avoid personal assault.
3. Identify and demonstrate self-protection or self-defense behaviors and techniques.	• Self-defense instructor discusses and demonstrates self-protection and self-defense behaviors. • Students discuss protection and defense concepts, and, with approval and instruction, practice self-defense behaviors with self-defense instructor. • Class lists on the chalkboard self-protection or self-defense behaviors. • Students take a field trip to a self-defense school.	• Parents demonstrate to student how they believe they would defend themselves. • Parents and students visit self-defense school. • Self-defense instructor demonstrates self-defense and self-protection behaviors.

Objectives	Activities/Strategies	Adult/Peer Roles
4. Identify precautions to follow when dealing with strangers.	• Students discuss do's and don't's when meeting strangers. • Students take turns simulating interactions with strangers and then evaluating each other. • Students discuss what strangers could do to them if they are not cautious. • Students role-play appropriate behaviors upon meeting strangers. • Class lists on chalkboard precautions to follow when dealing with strangers.	• Parents and/or peers discuss the do's and don't's of meeting strangers. • Parents role-play with the student how they behave with strangers.
5. Identify potential safety hazards in the home.	• Students construct posters or a bulletin board with magazine pictures of poisonous substances. • Class discusses the dangers of swallowing these poisonous substances. • Students discuss the significance of locating and checking electrical outlets and cords, gas appliances, and light switches for safety. • Students discuss the dangers of electrical shock. • Students are shown what constitutes a household hazard. • Students maintain a scrapbook of pictures of household hazards. • Students collect a notebook of sources to correct hazards.	• Parents point out poisonous substances in the home. • Paramedics discuss poisonous hazards and individual responsibilities. • Representatives from the public utilities give home hazard presentations. • Gas company and electrical company representatives give presentation concerning potential utility hazards. • Parents discuss potential hazards in the home (e.g., stairways, electrical outlets, and flammables). • Insurance agent discusses household hazards and means of prevention.
6. List and demonstrate actions to take in the event of an emergency.	• Class discusses first aid techniques. • Techniques for specific emergencies are demonstrated. • Students role-play administering first aid to each other. • Class lists on chalkboard the vital information to be conveyed in emergency situations. • Students simulate emergency procedures at school (e.g., fire, tornado, etc.). • Students take field trip to Red Cross Emergency Center. • Students are shown how to extinguish different types of fires. • Students plan evacuation procedures for given situations (their own house, hypothetical situations, etc.). • Class discusses emergency phone numbers and procedures for summoning emergency assistance.	• Parents practice emergency drills in the home. • Nurse or paramedic demonstrates first aid. • Emergency squad presents its equipment and methods and discusses its training. • Red Cross instructor delivers training course. • Parents practice first aid techniques with the student at home. • Parents identify possible sources of fire in the home, as well as how to prevent and extinguish them. • Parents show the student the best means for exiting various parts of the house in the event of serious fire. • Family practices fire drills. • Parents discuss severe weather conditions and safety procedures.

DAILY LIVING SKILLS

Domain: Daily Living Skills
Competency: 4. Raising Children and Meeting Marriage Responsibilities
Subcompetency: 17. Demonstrate Physical Care for Raising Children

Objectives	Activities/Strategies	Adult/Peer Roles
1. List physical responsibilities involved in child care.	• Class lists on chalkboard the responsibilities in raising children. • Students role-play a family situation with a child, which includes diapering, feeding, stimulation, etc. • Class discusses economic responsibilities of family life. • Class discusses the importance of prenatal care and nutrition.	• Parents identify their responsibilities for maintaining the welfare of children. • Parents assist student in identifying those occasions in which children need assistance from older family members. • Staff from child care center explains physical responsibilities involved in child care.
2. Given a hypothetical situation, demonstrate basic safety measures for a child who has ingested poison or is severely cut.	• Class identifies poisons found in the home. • Class discusses safety hazards for children in the home (e.g., medicine bottles, razor blades, detergent, etc.). • Student role-plays emergency situation and procedures for a child who has ingested poison or has been cut severely. • Class lists on chalkboard the emergency procedures for a child who has ingested poison or has been cut severely. • Class discusses obtaining emergency assistance for a child who has ingested poison or has been cut severely. • Students take a field trip to area poison emergency center.	• Parents instruct the student in the proper storage of poisonous substances, medications, and sharp objects. • Parents discuss with student the measures they take when a child ingests poison or is cut severely. • Nurse or paramedic demonstrates immediate first aid for a child who has ingested poison or has been cut severely.
3. Identify common childhood illnesses and a symptom and treatment for each.	• Students construct a "symptom chart" for each common disease. • Class lists on chalkboard the common childhood illnesses and the symptoms they experienced. • Students practice using thermometers, vaporizers, etc. • Class discusses disease prevention techniques in the home. • Students construct a baby health bulletin board.	• Pediatrician or nurse discusses childhood illnesses. • Nurse assists students in solving hypothetical child health problems. • Nursery personnel describe their methods, experiences, and training.
4. Identify basic stages of child development and a characteristic of each.	• Students observe pictures of children at different developmental levels (infant, toddler, preschool, school age, etc.), and list notable characteristics of children at those levels. • Students go on a field trip to a day-care center, nursery school, Head Start, or public school to observe levels of development. • Class discusses physical growth and development skills. • Class discusses appropriate growth for young children. • Class lists on chalkboard the basic stages of child development.	• Personnel from day-care center discuss growth and development of a child and the impact on the family. • Parents discuss the student's own growth sequence, using photographs of the student at different levels. • Parents encourage the student to observe a child's development.

Objectives	Activities/Strategies	Adult/Peer Roles
5. Identify potential dangers to children outside the home.	• Class discusses several outside-the-home dangers to children (playing with matches, playing in hazardous areas, becoming friendly with strangers, accepting candy or rides from strangers). • Students identify community sources that can assist parents with hazardous conditions or situations. • Class lists, on the chalkboard or newsprint, potential dangers to children outside the home.	• Parents discuss with students safety precautions to take when playing outdoors. • Members of several community agencies (police, fire protection, animal control) discuss hazards and ways to prevent them
6. Demonstrate procedures for care of child's physical health.	• Students are given a demonstration of pre-natal care: medical checkups, proper diet. • Students go on a field trip to a nursery to observe children and techniques of child care. • Basic toilet training techniques are demonstrated. • Students perform proper infant stimulation exercises and identify the reasons for such activities. • Students go on a field trip to a supermarket to select items suitable for infant or child diet. • Proper methods of physically handling infants and children are demonstrated. • Students select appropriate clothing for children relative to the seasons. • Class discusses the need for regular medical checkups for children. • Students practice bathing an infant or child, using a doll in a bassinet or tub. • Class discusses the advantages of breast-feeding and bottle-feeding for infants.	• Pediatrician or nurse from baby clinic discusses ways to enhance child's well being through proper care. • Parents allow the student to assist in taking care of younger family members. • Parents show the student proper methods of feeding, changing, and bathing young children. • Other adults with children encourage the student to observe how they perform certain aspects of child rearing (e.g., breast-feeding, infant stimulation, sickness prevention, etc.).

Domain: Daily Living Skills
Competency: 4. Raising Children and Meeting Marriage Responsibilities
Subcompetency: 18. Know Psychological Aspects of Raising Children

Objectives	Activities/Strategies	Adult/Peer Roles
1. Identify changes when a child enters the family.	• Class discusses children's role in the family. • Students discuss what they feel would be a parent's perception of a child in the family. • Students list ways in which a family serves the needs of children. • Students discuss their feelings and experiences as younger siblings entered the family.	• Parents discuss the effect of a child's entry into the family. • Parents model positive child-rearing behavior in the home. • Child psychologist explains healthy family relationships.

DAILY LIVING SKILLS

Objectives	Activities/Strategies	Adult/Peer Roles
2. Name psychological needs of the child and tell how these can be provided.	• Students describe what they need from their family. • Class discusses the child's needs for love, understanding, physical contact, structure, play, etc. • Students engage in positive interaction with a child and evaluate each other. • Students list emotions and identify them in pictures of children. • Class lists on chalkboard children's psychological needs.	• Personnel from a child guidance center discuss aspects of the child's psychological development. • Parents discuss basic emotional needs with student. • Parents discuss with student how they attempt to meet the psychological needs of their children.
3. Identify parental responsibilities involved in the psychological care of the child.	• Students role-play as parents and list things they must do or be aware of in regard to a child's psychological development (giving love, being consistent in working with the child, etc.). • Class discusses the changes in parent-child relationships as the child gets older and less dependent. • Students discuss how their own relationships with their parents have changed. • Students observe growth patterns of younger siblings. • Students go on a field trip to a day care nursery to observe parent responsibilities as carried out by community agencies. • Class lists on chalkboard the parental responsibilities involved in the psychological care of the children.	• Child psychologist, social worker, and nurse discuss adult responsibilities to children. • Parents discuss with the student their roles as parents. • Representatives from family service agencies discuss effective means of fulfilling adult responsibilities. • Parents identify ways that other adults meet responsibilities with children.
4. Identify common family problems and a way of dealing with each of the problems.	• Students go on a field trip to a child guidance clinic or welfare office. • Class lists agencies that offer assistance to troubled families in the community (e.g., legal services, homemakers, counselors, day care, family mental health). • Students practice locating and contacting assisting persons and agencies. • Class discusses other family members as a source of support and assistance in time of family stress. • Class lists on chalkboard the potential family problems and how they may have been caused (e.g., health problems, child neglect and abuse, developmental problems, separation problems involving death, parent returning to work, divorce, emotional problems, financial stress). • Class discusses possible solutions to the list of potential problems.	• Representatives from a child guidance clinic, day-care, Head Start, welfare, legal services, etc., describe their agency's assistance to families. • Counseling personnel describe problems that can occur in families and offer suggestions for prevention. • Parents discuss kinds of problems that have occurred in the family.

Domain: Daily Living Skills
Competency: 4. Raising Children and Meeting Marriage Responsibilities
Subcompetency: 19. Demonstrate Marriage Responsibilities

Objectives	Activities/Strategies	Adult/Peer Roles
1. Identify reasons for marriage.	• Class discusses the comparisons and differences between being married and being single. • Class has a workshop on decision-making and values clarification. • Students list adjustments they feel would be necessary in marriage. • Class lists on chalkboard the activities a single person engages in to maintain self-sufficiency (i.e., washing clothes, paying bills, cooking, cleaning, working, etc.). • Class lists on chalkboard the activities that are shared by couple (i.e., cleaning, shopping, parenting, etc.). • Class lists on chalkboard the adjustments they feel would be necessary in marriage. • Class discusses conflict resolution in marriage. • Students examine personal characteristics that may be in need of change as an adult, whether married or single.	• Marriage counselor or clergyman discusses the necessity of adjustment in an institute relationship. • Parents discuss with student their adjustments from being single to being married. • Parents discuss the ways in which they adjusted to develop a better relationship.
2. Identify a personal responsibility in marriage.	• Small groups and the class discuss sharing emotions with one's mate. • Class discusses ways in which one person can continue with his own goals without excluding the other. • Class discusses the nature of a commitment to another person. • Class lists on chalkboard the personal responsibilities in marriage.	• Married couples discuss with the class what they consider to be the responsibilities of marriage. • Marriage counselor or social worker discusses ways in which people are able to grow as individuals while being part of a relationship.
3. Identify joint responsibility in marriage.	• Students role-play class members' ideas about the roles of husband and wife in a marriage. • Class discusses the emotional, economic, and social needs shared by both partners. • Class discusses sexual and child rearing responsibilities. • Class receives instruction on open communication about sexual matters, attitudes, etc. • Class discusses the religious and secular values held by marriage partners. • Class lists on chalkboard the joint responsibilities in marriage.	• Married couples discuss with the class what they have felt to be joint responsibilities. • Parents discuss the idea of joint responsibilities with the student. • Marriage counselor discusses difficulties that arise when joint responsibilities go unmet.

Domain: Daily Living Skills
Competency: 5. Buying, Preparing, and Consuming Food
Subcompetency: 20. Purchase Food

Objectives	Activities/Strategies	Adult/Peer Roles
1. Construct a weekly shopping list within a budget.	• Class discusses organizing a shopping list (e.g., weekly essentials, milk, eggs, meat, etc.). • Class lists meats by generic names (beef, poultry, fish, pork, etc.). • Teacher demonstrates constructing a weekly shopping list within a given budget. • Class lists a weekly shopping list on chalkboard. • Students practice making an actual list and discuss their rationale with other students. • Students pretend to buy listed items, based on a given amount of money. • Students develop weekly shopping lists, and on a field trip to a grocery store indicate the prices of the items on their lists.	• Parents explain their shopping list for the week. • Student takes part in actual construction of the list. • Peers or young adults discuss their experience with using a budget. • Parents discuss their weekly budget with the student. • Home economist explains the importance of developing a weekly shopping list within her budget.
2. List characteristics of perishable foods.	• Teacher demonstrates what to look for when purchasing meat, dairy products, vegetables, etc. • Students make a scrapbook of pictures of different foods. • Class discusses seasonal foods and the economics of purchasing them. • Class discusses the expiration dates on perishables (milk, bread, etc.) in grocery stores. • Students are shown how to determine freshness in fruits, vegetables, breads, meats, etc. • Class lists perishable foods on the chalkboard. • Students take field trip to grocery store to identify perishable foods.	• Parents and student go on shopping trips to select fruits, vegetables, meats, etc. • Parents and student discuss seasonal foods and expiration dates. • Parents allow the student to select foods. • Produce or meat department managers of grocery stores discuss quality of perishable foods.
3. Identify types and cuts of meat, fish, and poultry.	• Students are shown the kinds of meat and fish, and the ways to identify different cuts of meat, cost of different cuts, etc. • Students discuss chart from grocery store meat department that displays different cuts of meat and fish. • Students construct a scrapbook of pictures of different kinds of meat and fish. • Students take a field trip to a meat- or fish-packing plant or to a market to examine the types and sizes of cuts. • Students compare nutritional values and costs of various types and cuts of meats (e.g., a roast is as nutritional as a steak but is less costly per pound). • Class lists on chalkboard different types of meat, fish, and poultry.	• Parents discuss different kinds of meat and fish they commonly purchase, including price, cuts, and amount required per person. • Parents help the student identify different cuts of meats through pictures in cookbooks and magazines. • Butcher discusses meats, fish, materials, and training.

Objectives	Activities/Strategies	Adult/Peer Roles
4. Identify how to use newspaper ads to take advantage of sales.	• Class discusses the pros and cons of taking advantage of specials and stores that offer specials. • Students get ads and role-play items for purchase. • Students take field trip to grocery stores to compare regular and sale-priced items. • Students discuss why they would or would not shop at each of the stores.	• Parents explain the use of newspaper ads to select items for weekly purchases. • Representative of consumer products discusses reading food ads. • Students accompany parents on grocery shopping trips to help identify sale and non-sale items.

Domain: Daily Living Skills
Competency: 5. Buying, Preparing, and Consuming Food
Subcompetency: 21. Clean Food Preparation Areas

Objectives	Activities/Strategies	Adult/Peer Roles
1. Identify the importance of personal hygiene in food preparation areas.	• Students discuss reasons for personal cleanliness when around areas where food is prepared. • Students discuss the importance of keeping hands clean and wearing a hairnet or hat when handling food. • Students discuss diseases resulting from contamination of food and poor sanitary conditions. • Students take a field trip to a place where food is prepared to hear firsthand the importance of personal hygiene (e.g., hospital cafeteria, restaurant kitchen). • Class lists on chalkboard the reasons for good personal hygiene in food preparation areas.	• Parents stress personal hygiene when preparing meals. • County health inspector speaks to class on personal hygiene and food preparation.
2. List reasons for cleaning work area and materials after food preparation.	• Class discusses the reasons for cleaning up immediately after a meal (e.g., neatness, cleanliness, health). • Class discusses proper step-by-step procedures involved in clean-up (e.g., wrapping and storing leftovers, clearing table, scraping plates, etc.). • Class lists on chalkboard the reasons for cleaning work area and materials after food preparation.	• Parents explain aftermeal clean-up procedures. • Parents involve student in the actual clean-up process. • Counter personnel or bus boys discuss clean-up procedures.

DAILY LIVING SKILLS

Objectives	Activities/Strategies	Adult/Peer Roles
3. Identify and demonstrate appropriate cleaning procedures.	• Students are shown the procedures used to clean the work area and appliances used in food preparation (e.g., store, kitchen sink, kitchen table, refrigerator, counters, etc.). • Class discusses the type of cleaners (e.g., steel wool, cloths, cleansers, dish soap, etc.) to be used for each job. • Class discusses how often different clean-up jobs must be performed (e.g., daily, weekly, etc.). • Students go on field trip to a cafeteria or restaurant to observe kitchen procedures. • Appropriate cleaning materials are displayed in the class. • Class lists appropriate cleaning procedures on the chalkboard.	• Parents demonstrate proper procedures for cleaning work areas and appliances. • Parents include the student in actual clean-up procedures. • Kitchen personnel of cafeteria or restaurant demonstrate procedures, materials, and appliances.
4. Identify and demonstrate appropriate waste disposal procedures.	• Students discuss materials to be placed in garbage or disposal unit and proper placement in trash cans. • Students discuss how to set out garbage cans for trash pick-up. • Students discuss the consequences of neglect of waste or improper disposal of waste. • Students take part in trash removal and garbage disposal in home economics class or cafeteria. • Class lists on chalkboard the appropriate waste disposal procedures.	• Parents explain to the student how, when, and where to remove different kinds of trash. • Student is given the responsibility of disposing of waste in the appropriate receptacles after meals. • Sanitation personnel discuss proper preparation of trash, as well as their job duties and preparation.

Domain: Daily Living Skills
Competency: 5. Buying, Preparing, and Consuming Food
Subcompetency: 22. Store Food

Objectives	Activities/Strategies	Adult/Peer Roles
1. Identify the need for proper food storage.	• Students discuss the reasons for food storage (e.g., spoilage, disease, bugs, etc.). • Students are shown pictures or other demonstrations of what happens to food that is improperly stored. • Students discuss the consequences of eating spoiled food. • Students make a scrapbook on proper method for storing different types of food. • Classroom bulletin board illustrates food storage. • Class lists on chalkboard the reasons for proper food storage.	• Parents explain to the student the reasons that some foods need refrigeration or storage. • Personnel from a food packaging firm discuss the reasons for proper storage of food.

Objectives	Activities/Strategies	Adult/Peer Roles
2. Identify appropriate food storage techniques.	• Teacher identifies the proper methods for storing food (e.g., wrapping, refrigeration, freezer, etc.). • Students identify the location of food storage. • Students discuss the length of time for storage of food before consumption. • Students construct bulletin board illustrating proper methods of food storage. • Class lists on chalkboard foods that require storage and the techniques for storage. • Students take a field trip to a food package and storage firm.	• Parents demonstrate proper methods for storing different kinds of food. • Parents discuss how long different kinds of foods may be safely stored. • Personnel who work in food packaging and storage discuss methods of training.
3. Identify appearance of foods when they have spoiled.	• Teacher demonstrates different ways to identify spoiled foods (e.g., smell, appearance, taste, etc.). • Students participate in an exercise that asks them to identify spoiled foods. • Students construct bulletin board depicting different types of food spoilage. • Class lists food spoilage indicators on chalkboard.	• Parents explain different ways in which food can be spoiled. • Parents discuss different ways to identify spoiled foods. • Nurse or paramedic demonstrates the dangers of spoiled foods, ways to identify them, and treatment in case one has eaten spoiled food.
4. Identify and demonstrate food storage procedures.	• Students discuss foods which need to be stored. • Students demonstrate the proper food storage procedures for such items as eggs, meat, vegetables, cereals, cakes. • Class lists food storage procedures on chalkboard.	• Parents demonstrate appropriate food storage procedures daily. • Parents assist the student in practicing appropriate food storage procedures. • Cafeteria supervisor discusses proper storage.

DAILY LIVING SKILLS

Domain: Daily Living Skills
Competency: 5. Buying, Preparing, and Consuming Food
Subcompetency: 23. Prepare Meals

Objectives	Activities/Strategies	Adult/Peer Roles
1. Identify food preparation procedures.	• Students are given demonstrations of the preparation of vegetables, meats, fruits, etc. • Students are given demonstrations of the different methods of cooking (e.g., boiling, baking, frying, etc.). • Students take part in actual food preparation. • Students go on a field trip to a school or community kitchen to observe cooking methods. • Students discuss which techniques to use for which foods and why (e.g., frying is faster but adds calories). • Students discuss the importance of proper food preparation techniques (e.g., undercooking or overcooking foods is nutritionally improper). • Class lists on chalkboard the procedures for several food preparation techniques.	• Parents and/or peers demonstrate the preparation of different foods. • Cook demonstrates basic techniques in food preparation.
2. Identify and demonstrate the use of basic appliances and tools.	• Students list kitchen appliances and utensils found in their homes. • Kitchen appliances and utensils and their use are demonstrated. • Students role-play preparation of meals and decide which appliances or utensils to use. • Bulletin board contains pictures of appliances and utensils. • Students go on field trip to the school kitchen. • Class lists on chalkboard the basic appliances and utensils and their uses.	• Parents demonstrate the appliances and utensils in their kitchens. • Cook demonstrates utensils and appliances found in cafeteria or restaurant.

Objectives	Activities/Strategies	Adult/Peer Roles
3. List basic recipe abbreviations and cooking terms.	• Students discuss basic terms such as baste, simmer, marinate, measure, cup, pound, tablespoon, etc., and their abbreviations. • Students discuss wall chart illustrating measures with representative pictures. • Students collect a scrapbook of terms and measures. • Teacher and class demonstrate the basic terms. • Students make flashcards to identify knowledge of food preparation. • Students measure different quantities of liquids and solids. • Teacher demonstrates the use of a recipe card or cookbook in preparing meals. • Students collect recipes from local media and place on bulletin board. • Students follow a set of written instructions in preparing or pretending to prepare a meal. • Class lists on chalkboard the basic recipe abbreviations and cooking terms.	• Parents and/or peers identify terms used in cookbooks and ensure that the students understand what they mean (e.g., baste, simmer, measure, fill, tsp, tbsp, etc.). • Parents or peers demonstrate liquid and solid measures in the kitchen. • Parents encourage the student to do the measuring during actual meal preparation. • Parents or peers demonstrate simple directions in a cookbook or recipe. • Cook discusses the use of recipes.
4. Practice kitchen safety procedures.	• Students compile a scrapbook of the various kitchen hazards and emergencies. • Class discusses safety procedures in food preparation (knife handling, electrical appliance use, turning pot handle to rear of stove, etc.). • Students are shown simple first aid for minor burns. • Students role-play receiving minor burns and applying simple first aid procedures. • Teacher demonstrates how to avoid kitchen fires and how to extinguish different types of fires. • Class lists on chalkboard several kitchen safety procedures.	• Parents demonstrate for the student the hazards that are present in the kitchen, how accidents can happen, and what to do when they happen. • Nurse or paramedic discusses first aid for minor burns.
5. Prepare a full-course meal for one or more people.	• Prepare a complete meal for one or more people. • Students are given a demonstration of the preparation of an entire meal. • Students construct a scrapbook of favorite meals.	• Parents involve the student in actual food preparation and meal planning. • Parents allow the student to plan and prepare simple meals on a regular basis.

DAILY LIVING SKILLS

DAILY LIVING SKILLS

Domain: Daily Living Skills
Competency: 5. Buying, Preparing, and Consuming Food
Subcompetency: 24. Demonstrate Appropriate Eating Habits

Objectives	Activities/Strategies	Adult/Peer Roles
1. Identify the need for proper manners and eating behavior.	• Class discusses why one should display proper eating behaviors. • Proper etiquette and eating behavior are demonstrated (e.g., requesting food, proper use of utensils, placement of napkin, etc.). • Students role-play eating a meal using proper etiquette. • Students take a field trip to a restaurant to practice etiquette. • Class lists on chalkboard the reasons for proper manners and eating behaviors.	• Parents explain their understanding of proper table manners. • Parents demonstrate proper table manners and use of utensils.
2. Identify and demonstrate proper manners and eating behavior at a meal.	• Students are instructed in the proper way to eat a meal (e.g., how to cut meat, serve oneself, pass food, request seconds, etc.). • Students role-play eating a meal. • Students discuss the most and least difficult areas of etiquette experienced during role-playing. • Students design an evaluation checklist of etiquette to be adhered to during meals. • Students eat a meal while being videotaped (tape could be used to correct errors). • Students take a field trip to a local restaurant, eat a meal, and critique each other using guidelines for evaluation designed by the class.	• Parents develop a hierarchy of eating skills and manners for the student; the hierarchy could be used as a checklist of which skills the student already has and which skills he or she needs. • Home economist works with the student and parents on identifying and developing appropriate eating skills.
3. Identify and demonstrate the proper way to set a table and serve food.	• Students are shown the proper methods of setting a table and serving different types of food (e.g., use of hot pads, appropriate serving dishes, how to carve different meats, etc.). • Students role-play setting the table and serving foods. • Class lists the process for setting a table and serving food.	• Parents and/or peers demonstrate the proper methods of setting the table. • Parents and/or peers demonstrate the proper way to serve foods. • Parents involve the student in setting the table and serving meals at home. • Home economist demonstrates serving food.
4. Identify and demonstrate proper manners and eating behavior at a public place.	• Class lists on chalkboard the do's and don'ts of eating at a restaurant (e.g., reading a menu, ordering, tipping, etc.). • Students role-play eating in a restaurant in class. • Class tours different types of restaurants. • Class discusses the prices and kinds of foods served at different types of restaurants. • Class takes a field trip to eat at a local restaurant.	• Parents discuss with student the proper manners to display when dining out. • Parents have the student accompany them when they dine out. • Parents monitor the student's behavior in this situation and correct inappropriate behaviors. • Head waiter discusses the do's and don't's of dining out.

Domain: Daily Living Skills
Competency: 5. Buying, Preparing, and Consuming Food
Subcompetency: 25. Plan and Eat Balanced Meals

Objectives	Activities/Strategies	Adult/Peer Roles
1. List the basic food groups required in each meal.	• Students identify different kinds of food and food products and sort them into food groups. • Class discusses various ways to combine these foods to make a balanced meal. • Students take a field trip to markets to identify food groups. • Dietitian from school explains the use of food groups in school menu. • Class lists on chalkboard the basic food groups required in each meal.	• Parents and student identify different kinds of food and sort them into food groups. • Parents discuss with student the purpose of eating balanced meals. • Parents and student go through list, select foods from food groups, and design a balanced meal. • Students help parents select groceries.
2. Identify appropriate foods eaten at typical daily meals.	• Class constructs bulletin board illustrating food products with food groups. • Class discusses what constitutes a balanced nutritious breakfast, lunch, and dinner. • Class discusses how breakfast, lunch, and dinner are the same and how they are different. • Students make up balanced breakfast, lunch, and dinner menus for an entire week. • Class discusses which foods constitute a good snack and which are junk foods.	• Parents involve the student in weekly menu planning sessions (including grocery shopping). • Dietitian discusses foods used for morning, afternoon, and evening meals and junk foods.
3. Plan a day's meals within a given budget.	• Class discusses the costs of food items. • Teacher explains how to take advantage of specials at the grocery store. • Students are given play money and allowed to shop for weekly food needs at a mock store in class. • Students collect coupons and discuss advantages. • Students are given a fixed budget per day and asked to select foods in planning breakfast, lunch, and dinner within that budget (may use coupons). • Class discusses buying prepared, packaged, or convenience foods versus making food items from scratch.	• Parents involve the student in menu planning and shopping (may use coupons). • Parents give the student money and allow him or her to plan his or her own menu and purchase necessary goods. • Home economist gives tips on meal and menu planning. • Grocery store manager discusses shopping and saving techniques.

DAILY LIVING SKILLS

Domain: Daily Living Skills
Competency: 6. Buying and Caring for Clothing
Subcompetency: 26. Wash/Clean Clothing

Objectives	Activities/Strategies	Adult/Peer Roles
1. Identify the following laundry products and their uses: bleaches, detergents, and fabric softeners.	• Students bring to school magazine pictures of laundry products for a collage. • Teacher demonstrates the major types of laundry products by category and brand name (e.g., bleaches, Clorox; detergents, Tide; softness, Sta-Soft). • Students list on chalkboard which laundry products are used for what purposes. • Demonstrations or films show how each product is best used. • Students role-play choosing the appropriate product for a particular job.	• Parents or peers identify laundry products in their home and how they are used. • Parents allow the student to choose and measure the type of product required for a particular washing.
2. Identify and demonstrate appropriate laundering procedures for different types of clothing.	• Students discuss washing and drying temperatures recommended for specific fabrics. • Class has demonstrations or films of operating a washer and dryer, hand washing, and removing spots from clothing. • Students participate in the above procedures. • Students list on chalkboard the cleaning techniques for certain fabrics (e.g., dry cleaning for wools, etc.). • Students select appropriate laundering products for particular fabrics. • Students read cleaning labels in clothing and sort clothing by types of cleaning techniques required.	• Parents or peers demonstrate how to perform the various laundering procedures. • Laundering expert demonstrates and explains these procedures.
3. Demonstrate use of laundry facilities at a laundromat.	• Students are given a demonstration of coin-operated washers and dryers. • Students take a field trip to a laundromat for a demonstration of the various machines. • Students wash and dry a load of laundry at a laundromat.	• Parents or peers take the student to a laundromat to do laundry. • Laundromat owner explains the various cleaning services available at his or her establishment.

Domain: Daily Living Skills
Competency: 6. Buying and Caring for Clothing
Subcompetency: 27. Purchase Clothing

Objectives	Activities/Strategies	Adult/Peer Roles
1. List basic articles of clothing.	• Students list on chalkboard all articles of clothing that constitute a basic wardrobe (including optional items). • Students discuss what they would want to include in their basic wardrobe. • Students construct a bulletin board depicting basic wardrobe items.	• Parents or peers explain articles of clothing that constitute a basic wardrobe. • Parents or peers have the student make up a list of items he or she would like to have in his or her basic wardrobe. • Seamstress or fashion expert demonstrates different articles of clothing required in a basic wardrobe.

Objectives	Activities/Strategies	Adult/Peer Roles
2. Identify personal body measurements and clothing sizes.	• Teacher demonstrates how body measurements relate to having clothing fit properly. • Students are shown how to determine if an article of clothing fits properly. • Class discusses how measurements can change with growth and weight loss or weight gain. • Students are shown how to identify clothing tags. • Students make lists on chalkboard of personal clothing sizes.	• Parents or peers demonstrate how to take body measurements. • Parents or peers discuss how body measurements can change. • Parents or peers show how to read clothing labels. • Parents and student take trip to clothing store to examine clothing tags and try on merchandise for proper fitting.
3. List major clothing categories by dress, work, casual, sports, school.	• Teacher discusses the purpose of each type of clothing and shows pictures of each type. • Students cut out pictures of people wearing different types of clothing for specific activities. • Students discuss why and when to wear each type of clothing. • Students see films of situations for which each type of clothing might be appropriate.	• Parents or peers discuss the different categories of clothing, and why and when each type may be worn. • Parents or peers help the student identify the characteristics of each type of clothing.
4. Given a hypothetical budget, select a school wardrobe.	• Home economics teacher demonstrates construction of a clothing budget. • Students cut out clothing sale ads and put them on the bulletin board. • Students discuss what items of clothing are most essential for their wardrobe (basic clothing items). • Students use mock store and play money to shop for their wardrobes. • Students discuss the economics of clothing purchases (color selection so various articles can be interchanged to make varied outfits). • Teacher discusses ways to identify good workmanship (hence, longer life) of clothing articles.	• Parents explain their clothing budget. • Student accompanies parents or peers on shopping trips. • Parents help the student plan for a shopping trip by making a list of clothing needs. • Parents explain what comparison shopping means and show examples of this during shopping trip. • Student purchases his or her own clothing when accompanied by a parent or peer. • Peers help the student identify clothing sale ads in the newspaper.
5. State the importance of matching colors and fabrics.	• Teacher discusses with student the images conveyed to others due to one's dress or appearance. • Class discusses feelings of mixing plaids with stripes and other combinations. • Class discusses mixing of fabrics (e.g., cotton, wool, silk, etc.).	• Parents or peers discuss with student the importance of appropriate dress as related to one's image and in gaining respect from others. • Parents assist the student in selecting matching colors and fabrics.

DAILY LIVING SKILLS

Domain: Daily Living Skills
Competency: 6. Buying and Caring for Clothing
Subcompetency: 28. Iron, Mend, and Store Clothing

Objectives	Activities/Strategies	Adult/Peer Roles
1. Identify and demonstrate proper ironing procedures for common fabric.	• Teacher demonstrates proper ironing techniques for specific articles of clothing (how to iron shirts, pleats, flatwork, etc.). • Teacher demonstrates what happens to fabric when the wrong temperature is used on fabrics (using fabric scraps). • Students identify fabrics and match with proper ironing temperatures. • Teacher demonstrates the proper method used to iron each type of fabric (e.g., temperature setting, use of starch or sizing, etc.). • Students construct a notebook of different kinds of fabrics and proper methods of ironing. • Students practice ironing different articles of clothing.	• Parents instruct and supervise the student in ironing to ensure proper temperatures are being used. • Someone with expertise in alterations speaks to the class on ironing, including using proper temperatures. • Parents or peers identify different types of fabrics by sight, touch, and labels. • Parents or peers demonstrate proper method of ironing different fabrics. • Student assists parents in ironing.
2. Demonstrate appropriate safety precautions for using ironing equipment.	• Teacher demonstrates the use and the maintenance of a steam iron, dry iron, and aerosol products. • Teacher identifies parts of a steam iron and dry iron. • Students practice using a steam and dry iron. • Students demonstrate storage procedures for ironing equipment and proper use of aerosol products.	• Parents or peers demonstrate the use and maintentance of a steam iron, dry iron, and aerosol products. • Student assists parents in ironing and equipment maintenance.
3. Identify when, how, and where to store clothing.	• Teacher demonstrates the storing of clothing, how it is done, when it should be done, and where clothing should be stored (e.g., how to organize a closet, covering garments in plastic, use of mothballs, etc.). • Students visit firms that store household items, including clothing.	• Parents demonstrate storing clothing. • Worker in storage conducts discussion with students about storing clothes.
4. Identify and demonstrate procedures for mending clothing.	• Teacher demonstrates the use of a needle and thread and a sewing machine to perform mending. • Students practice matching color of thread and cloth, and pinning and basting cloth. • Students discuss the reasons for the techniques. • Students practice various mending chores. • Teacher demonstrates different ways to repair torn fabric. • Students practice these different methods. • Class discusses the best method of repair for each kind of tear and each fabric.	• Parents or peers demonstrate to the student how to match thread and cloth color and how to pin and baste cloth before sewing. • Seamstress (or parent) demonstrates techniques to the student. • Parents or peers demonstrate hand and machine methods of performing simple mending. • Parents or peers demonstrate different methods of fabric repair to the student. • Seamstress (or parent) demonstrates the different kinds of stitches that can be used to make repairs and emphasizes the best methods of repair for each kind of tear and fabric.

Domain: Daily Living Skills
Competency: 7. Exhibiting Responsible Citizenship
Subcompetency: 29. Demonstrate Knowledge of Civil Rights and Responsibilities

Objectives	*Activities/Strategies*	*Adult/Peer Roles*
1. Identify basic civil rights when being questioned by law enforcement officials.	• Class discusses an individual's inalienable rights. • Students work in pairs and list the rights they feel they have. • Students discuss what one should do if arrested. • Teacher lists basic rights on chalkboard. • Class takes a field trip to local police station for discussion of civil rights and responsibilities of every individual as an adult citizen.	• Parents discuss the importance of knowing basic rights. • Parents point out citizen's rights that are discussed in newspapers, magazines, and news programs. • Law enforcement official or a member of the American Civil Liberties Union discusses a citizen's rights if he or she is arrested.
2. Locate resources where one can acquire legal aid.	• Teacher presents resources for legal aid (e.g., United Way Community Directory). • Class works as a unit to locate places where students can receive legal aid. • Class discusses the role of a lawyer in legal situations.	• Parents discuss where they have received legal assistance. • Speaker from legal aid society presents resources for assistance.
3. Identify actions to take when a crime has been witnessed.	• Class discusses whether or not one should speak to authorities when he or she witnesses a crime. • Class takes a field trip to a police station to discuss citizen action to take when a crime has been committed. • Students collect articles that report cases in which citizens took responsible action.	• Lawyer discusses how to fulfill citizen obligations in specific situations. • Parents model responsible behavior under the law. • Law enforcement official discusses and demonstrates the appropriate report of a crime.
4. List basic civil rights.	• Teacher lists on chalkboard our basic constitutional rights. • Students role-play a citizen being denied his or her basic rights. • Students discuss specific rights in the Bill of Rights and what they understand about them.	• Representatives from Civil Liberties Union discuss student's rights. • Historian or constitutional law instructor discusses civil rights.
5. Identify who must register with the selective service.	• Students discuss the current draft policy and the prior draft policy. • Students discuss the rationale for the draft and express their opinions concerning conditions for being drafted. • Students discuss the possibility of females being drafted in the future. • Students take field trip to local selective service office.	• Recruiter speaks to the class regarding the current status of the selective service, future possibilities, and the role of inductees at present. • Parents and/or peers discuss their military experiences with the student.

DAILY LIVING SKILLS

Objectives	Activities/Strategies	Adult/Peer Roles
6. Identify when eligible individuals must register.	• Teacher explains intent of potential draftees registering when they become of age. • Students debate the age of potential draftees in reference to the teacher's explanation of intent.	• Recruiter speaks to the class regarding their need to register with the selective service when they become of age (18 years old).
7. Locate the address of the selective service or recruitment office nearest the student's home.	• Students look in the telephone book for local selective service offices and write their addresses on chalkboard. • Students use information from the local armed forces recruiter to locate selective service or recruiting offices.	• Parents and student locate the address of the selective service offices in the telephone book.

Domain: Daily Living Skills
Competency: 7. Exhibiting Responsible Citizenship
Subcompetency: 30. Know Nature of Local, State, and Federal Governments

Objectives	Activities/Strategies	Adult/Peer Roles
1. Identify the purpose of government.	• Teacher explains the purpose of government. • Students collect news clippings or pictures that represent government and display them on posterboard. • Students discuss the influence or role of government in their daily lives (e.g., regulate quality of food and drugs). • Students discuss areas of their lives in which they believe government should not be influential (e.g., religious affiliation, etc.).	• Parents or peers discuss their understanding of the purpose of the government. • Parents or peers encourage the student to read or watch the news. • Parents or peers discuss the student's understanding of news events related to government.
2. Define democracy and representative government.	• Teacher presents the concepts of democracy and representative government. • Class lists on chalkboard vocabulary words representative of government. • Class discusses the way these principles affect us. • Class conducts democratic election of a president and other officers. • Students visit government offices. • Students visit local postal system as an example of government service. • Class talks with members of the student council.	• Elected official or civil servant presents examples of the principles of democracy and representative government. • Instructor in government law makes presentation to class.

DAILY LIVING SKILLS

Objectives	Activities/Strategies	Adult/Peer Roles
3. Identify the branches of government, their functions, and one major official of each branch of government.	• Teacher describes and lists on chalkboard the three branches of government. • Class discusses the functions of the three branches of government. • Class identifies titles of government officials in each branch of government • Class constructs a bulletin board which represents the responsibilities of each branch. • Students collect news articles about the different branches of government. • Students take a field trip to a court and a legislative body.	• Elected official or civil servant presents the organization and functions of government.
4. Identify one way states might be different without a federal government.	• Class discusses the Constitution and the Declaration of Independence. • Teacher places reproductions of the documents on the bulletin board. • Class discusses how these documents affect us. • Class discusses the purposes of the federal government (i.e., provide money to states for support services, building maintenance; pass laws, etc.). • Class discusses what the states would be like without a federal government.	• Parents buy reproductions of the documents and read them through with the student. • Parents discuss with student the capacity and function of federal government.
5. Identify one duty of each level of government.	• Students identify the three levels of government (local, state, and federal) and write them on the chalkboard. • Students discuss the differences between the levels of government and list them on the chalkboard. • Class takes field trips to local, state, and federal offices for tours and presentations. • Class discusses responsibilities of each level of government and effects upon us (i.e., housing, taxes, building and construction, public schools, etc).	• Parents discuss with student the differences and responsibilities of the three levels of government. • Local law instructor discusses levels of government with class.

Domain: Daily Living Skills
Competency: 7. Exhibiting Responsible Citizenship
Subcompetency: 31. Demonstrate Knowledge of the Law and Ability to Follow the Law

Objectives	Activities/Strategies	Adult/Peer Roles
1. List types of local law.	• Teacher describes and gives examples of local laws which students should be familiar with (e.g., property, traffic, etc.). • Students list on chalkboard examples of reasons such local laws are needed. • Students role-play a situation in which such laws are heeded or abused.	• Parents emphasize the importance of local laws. • Policeman speaks on the importance of local laws.

DAILY LIVING SKILLS

Objectives	Activities/Strategies	Adult/Peer Roles
2. Identify possible consequences of violating laws.	• Teacher describes and lists on the chalkboard the penalties for breaking different laws. • Students work in pairs and list all possible penalties. • Students construct a bulletin board which illustrates several major infractions and their penalties. • Students discuss appropriateness of consequences for infractions of laws and offer alternative suggestions.	• Parents or peers explain why it is necessary to obey laws. • Lawyer, judge, or law enforcement officer talks about the penalties for breaking different laws.
3. List basic reasons for government and laws.	• Class discusses the function of laws. • Class discusses the distinction between government and laws. • Students go to a meeting of an elected body in session. • Teacher discusses basic laws.	• Parents or peers explain the reasons for a law and how it affects them. • Parents or peers discuss how laws change. • Lawyer, judge, or law enforcement officer discusses the basic ideas of law.
4. Explain and demonstrate the basic court system and its procedures.	• Teacher discusses the basic court procedures. • Class discusses the hierarchy of courts in the state–federal system. • Class discusses settling a dispute outside of court. • Students visit a court in session. • Class conducts a mock trial. • Class discusses trial by jury or judge. • Class discusses the appeal process. • Class discusses the function of local courts in relation to everyday living.	• Parents take the student to see a court proceeding. • A judge or lawyer explains the court system.

Domain: Daily Living Skills
Competency: 7. Exhibiting Responsible Citizenship
Subcompetency: 32. Demonstrate Knowledge of Citizen Rights and Responsibilities

Objectives	Activities/Strategies	Adult/Peer Roles
1. Locate community services available to citizens.	• Class discusses and lists on chalkboard the types of service available in the community. • Students look through the newspaper, listen to radio and television, and record a list of the community services. • Teacher and students work together using the phone book to locate services. • Students take field trips to several services. • Students discuss the services they feel are needed.	• Representatives from community services discuss the various services offered. • Parents and the student visit community departments to explore services.

Objectives	Activities/Strategies	Adult/Peer Roles
2. List major responsibilities of citizens.	• Students discuss and list on chalkboard what constitutes a "good" citizen. • Students collect articles that represent the responsibilities of citizenship and display them on posterboard.	• Parents or peers discuss responsibilities of a citizen. • Parents take the student with them when they vote, pay taxes, attend community meetings, etc. • Local official discusses the rights and responsibilities of a citizen to local government.
3. Identify voting requirements and demonstrate procedures.	• Students construct a mock voting booth. • Students display sample ballots on posterboard. • Students construct a bulletin board of upcoming elections and pictures of candidates (using newspaper clippings and materials from party headquarters). • Students call or write registrar of voters for information on voting requirements. • Students visit a voting booth on an election day. • Students practice voting with sample ballots and instruction forms. • Students hold a mock election.	• Representatives such as city clerk, registrar of voters, etc., discuss the particular requirements and procedures necessary for voting. • Parents allow the student to accompany them when they go to vote.
4. Identify why it is important to be an informed voter.	• Class discusses the responsibilities of an informed voter. • Students work in pairs and list possible implications surrounding voting choices. • Students collect articles about different candidates and keep a scrapbook. • Class discusses propaganda and campaign tactics. • Class discusses all types of elections and the need to be informed (i.e., from local school levy issues to national issues).	• Parents or peers encourage the student to watch news and candidate specials on television. • Parents or peers discuss the stances of candidates and possible implications of their election. • Representatives of the candidates present their positions. • Representatives of the League of Women Voters present information about candidates and issues.
5. List the dates for primary and general elections, and demonstrate procedures for registration.	• Students complete mock registration forms. • Students construct a bulletin board which states necessary steps when registering to vote. • Students discuss voting dates for primary and general elections.	• Parents take the student with them when they go to register to vote. • Registrar of Voters discuss procedures and forms.
6. Identify sources that inform the voter about election issues.	• Organization (e.g., The League of Women Voters) presents information on election issues. • Students clip articles from newspapers and magazines on election issues. • Students discuss current events which are relevant election issues. • Teacher reads articles aloud to the class. • Teacher lists on chalkboard the pros and cons of an election issue, as students discuss them.	• Parents discuss ways to locate information on election issues. • Guest speaker from the League of Women Voters discusses ways to locate information on election issues. • Guest speaker from the local newspaper explains how newspapers obtain information on election issues.

DAILY LIVING SKILLS

Domain: Daily Living Skills
Competency: 8. Utilizing Recreational Facilities and Engaging in Leisure
Subcompetency: 33. Demonstrate Knowledge of Available Community Resources

Objectives	Activities/Strategies	Adult/Peer Roles
1. List sources of information about specific recreational activities.	• Students compile a listing of recreational activities from newspapers, magazines, television, and personal observation. • Students construct a bulletin board depicting the various activities. • Class discusses favorite activities. • Class takes field trips to YMCA/YWCA, community centers, civic center, playground, park, etc. • Different students present the activities available through community agencies. • Students compile a notebook of sources. • Students identify prerequisites of participation (e.g., membership, physical exam, etc.).	• Recreation workers, arts and crafts personnel, YMCA/YWCA personnel, church youth group members, etc., make presentations to the class. • Parents or peers identify preferred community activities.
2. List activities appropriate to each season of the year.	• Students list on chalkboard activities appropriate for each of the four seasons. • Students discuss sports events they participate in and the time of year they participate. • Teacher contacts the local parks and recreation department for a list of the seasonal programs.	• Parents encourage the student to participate in individual and group activities. • Local sports announcer discusses seasonal sports activities. • Parents assist the student in enrolling (if necessary) in a fitness program.
3. Locate recreational facilities and equipment in the community.	• Students look in local telephone book under "recreation" or related topic for listing of community activities. • Students take field trip to facilities. • Students demonstrate the ability to use a facility and equipment (e.g., swimming pool, gymnastic apparatus, etc.) under the supervision of authorized adults. • Students develop a recreational plan suited to their own personal interests and needs. • Fitness expert demonstrates proper use of facilities and equipment. • Students make phone inquiries about availability of various recreational facilities.	• Facility personnel demonstrate proper facility usage. • Parents or peers demonstrate proper techniques for using equipment. • Representative from community parks and recreation department tells students about facilities and opportunities.
4. Participate in recreational activities outside the home.	• Class constructs a large-scale area map indicating the location of all facilities and activities offered. • Students take a trip around the area to see facilities. • Students obtain membership or participate in one or more of the identified activities and organizations. • Students construct bulletin board depicting involvement in community recreation.	• Parents or peers assist the student in finding the location of activities, establishing means of transportation, and engaging in activities. • Recreation personnel give periodic presentations about new programs of activities.

Domain: Daily Living Skills
Competency: 8. Utilizing Recreational Facilities and Engaging in Leisure
Subcompetency: 34. Choose and Plan Activities

Objectives	Activities/Strategies	Adult/Peer Roles
1. List personal leisure activities.	• Students discuss how interest and abilities are a part of deciding favorite activities. • Students list on chalkboard personal leisure activities. • Students discuss differences between leisure and nonleisure activities. • Students make a chart of leisure-time activities. • Students discuss why they have chosen particular activities. • Students participate in new leisure activities.	• Parents or peers help the student evaluate favorite activities. • People with unique recreation interests discuss and demonstrate their experiences with the class (e.g., judo, karate, skydiving, etc.).
2. List costs, times, locations, and physical requirements of activities.	• Class lists on chalkboard the cost, location, and time factors involved in various forms of recreation. • Class discusses the way in which cost, time, and location influence one's choice of activity. • Students collect cost, time, and location factors in a notebook for future reference. • Students choose a common recreational activity, research the cost and physical requirements of that activity, and report findings to the class. • Students match on chalkboard physical requirements and financial costs with common recreational activities.	• Parents or peers help the student plan a budget that incorporates recreational expenses. • Parents assist the student in determining the cost of participation in a specific recreational activity. • Representatives of particular activities discuss the costs, time, and location considerations involved in an activity. • Parents or peers assist the student with transportation to and from activities. • Parents assist the student in determining if he or she is physically ready for the recreational activity and if he or she has enough money to participate in the activity.
3. Develop individual plan of leisure activities.	• Students list on chalkboard leisure activities, arrangements to be made, and times and days to engage in activities. • Students complete individual plans for a given period of time. • Students create bulletin board which lists their plans and progress.	• Peers and young adults describe their experiences with activities and planning. • Parents assist the student in carrying out activities that student describes in his or her plans.

DAILY LIVING SKILLS

Domain: Daily Living Skills
Competency: 8. Utilizing Recreational Facilities and Engaging in Leisure
Subcompetency: 35. Demonstrate Knowledge of the Value of Recreation

Objectives	Activities/Strategies	Adult/Peer Roles
1. List differences between leisure that involves nonpaid work activity and relaxation.	• Students define work time on chalkboard. • Students define leisure time and leisure options. • Students demonstrate their hobbies. • Students explore possibilities for hobbies through visits to hobby stores, craft exhibits, sports shows, etc.	• Local hobby enthusiasts give class displays or demonstrations. • Parents discuss leisure time activities. • Parents encourage the student to develop specific leisure time activities which hold the student's interest.
2. List ways in which recreation affects both physical and mental health	• Class discusses the pleasures of free time. • Class lists on chalkboard indications that there is a need for leisure time (i.e., bored at work, tired, listless, stressed out, etc.). • Class discusses the need for a "time out" recreational period when feeling emotionally and physically stressed. • Class discusses the role of recreation in developing the ability to socialize and work cooperatively with others. • Class creates a bulletin board which illustrates various kinds of recreation.	• Parents discuss with the student the value of time away from school or work. • Parents discuss how periods of recreation have a positive bearing upon their emotional and physical functioning. • Parents or peers involve the student in their leisure time activities.
3. List personal requirements of leisure time.	• Teacher presents on chalkboard daily schedules of certain types of employment. • Students role-play or simulate sedentary employment in the class to compare these activities to leisure time activity. • Class discusses physical activities which provide physical and emotional change. • Students list on chalkboard the physical activities a person can do independently (bicycling, jogging, swimming, etc.), and the requirements to engage in the activity (i.e., stamina, endurance). • Students explore a variety of hobbies and select one that they can use as a leisure activity. • Class discusses the decisions in selecting leisure. • Students report on leisure activities.	• Parents discuss options that the student can exercise in leisure time. • Peers and young adults discuss their use of leisure time. • Parents encourage the student to participate in physical activity. • Parents provide opportunities for the student to join in family leisure-time activities. • Parents relate individual and group activities in which they engage.

Domain: Daily Living Skills
Competency: 8. Utilizing Recreational Facilities and Engaging in Leisure
Subcompetency: 36. Engage in Group and Individual Activities

Objectives	Activities/Strategies	Adult/Peer Roles
1. Identify reasons for participating in group activities.	• Students observe several activities involving varying numbers of participants. • Class discusses making friends in a recreational setting. • Class discusses the value of incorporating friends and people with similar interests into recreational activities. • Students engage in activities and record the names of fellow participants on a classroom bulletin board. • Students participate in a group activity (e.g., softball) and in an individualized activity (e.g., swimming) and compare on chalkboard the two, with regard to social contact, group support, feelings of belonging, etc. • Class discusses their motivations for participating in group activities, and what they hope to gain.	• Adult participants from several activities discuss advantages and disadvantages, with regard to the number of participants in group. • YMCA/YWCA member discusses advantages of group activities. • Parents discuss their motivations for participating in group activities. • Parents point out ways in which contact with others leads to increased feelings of competency.
2. Identify and demonstrate knowledge of rules of group activities.	• Small groups of students learn the rules of different games and activities and explain them to the class. • Class plays the game or activity according to the rules. • Class discusses the necessity of rules in activities and group cooperation. • Each student gets a chance to be "referee" for a game or activity.	• Local umpire, scorekeeper, or referee discusses the reasons for rules in games and activities. • Athletes and coaches discuss abiding by rules. • Parents compare rules for games to other areas of life.
3. List qualities of good sportsmanship.	• Students observe sports events and note instances of good and poor sportsmanship. • Students role-play an activity where participants exhibit good and poor sportsmanship and discuss feelings generated by each. • Class discusses the need for cooperation in recreational activities.	• Athletes discuss their views on what constitutes good sportsmanship. • Coaches discuss the idea that winning isn't everything in activities. • Parents point out how good sportsmanship is similar to group cooperation in the family. • Parents discuss their attitude towards athletes who display poor sportsmanship.
4. Identify and demonstrate the proper care of sports equipment.	• Students visit a local sporting goods store. • Students identify and examine various equipment used in games and activities. • Students are given a demonstration of the maintenance and storage of equipment. • Students bring their sports equipment to class and discuss how they take care of their equipment. • Students are shown the potential safety factors in using equipment. • Fitness expert demonstrates proper use of equipment.	• Personnel of sporting goods store demonstrate the proper use of equipment. • Parents demonstrate proper use of equipment available in the home. • Equipment repairman from local team demonstrates skills and materials.

DAILY LIVING SKILLS

Objectives	Activities/Strategies	Adult/Peer Roles
5. Identify general safety rules of physical activities.	• Class discusses potential dangers of physical activities. • Students discuss activity behaviors which lead to injuries. • Class discusses rules which prevent potential injuries from occuring.	• Parents discuss with student purpose of safety rules with activities. • Coach, referee, or athletic director discusses the importance of safety with sports.

Domain: Daily Living Skills
Competency: 8. Utilizing Recreational Facilities and Engaging in Leisure
Subcompetency: 37. Plan Vacation Time

Objectives	Activities/Strategies	Adult/Peer Roles
1. Identify financial considerations involved in planning a vacation.	• Students get travel folders from vacation areas and compare prices. • Students list on chalkboard all possible costs in a family vacation. • Class discusses and lists on chalkboard expenditures when vacationing. • Students estimate from mock financial information how much can be spent for a vacation. • Students plan, from mock financial information, a vacation budget.	• Representative from a travel agency lists on chalkboard the approximate expenses of different vacations. • Bank personnel discuss ways to save money for vacation activities. • Parents discuss their vacation expenditures and finances with the student.
2. List time considerations involved in planning a vacation.	• Teacher discusses vacation possibilities, with regard to the transportation time involved. • Students list on chalkboard the vacation sites available within the local area, in the event of limited time. • Students discuss ways of breaking up blocks of time into smaller vacation periods.	• Representative from travel agency discusses time as a factor in planning. • Representative from parks and recreation department discusses vacation options that exist in the general area (short-term vacations). • Parents plan vacation activities in the local area for the family.
3. List possible vacation activities.	• Students discuss what a vacation means to them. • Students construct a vacation and travel bulletin board with information received from vacation sites (e.g., brochures, magazine pictures, travel posters, etc.). • Students plan a mock vacation to a place where they could pursue the activity of their choice (e.g., camping, fishing, historical visitations, etc.). • Students take field trips to local vacation sites. • Students list on chalkboard the activities that can be done on a day trip. • Students write to state offices to obtain information on recreational opportunities at park facilities.	• Representatives from state or local department of parks and recreation discuss a variety of vacation possibilities. • Personnel from the local YMCA/YWCA discuss group vacations. • Parents structure a number of activities for family members.

Objectives	Activities/Strategies	Adult/Peer Roles
4. Locate resources available for help with making vacation plans.	• Students collect a notebook with sources of information about vacation spots, agencies, travel routes, estimating costs, etc. • Students take a field trip to the local Chamber of Commerce for resource information.	• Travel agent discusses sources of information. • Representative from AAA presents information on planning trips.
5. Construct a proposed vacation plan, including cost, time, transportation, facilities, and activities.	• Students plan a hypothetical trip or summer vacation using brochures, maps, guide books, etc. • Students determine cost, time, transportation, facilities, activities involved, and arrangements to be made for a hypothetical trip. • Students develop a list of local day trip opportunities.	• Parents plan a family vacation with the student. • Parents allow student to accompany them to local travel agent.

Domain: Daily Living Skills
Competency: 9. Getting Around the Community
Subcompetency: 38. Demonstrate Knowledge of Traffic Rules and Safety

Objectives	Activities/Strategies	Adult/Peer Roles
1. Identify the purpose and demonstrate procedures for pedestrian safety signs.	• Students go on a field trip, identify various pedestrian street signs, and describe the significance of each sign. • Students perform various pedestrian procedures and observe others as they do so.	• Police officer discusses and demonstrates procedures when using pedestrian signs, and emphasizes potential consequences of disobedience. • Parents or peers take the student for walks and have him or her point out signs and procedures and demonstrate his or her ability to comply with them.
2. List reasons for common traffic and safety rules and practices.	• Students take a field trip to the traffic control center at the local police department. • Students list on chalkboard the hazards to motorists and pedestrians. • Students discuss the hypothetical situation of a community without traffic or safety rules. • Students relate traffic or safety rules in the community to various rules and procedures in class or school.	• Police officer demonstrates traffic and safety rules. • Parents discuss what happens when people do not obey traffic safety rules.
3. Identify vehicle safety signs of the driver's education sign test.	• Students take a field trip through city to identify the vehicle safety signs and the procedures for conforming to them. • Students construct posters depicting traffic signs. • Teacher quizzes students with the posters. • Students read and discuss appropriate selections from the state driver's license manual regarding traffic signs.	• Parents or peers take the student for rides and point out the signs and procedures necessary for safe travel. • Police officer discusses the necessity of people obeying traffic regulations. • Parents or peers model positive behavior by adhering to rules of the road.

Domain: Daily Living Skills
Competency: 9. Getting Around the Community
Subcompetency: 39. Demonstrate Knowledge and Use of Various Means of Transportation

Objectives	Activities/Strategies	Adult/Peer Roles
1. Identify types of transportation available in the community.	• Class lists on chalkboard the local transportation facilities. • Students take a field trip to local transportation facilities (e.g., taxi stand or office, bus and train stations, airport). • Class constructs a bulletin board of transportation facility locations in their community. • Class discusses reasons for choosing certain forms of transportation.	• Representative of state department of transportation leads class discussions. • Parents point out all transportation modes available in the student's locality. • Representative operators of transportation discuss their tasks and training.
2. Identify reasons transportation is needed and the type most appropriate.	• Students list on chalkboard the types of transportation they use. • Students discuss the best means for transporting themselves to particular places in the community. • Teacher devises hypothetical situations in which students have to find the most appropriate way of getting to particular places.	• Persons who carpool discuss advantages of sharing transportation. • Parents or peers discuss their means of travel to and from work. • Parents assist in identifying the most appropriate ways of travel for their own needs.
3. Identify and demonstrate procedures to take a train, interstate bus, taxi, airplane.	• Students buy a bus ticket, deposit it, and take a bus ride. • Students call a taxi, pay the fare, and ride to their destination. • Airline representative explains procedures for making flight reservations, buying tickets, and boarding plane. • Students role-play activities relating to transportation.	• Class holds discussion with bus driver, cab driver, train conductor, airplane stewardess or pilot, and ticket agents from various types of transportation. • Peers accompany the student on various means of transportion.

Domain: Daily Living Skills
Competency: 9. Getting Around the Community
Subcompetency: 40. Find Way Around the Community

Objectives	Activities/Strategies	Adult/Peer Roles
1. Given a picture of a numbered house, identify numbers of houses on either side.	• Students tour nearby streets to observe the numbering sequence of houses. • Teacher devises a map in which students fill in missing house numbers. • Students find out the addresses of others living on their own street and deduce the way in which their own streets are numbered.	• Parents or peers take the student on a walking tour of neighborhood to identify numbering systems. • City or community planner discusses the overall design for the community.

Objectives	Activities/Strategies	Adult/Peer Roles
2. Given city and state maps, identify directions, symbols, and distance.	• Students construct on posterboard a large-scale localized map or obtain one from the city planning office. • Students study a local street map and then go to the area to investigate it. • Students design a model of a neighborhood, putting in streets, numbers, etc. • Class discusses the necessity of using maps. • Students read state road maps to understand symbols, compute distances, compare time and distance, and describe alternate routes.	• Parents or peers obtain local maps and go over them with the student at home. • Parents or peers take the student in a car and follow the map route while the student observes the map.
3. Identify basic community resources.	• Students clip and paste newspaper advertisements of resources available to the public, and arrange them on the bulletin board. • Students identify signs and symbols that give them direction, information, or guidance in everyday functioning (e.g. crosswalk and street signs).	• Parents and student obtain community directory information from their local mental health association or United Way organization.

Domain: Daily Living Skills
Competency: 9. Getting Around the Community
Subcompetency: 41. Drive a Car

Objectives	Activities/Strategies	Adult/Peer Roles
1. Given driving problems related to weather, demonstrate knowledge of appropriate technique.	• Students list on chalkboard the manual operations and expectations for each weather condition. • Students list on chalkboard the state laws regarding driving in particular conditions and the necessary vehicular equipment (e.g., snow tires).	• Parents discuss the need for insurance. • Highway patrolman presents procedures to follow in case of an accident. • Local insurance agent discusses car insurance with the class. • Parents discuss with the student what to do.
2. Describe appropriate procedures to follow after being involved in an accident.	• Students practice contacting the highway patrol and ambulance. • Students role-play exchanging information with other drivers and contacting their insurance companies. • Students are shown how to signal other drivers, use danger markers, light flares, etc. • Students go over basic emergency first aid. • Students are instructed about the advantages of having insurance. • Students role-play an accident situation.	• Parents discuss the need for insurance. • Highway patrolman presents procedures to follow in case of an accident. • Local insurance agent discusses car insurance with the class. • Parents discuss with the student what to do in case of an accident.

DAILY LIVING SKILLS

Objectives	Activities/Strategies	Adult/Peer Roles
3. Identify everyday basic driving knowledge.	• Students participate in driver education classes. • Driving instructors have students practice maneuvers in the parking lot and use simulated driving machines. • Students gain street experience from a licensed adult (teacher, driving instructor, etc.). • Students are given a mock driving test to find their weak areas. • Students role-play driving situations with each other.	• State driving instructor works with the class in certain areas. • Parents and other adults with licenses take the student out to practice driving skills. • Parents or adults model appropriate driving skills. • Peers relate their experiences with the driving exam.
4. Demonstrate proficiency on the written portion of the operator's exam.	• Teacher abstracts concepts from a test manual and gives a mock written exam. • Students construct traffic signs and traffic lights from posterboard, and identify rules. • Students make a game out of holding up traffic signs and identifying the purpose of each sign. • Class goes over the manual in small groups, concentrating on the more difficult aspects of written material.	• Licensing inspectors hold workshop and distribute written information. • Parents go over information with the student at home. • Peers relate their experience pertaining to the written exam.

PERSONAL-SOCIAL SKILLS

Domain: Personal–Social Skills
Competency: 10. Achieving Self-Awareness
Subcompetency: 42. Identify Physical and Psychological Needs

Objectives	Activities/Strategies	Adult/Peer Roles
1. List basic physical needs.	• Students list on chalkboard the needs for human survival (oxygen, food, water, sleep, warmth). • Students discuss other survival needs (shelter, reproduction of species, security from physical harm, etc.). • Students construct a bulletin board showing necessary ingredients for human survival (food, shelter, clothing).	• Nurse or doctor illustrates, using visual aids, the body's needs, and discusses how they are satisfied and maintained. • Archeologist or anthropologist discusses how ancient people met and modern people meet basic survival needs. • Parents assist the student in identifying ways in which his or her own basic needs are met (e.g., three meals a day, a house that keeps out the elements, etc.).
2. Identify ways to meet physical needs.	• Students discuss ways to obtain clothing, shelter, food, etc. • Students discuss how these needs are best obtained (e.g., work, sewing, buying, building, gardening, etc.).	• Parents demonstrate and model ways to achieve physical needs. • Guest speakers from the community discuss services their agencies provide relating to physical needs.
3. List basic psychological needs.	• Class identifies and lists on chalkboard such needs as love, security, trust, self-worth, acceptance, etc. • Students identify needs in reference to their own life experiences (e.g., parents and students meeting each other's needs). • Class discusses how people go about meeting psychological needs through relationships, growth experience, social or political activities, etc. • Class discusses the feelings of loss when these needs are unmet.	• Counselor discusses the ways in which parents satisfy the student's psychological needs, and how the student satisfies the parents' needs. • Parents assist the student in identifying activities that fulfill psychological needs.
4. Identify ways to meet psychological needs.	• Students identify and list on chalkboard the characteristics desirable in a friend, mate, parent, teacher, etc., who would be instrumental in helping meet their psychological needs. • Students use value clarification strategies to identify ways to meet psychological needs.	• Parents provide love, security, praise, and encouragement to the student. • Guest speaker from mental health field discusses available services. • Peers provide for psychological needs by offering friendship.

PERSONAL-SOCIAL SKILLS

Domain: Personal–Social Skills
Competency: 10. Achieving Self-Awareness
Subcompetency: 43. Identify Interests and Abilities

Objectives	Activities/Strategies	Adult/Peer Roles
1. Identify abilities common to most people.	• Students discuss and define the term "ability." • Students list on chalkboard the activities they participate in which reflect personal abilities. • Class lists on chalkboard those abilities they believe are representative of most people. • Each group of students from class designs an ability test and administers it to the other class members. • Each student selects an area where he or she shows weakness, and with help from the teacher devises a program to improve in that area. • Class discusses the idea that study and practice can increase a student's level of ability. • Students take a field trip to job sites to observe workers' abilities.	• Various workers demonstrate interests and abilities in their jobs. • Parents/peers discuss abilities they need to perform their jobs. • Parents and the student construct on posterboard an abilities program that can be conducted in the home.
2. Identify interests common to most people.	• Students discuss and define the term "interests." • Class constructs a poster indicating major areas of interest in class. • Students bring in hobbies or outside interests and share them with the class. • Students list on chalkboard hobbies and interests, and decide which of them are common to most people. • Each student conducts a one-week experiment with a new common activity and reports back to the class. • Students list on chalkboard activities, hobbies, and subjects which they are interested in learning.	• Hobby enthusiast discusses and displays his or her interests (stamps, coins, models, etc.). • Parents take the student to hobby shop, athletic activities, libraries, etc., to expose the student to a variety of potential interests. • Parents select an activity, interest, or hobby for the family.
3. Demonstrate goal setting in relation to pursuing an interest or ability and show how goals are attained.	• Students establish and list on chalkboard immediate and long-range goals that they would like to work toward. • Students divide into groups and discuss the steps involved in reaching their goals. • Student groups assess the kinds of abilities and interests necessary for accomplishing their goals. • Students reassess interest/ability levels in relation to goals (also in relation to other students). • Students discuss the self as a variable in attaining a goal: what a person can do, will do, can learn to do, etc. • Students play "This is Me" game, listing as many interests, abilities, and preferences as	• Parents discuss goals that they have had, how they have succeeded in them (or failed), and how they had to modify their plans. • Peers and young adults discuss present and future goals.

Domain: Personal–Social Skills
Competency: 10. Achieving Self-Awareness
Subcompetency: 44. Identify Emotions

Objectives	Activities/Strategies	Adult/Peer Roles
1. Identify common emotions (fear, love, hate, sadness).	• Students identify emotions from pictures. • Students list on chalkboard what they do when they feel angry, happy, sad, afraid, etc.). • Students describe their experiences with anger, joy, fear, etc., and any resulting physical changes. • Students role-play expressing their emotions through verbal messages. • Students express their list of feelings through nonverbal gestures. • Students construct a bulletin board which shows faces and situations that demonstrate emotions. • As the teacher reads a story, students supply the appropriate emotional state of the characters.	• Psychologist or counselor discusses emotions and how they affect us. • Members of a performing arts company role-play a variety of human emotions. • Doctor or nurse discusses physical changes in the body during different emotional states. • Parents discuss cues they observe when the student is feeling happy, angry, sad, etc. • Parents discuss the different types of emotions people experience and help the student list situations that might prompt particular emotions.
2. List ways in which one's emotions affect the behavior of self and others.	• Students structure open-ended problem situations along the lines of "If I said (did) this, how would you feel?" • Pairs of students are given a list of feelings and responses in which one student is asked to pantomime the feeling and the other respond to the feeling while the class observes. • Students discuss the fear of expressing one's feelings to others and the rational and irrational consequences of disclosure.	• Parents express how they feel when a student behaves in a particular way.
3. Identify ways in which one may cope with emotions.	• Students discuss problem-solving techniques that assist them in coping with their feelings. • Students list on chalkboard the options that exist in particular emotional situations. • Teacher observes if each student is able to exercise control, utilize options, and deal directly with feelings. • Teacher and students practice stress-management techniques in learning how to cope with emotions (e.g. breathing exercises, progressive relaxation techniques, time-out, physical exercise).	• Mental health personnel discuss and demonstrate how to release tension appropriately. • Artist discusses the value of the arts as creative emotional expressions. • Parents model effective coping skills. • Parents point out options that exist for the student when dealing with difficult situations.

PERSONAL-SOCIAL SKILLS

Objectives	Activities/Strategies	Adult/Peer Roles
4. Differentiate particular emotions in self and others.	• Students describe their experiences with anger, joy, fear, etc., and what they felt inside their bodies (physical changes). • Students role-play expressing emotions through verbal messages—content, tone, speed. • Students role-play expressing emotions through nonverbal cues—facial expressions, posture, rigidity or flexibility of movement. • Students supply the appropriate emotional state to a story or character read by the teacher.	• Members of a performing arts company role-play a variety of human emotions. • Doctor or nurse discusses physical changes in the body during different emotional states. • Parents discuss cues they observe when the student is feeling happy, angry, sad, etc.

PERSONAL-SOCIAL SKILLS

Domain: Personal–Social Skills
Competency: 10. Achieving Self-Awareness
Subcompetency: 45. Demonstrate Knowledge of Physical Self

Objectives	Activities/Strategies	Adult/Peer Roles
1. Identify major systems of the body.	• Students complete a physical exercise to feel the presence of certain muscles (doctor approval recommended). • Students attempt to identify muscle groups by listing them on the chalkboard. • Students list on chalkboard the major organ systems and their functions. • Teacher discusses muscle action and the functions of the skeletal system. • Teacher discusses the major systems of the human body (respiratory, circulatory, digestive, etc.). • Students are given a demonstration of the voluntary and involuntary responses of the body. • Students discuss body image and their perceptions of their bodies. • Students bring to class pictures of the major systems of the body.	• Nurse or professional describes the functions of internal organs. • Artist demonstrates the role of muscle groups in a painting or drawing.

Objectives	Activities/Strategies	Adult/Peer Roles
2. List personal physical characteristics.	• Students list on chalkboard physical characteristics such as the color of eyes, hair, height, weight, shoe size, birthmarks, etc. • Students discuss the differences in physical characteristics and their personal meaning. • Students discuss what they like most about their own bodies and what they wish was different (height, weight, etc.). • Students discuss changeable and unchangeable physical characteristics, and positive ways to accept the unchangeable characteristics. • Students discuss the concept and positive aspects of human uniqueness (genetic factors). • Students construct a bulletin board which illustrates different physical characteristics.	• Parents discuss positively ways in which the student is unique.
3. Describe typical physical characteristics and dimensions.	• Students clip pictures from magazines and identify what society considers normal physical characteristics. • Students discuss and agree upon what they consider to be normal physical characteristics. • Teacher explains, using a visual diagram, what is considered normal weight according to height.	• Parents support the student's efforts in acquiring physical dimensions desirable for certain heights and body frames. • Doctor or nurse speaks on normal physical characteristics. • Parents model acceptance of physical differences, particularly those differences not considered to be normal.
4. Identify major parts of the body.	• Students complete an exercise to feel the presence of certain muscles (doctor approval recommended). • Teacher discusses muscle action and the functions of the skeletal system. • Students and teacher list on chalkboard the internal and external body organs. • Students are given a demonstration of the voluntary and involuntary responses of the body. • Students discuss body image and their perceptions of their bodies. • Students bring to class pictures of the major parts of the body. • Students take a field trip to a natural science museum to learn about the body.	• Nurse or professional describes the functions of parts of the body. (A skeleton is brought in for demonstration.) • Artist demonstrates in a drawing the role of muscle groups.

PERSONAL-SOCIAL SKILLS

Domain: Personal–Social Skills
Competency: 11. Acquiring Self-Confidence
Subcompetency: 46. Express Feelings of Self-Worth

Objectives	Activities/Strategies	Adult/Peer Roles
1. List positive physical and psychological attributes.	• Teacher writes on chalkboard "I feel good because . . .," and asks students to complete the sentence. • Students make a personal coat of arms on posterboard, using pictures and symbols to represent positive areas in their lives. • Students discuss their favorite interests to the class, and the class responds by asking questions. • Students compose self-portraits and then create stories to accompany them. • Class discusses having the right to feel good.	• Parents discuss with the student the idea that the student has worth as a human being. • Peers point out areas in which the student should feel good about himself or herself.
2. Express ways in which positive attributes make him/her feel good.	• Students write "I am a worthwhile person because …" • Teacher reads statements of each student's positive qualities, and class members guess the student's identity.	• Parents exchange "I feel good about myself" statements with the student. • Young adults discuss their successes in adult life.
3. List the characteristics necessary to feel good about oneself.	• Class discusses the need to believe in oneself, to value one's own achievements, and to accept one's own limitations while trying to overcome them. • Class discusses ways of taking pride in one's appearance, behavior toward others, and capabilities. • Students role-play self-confident people, and people with little self-worth.	• Parents list with the student what they consider to be necessary ingredients in feeling good about oneself. • Peers assist the student with a particular skill or talent that the student would like to develop.
4. Describe ways in which the actions of others affect one's feelings of self-worth.	• Students role-play situations in which praise and reinforcement affect one's feelings of self-worth and situations in which scorn and ridicule affect one's self-worth. • Students discuss how others make them feel good and how they return the feeling. • Class discusses how attitude, mood, facial expression, etc., can affect one's feelings.	• Peers discuss with the student how they make the student feel worthwhile in non-school settings. • Parents ask for the student's opinions and suggestions regarding family affairs, indicating that the student's ideas and feelings are valued.

PERSONAL-SOCIAL SKILLS

Domain: Personal–Social Skills
Competency: 11. Acquiring Self-Confidence
Subcompetency: 47. Describe Others' Perception of Self

Objectives	Activities/Strategies	Adult/Peer Roles
1. List potential reactions of others to oneself.	• Class discusses the concept and effects of prejudice. • Students list on chalkboard ways people can positively and negatively react to individual differences. • Students discuss differences among themselves, and their attitudes towards those differences. • Class discusses strategies to deal with people's reactions. • Students role-play responses to others' reactions of them.	• Young adults discuss reactions they have received in the past regarding their differences and how they dealt with the reactions. • Parents emphasize the value of the student as an individual, despite any limitations.
2. Construct a personal view of how others see oneself.	• Students list on chalkboard how they believe others perceive them. • Students discuss others' perceptions of themselves and receive feedback from classmates. • Each student role-plays himself or herself as seen by others in a variety of situations. • Student observes himself or herself on videotape and gets an idea how he or she acts, looks, and sounds to others.	• Parents assist the student in obtaining a self-concept by offering feedback regarding the student's behavior and attitudes. • Parents discuss with student what they consider desirable and undesirable qualities. • Parents encourage the student to consider how the student's behavior and attitudes are perceived by others.
3. Describe the relationship between one's own behaviors and others' reactions.	• Students simulate situations in which certain behaviors elicit particular reactions from others. • Class discusses behaviors and the general reactions from others. • Class discusses situations and circumstances in which they are not responsible for others' reactions. • Counselor discusses the importance of students accepting the responsibility and consequences of their own behaviors. • Class discusses attitudes towards individuals who are and act irresponsible.	• Parents point out how they react to certain behaviors of others. • Counselor discusses with students, in individual or group sessions, the importance of accepting consequences of their behaviors.
4. Demonstrate awareness of individual differences in others.	• Students role-play different types of personalities (i.e., extrovert, introvert, chronic complainer). • Students discuss and list on chalkboard the differences in individuals (i.e., appearance, dress, personality). • Teacher or students construct a collage which illustrates the variety of individual appearances.	• Parents have a discussion with the student to help him or her become more aware of individual differences. • Parents model tolerance of the individual differences.

PERSONAL-SOCIAL SKILLS

Domain: Personal–Social Skills
Competency: 11. Acquiring Self-Confidence
Subcompetency: 48. Accept and Give Praise

PERSONAL-SOCIAL SKILLS

Objectives	Activities/Strategies	Adult/Peer Roles
1. Identify statements of praise in everyday activities.	• Students discuss their perceptions of praise, criticism, and neutral statements. • Teacher reads a variety of statements, and students indicate whether statement is of praise, criticism, or neutral. • Teacher or students read short stories in which characters behave in a manner that warrants praise. • Teacher and students create a display on a bulletin board which illustrates instances where praise would be appropriate. • Students role-play classroom, home, or play situations demonstrating the effective use of praise.	• Parents identify praise statements they use in the family environment. • Parents discuss their concept of criticism and neutral statements. • Salesperson, store manager, or coach discusses how he or she utilizes praise.
2. List appropriate and inappropriate responses to praise.	• Students are given tasks by the teacher and praised accordingly. • Students define areas in which they receive praise. • Students define a weak area and, with assistance, strengthen their abilities and receive the appropriate praise. • Students identify and list on chalkboard appropriate and inappropriate responses to praise or compliments. • Students practice accepting and giving praise in group situations at appropriate times. • Students practice delivering praise in everyday classroom situations.	• Parents role-play with the student, giving him or her opportunities to practice using praise. • Parents model effective praise behavior within the family environment. • Parents identify situations in which the student can give someone praise for his or her efforts, abilities, appearance, etc.
3. Respond to praise statements by others.	• Students discuss how they feel when someone praises them (e.g., awkward, proud, happy, embarrassed, etc.). • Students role-play ways to accept praise. • Students compare situations in which someone is sincerely praising the student and when someone is using praise as an ulterior motive (manipulation).	• Parents discuss ways the student can accept praise. • Parents model appropriate ways to accept praise. • Parents give the student praise, when appropriate, to provide him or her with an opportunity to practice reactions.
4. List the effects of praise on oneself.	• Students discuss their feelings after receiving and giving praise. • Class examines the manipulative effects of praise on someone's needs for attention and reinforcement. • Students role-play or see a videotape of a praise situation, and then they evaluate the effects of praise on the receiver. • Teacher presents incomplete stories in which students describe characters affected by praise.	• Counselor or psychologist discusses how praise tends to increase behaviors. • Parents compare situations in which someone is sincerely praising the student and when someone is using praise as an ulterior motive (manipulation).

Domain: Personal–Social Skills
Competency: 11. Acquiring Self-Confidence
Subcompetency: 49. Accept and Give Criticism

Objectives	Activities/Strategies	Adult/Peer Roles
1. Identify critical and/or rejecting types of statements.	• Students discuss their perceptions of criticism. • Teacher or students read short stories in which characters behave in a manner that warrants criticism, and students attempt to fit the response to the situation. • Class discusses the reasons people use criticism (positive and negative reasons). • Students construct bulletin board that illustrates situations in which criticism would be appropriate. • Class discusses the differences between constructive and destructive criticism.	• Parents identify how and when they use criticism in their relationships with the student. • Parents discuss criticism as being constructive and destructive.
2. List appropriate ways to respond to criticism and/or rejection.	• Students practice desensitizing exercises by hearing legitimate and constructive criticisms of themselves. • Students discuss the appropriateness of "acceptance of" but not "internalization of" criticism. • Students role-play situations in which they deliver critical comments to each other. • Students observe the modeling of constructive criticism on videotape and attempt direct imitation.	• Local politician discusses the need to accept criticism realistically but not personally (internalization). • Numerous owners, managers, and supervisors conduct a panel discussion on the role of criticism with employees. • Peers and young adults discuss their experiences with criticism on and off the job.
3. Respond appropriately to critical statements.	• Students list on chalkboard possible statements which could be construed as critical. • Students discuss ways to react to critical statements. • Students role-play situations in which critical statements are made to them.	• Parents model effective acceptance and giving of criticism in the home. • Parents model inappropriate responses to criticism.
4. List positive and negative effects of criticism.	• Students discuss situations in which they have received criticism for particular acts or statements. • Students list on chalkboard the feelings that result from criticism (i.e., rejection, lowered self-esteem, etc.). • Students role-play constructive criticism or particular acts and discuss the potential consequences. • Students role-play destructive criticism and discuss its possible consequences. • Students demonstrate the variety of reactions to criticism and discuss the reasons for such reactions. • Students discuss the role of constructive criticism to improve a person's ability.	• Coaches discuss criticism as it assists athletes in improving their performance. • Athletes discuss their responses to criticism in terms of their athletic performance. • Psychologist or counselor discusses the negative consequences of destructive criticism. • Parents discuss how they deal with criticism on the job. • Actors for a local company discuss how constructive criticism has assisted them in cultivating their acting skills.

PERSONAL-SOCIAL SKILLS

Domain: Personal–Social Skills
Competency: 11. Acquiring Self-Confidence
Subcompetency: 50. Develop Confidence in Oneself

Objectives	Activities/Strategies	Adult/Peer Roles
1. Identify and describe positive characteristics of oneself in a variety of areas.	• Students list on chalkboard all the areas in which they can evaluate performance (e.g., schoolwork, assigned classroom job, work, personal activities). • Students discuss how regularly re-evaluating their own capabilities and performance and making appropriate corrections is one way of maintaining positive self-concept. • Class discusses how working up to one's capabilities assists in establishing self-confidence. • Students or teacher evaluate student behaviors and offer constructive feedback.	• Student asks parents to evaluate his or her performance in household responsibilities. • Parents discuss positive characteristics of student. • Employers or supervisors discuss their evaluation of employees.
2. List appropriate ways to express confidence in oneself.	• Students discuss situations in which self-trust and self-reliance are important. • Teacher asks the student "judgment questions" which require the student to choose the correct response; then the teacher offers other answers, giving the student a chance to change his mind (objective: to assist the student in developing trust in judgment). • Class discusses experiences that strengthen or damage self-confidence. • Class discusses feelings associated with self-confidence and lack of self-confidence and emotional insecurity. • Students discuss the idea that failure at hard tasks should not undermine trust in one's own abilities. • Students discuss the role of trust in the self as reflected in the selection of friends. • Students list areas in which they trust themselves the most, and those areas where they consider themselves to have limitations.	• Parents reinforce feelings of competence in the student by praising positive accomplishments. • Peers identify the student's positive characteristics. • Parents discuss the importance of self-trust, particularly in situations in which group pressure is put on the student to conform to particular values, behaviors, or attitudes. • Employers or supervisors discuss the role of trust in oneself in the area of adequate work performance.
3. Make positive statements about oneself.	• Students list on chalkboard ways in which they can act in their own behalf (dressing, maintaining responsibilities). • Students discuss and list on chalkboard what they like about themselves. • Students practice assertiveness exercises. • Students discuss the importance of, and feelings associated with, standing up for oneself.	• Parents role-play self-assertiveness situations with the student (e.g., exchanging faulty merchandise). • Parents discuss what they like about themselves and the feelings associated with their descriptions. • Parents reinforce all self-reliant actions of the student in an effort to further the student's independence. • School counselor assists students in skills of self-reliance.

Objectives	Activities/Strategies	Adult/Peer Roles
4. Identify potential reactions of others to expressions of self-confidence.	• Students list on chalkboard ways in which others could respond to an expression of self-confidence. • Students discuss appropriate responses of others to expressions of self-confidence. • Students dramatize possible responses when others express self-confidence.	• Parents discuss the difference between an expression of self-confidence and bragging. • Counselor explains how a positive self-image can help a person. • Counselor and parents identify strengths in the student and help him or her find ways to respond to others when they express self-confidence.

Domain: Personal–Social Skills
Competency: 12. Achieving Socially Responsible Behavior
Subcompetency: 51. Demonstrate Respect for the Rights and Properties of Others

Objectives	Activities/Strategies	Adult/Peer Roles
1. Identify personal and property rights of others.	• Students visit a local court. • Students study an abbreviated version of the Bill of Rights. • Teacher reads situations in which an individual's rights are being violated, and students identify the violation on the chalkboard. • Students list what they feel are their individual rights. • Students role-play individuals receiving proper respect from others, and unfair treatment from others.	• Lawyer discusses the broad spectrum of legal rights of individuals. • Parents discuss the rights and responsibilities of each family member.
2. Identify reasons for respecting the rights and properties of others.	• Students list any object they value and discuss why they would not want it damaged. • Students identify objects they have purchased from their own resources and discuss the time it took to save money to obtain these items. • Students role-play using and abusing a belonging of another student, followed by a discussion of the owner's feelings about the other student's irresponsibility. • Students list on chalkboard the things they use in the course of the day that do not belong to them (school books, pencils, school owned equipment, etc.).	• Parents/peers show the student their favorite and most valuable possessions, and explain why they are valuable to them. • Peers discuss with the student that respect for others' possessions is part of keeping a lasting friendship.
3. Demonstrate respect for others and their property.	• Each student is given a situation to role-play, and the class evaluates the student's behavior in regard to respecting the rights of others. • Students list on chalkboard settings in which they can demonstrate respect for others.	• Young adults discuss the importance of respecting personal rights of others as it applies to their work situations. • Parents model effective behavior within the family context and point out instances of one family member respecting the rights of another member.

Objectives	Activities/Strategies	Adult/Peer Roles
4. List appropriate situation and procedures for borrowing the property of others.	• Students role-play a potential borrower and lender. • Students role-play a situation in which a student has damaged the borrowed article. • Students list on chalkboard situations in which they might have to borrow something from another person. • Students identify sources from which they borrow tools, household appliances, etc., and the average, acceptable amount of time those items are borrowed.	• Parents/peers discuss the importance of caring for others' possessions as one's own when borrowing. • Parents role-play borrowing situations with the student. • Peers discuss with the student their feelings about approaching another person to borrow something. • Managers of firms that loan tools, appliances, etc., discuss resources and rules for borrowing.

Domain: Personal–Social Skills
Competency: 12. Achieving Socially Responsible Behavior
Subcompetency: 52. Recognize Authority and Follow Instructions

Objectives	Activities/Strategies	Adult/Peer Roles
1. Identify common authority roles.	• Students list on chalkboard the authority roles that affect their environment (parents, teacher, principal, etc.) and discuss their purposes. • Students role-play authority figure and student interchanges. • Students list on chalkboard the authority roles in the community (police officer, elected officials, clergy, etc.) and discuss their importance. • Students role-play situations involving the student and authority figures from the general community. • Class constructs a bulletin board illustrating different authority figures at work.	• Police officer discusses his or her function as an authority figure. • Workers from the community (young adults and peers) discuss how they handle working with an authority figure (e.g., foreman, boss, etc.).

Objectives	Activities/Strategies	Adult/Peer Roles
2. Identify aspects of following instructions.	• Students discuss the way things would be if everyone did as they pleased. • Students list on chalkboard instructions they follow in school (e.g., where to go for fire drills, what chapters to read, etc.). • Students design picture cards (showing rules of order, safety, and convenience), mix them up, and place them in the appropriate category. • Students role-play situations in which one student follows given instructions and one does not, and then the class discusses the outcome with regard to time necessary to do the task over, possible safety hazards, and feelings of frustration. • Students observe instances of rules and instructions in business and industry. • Teacher assigns small groups of students different tasks which can only be completed by following instructions. • Each student is given sequential instructions for completing an assigned task. • Students discuss how to ask for more information if instructions are not clear. • Students role-play asking for more information. • One group of students constructs sequential instructions for completing particular tasks, for another group to complete.	• Parents discuss the importance of following instructions in family life. • Peers discuss problems caused when one student disregards the rules. • Swimming pool guard discusses the safety factors that are considered in instructions and rules for pool use. • Supervisors and workers from various industries discuss important rules, regulations, and procedures. • Parents give the student sequenced instructions and evaluate student's ability to properly handle them. • Peers and students practice following specific instructions by devising rules for a new game or new rules for existing games. • Craftsperson, cook, or auto mechanic demonstrates the importance of complying with specific directions or procedures.
3. Identify situation in which the individual has the right to disregard instructions from authorities.	• Students discuss possible personal reasons (injury, illness, etc.) which would make it necessary and acceptable to disregard instructions. • Teacher puts a variety of situations on the board and explains each; then students discuss in which situations it would be appropriate to disregard instructions (e.g., safety, unlawful acts). • Students discuss the effect of peer pressure when involved in situations in which it would be appropriate to disregard instructions (e.g., out-of-school activities, unlawful activities). • Students discuss and practice ways of communicating to others, and discuss the individual's reasons for noncompliance.	• Parents discuss consequences of possible harmful instructions (e.g., threat to physical safety). • Parents stress the importance of disregarding instructions and informing the proper authority of the reason for the disregard. (e.g., tell the teacher or coach you are sick or injured). • Authority figure commends a student for disregarding potentially harmful instructions.

PERSONAL-SOCIAL SKILLS

Domain: Personal–Social Skills
Competency: 12. Achieving Socially Responsible Behavior
Subcompetency: 53. Demonstrate Appropriate Behavior in Public Places

PERSONAL-SOCIAL SKILLS

Objectives	Activities/Strategies	Adult/Peer Roles
1. Identify appropriate behavior in public places.	• Students role-play one polite and one rowdy person; class serves as the public and discusses perceptions of both students. • Class discusses respecting the rights of others through manners and good behavior. • Students list on chalkboard their definitions of proper behavior. • Students and teacher construct a display on the bulletin board which illustrates proper behavior in public places.	• Parents/peers assist the student in developing proper manners and behavior around the home and reinforce the student for using the same in public. • Parents/peers model skills in their daily lives.
2. Identify and demonstrate appropriate behaviors when using transportation facilities.	• Students take field trips to a variety of transportation facilities (e.g., train station, bus station, airport). • Students role-play appropriate behavior while using a particular mode of transportation.	• Bus driver, taxi driver, or train conductor discusses appropriate behavior. • Parents/peers take the student on each mode of transportation and identify proper behavior.
3. Identify and demonstrate appropriate behaviors when using eating facilities.	• Students take field trips to several different types of dining places. • Students role-play dining in a restaurant, including ordering, paying the bill, and leaving a tip.	• Restaurant manager discusses appropriate behavior. • Parents instruct the student in how to behave in different situations.
4. Identify and demonstrate appropriate behaviors when using recreational facilities.	• Students take field trips to a bowling alley, skating rink, ball game, etc., to observe participant and audience behavior. • Students discuss participant and audience behaviors immediately upon return from field trip. • Students role-play behaviors that can lead to injury or present safety hazards. • Students discuss improper manners and behavior and their influence on enjoying recreation.	• Recreation personnel discuss safety factors and proper behavior at their facilities. • Parents take the student to a variety of recreational settings and identify appropriate behavior.

LESSON PLAN 7   **12.53.2P:7**

LCCE Objective 12.53.2. Identify and demonstrate appropriate behaviors when using transportation facilities.

Lesson Objective: The student will demonstrate appropriate public behavior when experiencing a transportation problem.

Instructional Resources: Worksheet **Transportation Role-Plays**

Lesson Introduction: We've talked about how to act when we use public transportation in normal, everyday situations. Today we're going to talk about what you might do if you have a problem while traveling. You'll have the chance to show appropriate behavior in several situations using role-plays.

School Activity: **Time: 1 session**

Task:

1. Divide the class into small groups and distribute Worksheet **Transportation Role-Plays.**
    *   Ask each group to review the 10 scenarios and discuss what would be appropriate to do and/or say in each case.
    *   Groups reach a consensus on each item.

2. Small groups report their consensus of the appropriate response for each question. Class evaluates each response as good or needing improvement.

3. Ask individual students to role-play two scenarios from the worksheet.
    *   Discuss responses after each role-play.
    *   At the end of the role-playing assessment, suggest guidelines for how to handle transportation problems:
        *   Be courteous
        *   Be considerate
        *   Be careful

Lesson Plan Evaluation:

Activity: Students will participate in role-plays of transportation problem situations.

Criteria: Student will role-play two appropriate behaviors.

Career Role: Family Member/Homemaker, Employee, Citizen/Volunteer, Avocational
Career Stage: Preparation

12.53.2P:7

TRANSPORTATION ROLE-PLAYS

Worksheet

Name _____   Date _____

Directions: Here are some problems that can happen when you use different kinds of transportation. Role-play what you would do in each of these situations.

1. Your taxi doesn't show up in time to get you to your job interview.

2. You don't have enough money to pay the taxi fare.

3. You get on the wrong bus and are late to work.

4. The bus leaves without you and you have someone expecting to pick you up at your destination.

5. You want to take the subway in a large, strange city but can't figure how much money you will need for the fare.

6. Your train leaves 4 hours late and your parents, who are 400 miles away, expect you to arrive on time.

7. The child sitting behind you on the bus is kicking your chair. You are trying to sleep.

8. Your plane lands late and you miss your connecting flight.

9. You are driving your car in a 35 miles per hour speed zone but the car in front of you is going 20 miles per hour. It is a no-passing zone.

10. You are riding on a bus and all the seats are taken. An elderly woman gets on.

Sample Lesson Plan from *Life Centered Career Education Daily Living Skills*, pp. 521–522.

Domain: Personal–Social Skills
Competency: 12. Achieving Socially Responsible Behavior
Subcompetency: 54. Know Important Character Traits

Objectives	Activities/Strategies	Adult/Peer Roles
1. Identify own acceptable character traits.	• Students list on chalkboard acceptable character traits, (e.g., honesty, cheerfulness, etc.). • In small group discussions each student states his or her own acceptable character traits and receives input from the teacher and other students as to how others perceive him or her. • Students complete a personal checklist or questionnaire of behavioral traits.	• Social worker or counselor conducts "who are you" workshops in class. • Parents/peers praise the student's traits. • Parents point out other adults who exhibit the same characteristics.
2. Identify acceptable character traits in others.	• In small group discussions, students identify positive qualities of classmates. • Teacher presents the lives of historical figures who demonstrated those same positive qualities and characteristics.	• Social worker or counselor conducts "who are you" workshops in class. • Parents identify acceptable traits in others. • Supervisor or foreman discusses acceptable traits of successful workers.
3. List character traits necessary for acceptance in group activities.	• Students participate in structured group activities that necessitate cooperation. • Students role-play cooperative behaviors. • Students list traits they find pleasing in others.	• Parents/peers discuss cheerfulness and cooperation as a necessity in everyday life. • Student observes various workers using these traits in their daily activities (e.g., bank teller, store clerk, etc.). • Various workers describe the necessity of cooperation on the job and provide examples.
4. List character traits that inhibit acceptance.	• Teacher presents incomplete stories of characters demonstrating certain traits; students complete the stories and discuss. • Students construct hypothetical characters to fit particular situations.	• Parents point out behaviors when they occur at home and when they are encountered outside of the home. • Supervisor, foreman, or personnel manager discusses behaviors that interfere with work performance and relations with fellow workers.

PERSONAL-SOCIAL SKILLS

Domain: Personal–Social Skills
Competency: 12. Achieving Socially Responsible Behavior
Subcompetency: 55. Recognize Personal Roles

PERSONAL-SOCIAL SKILLS

Objectives	Activities/Strategies	Adult/Peer Roles
1. Identify current roles.	• Students discuss their ideas of roles, understanding that all people fit into any number of roles. • Students list on chalkboard all the roles in which they are involved, and discuss the expectations for those roles. • Students create a display on a bulletin board that illustrates roles for the student in school, home, and community.	• Parents discuss their own roles within the family and assist the student in defining his or her role in the family. • Peers and the student discuss roles played outside the school (e.g., participant in sports group or team, member of a Sunday school or hobby group, etc.).
2. Identify possible future roles.	• Class discusses the responsibilities involved in future roles of spouse, parent, citizen, etc. • Class takes a field trip to the local Chamber of Commerce to learn about activities and organizations in the community. • Students list on chalkboard community activities in which they may participate. • Students go on a field trip to a city meeting on taxation, where they can observe concerned citizens in civic action.	• Parents discuss the responsibilities of family life. • Persons who have recently become parents discuss the change in their lives because of new roles. • Members of taxpayers committee discuss, with the class, their activities.
3. List roles of significant others.	• School personnel discuss the nature of their roles. • Students list on chalkboard persons in roles affecting the students' lives outside of the school (e.g., crossing guard, police officer, fireman, storekeeper, etc.).	• Persons from various areas of the work world discuss their influences on the lives of others. • Parents identify individuals performing the duties of their roles. • Parents discuss how others' roles affect them.
4. Describe the rights and obligations in personal roles as they interact with the roles of others.	• Students list on chalkboard their involvement in group activities. • Students role-play group interactions in which they are given a theme to act out. • A mock community meeting is held in class in which groups of students represent different points of view. • Students take a field trip to a local government meeting or social club meeting. • Class discusses the reciprocal nature of roles (e.g., teacher to pupil to teacher).	• Members of community, social, and fraternal groups discuss aspects of members in their respective groups. • Workers from the community discuss the interactions between their job and another person's job (e.g., carpenter and mason). • Athletes discuss teams as a form of a group and how the success of the team depends on the role of each member.

Domain: Personal–Social Skills
Competency: 13. Maintaining Good Interpersonal Skills
Subcompetency: 56. Demonstrate Listening and Responding Skills

Objectives	Activities/Strategies	Adult/Peer Roles
1. Identify proper listening and responding techniques.	• Students observe videotape of listening behaviors (e.g., eye contact, posture, gestures, etc.). • Students list on chalkboard the do's and don't's of a good listener (e.g., be patient, allow the speaker a chance to express himself or herself, avoid distractions, etc.). • Class evaluates each student's performance as a listener. • Teacher reads/speaks for several minutes, then asks students to summarize what has been said or to answer questions about the content. • Students conduct activities on how and when to ask questions. • Class discusses the student's right to ask questions. • Students role-play situations requiring the listener to ask questions. • Students write sentences on chalkboard as the teacher clearly reads them.	• Counselor or psychologist discusses the role of listening behavior when helping clients with problems. • Parents check the student's ability to demonstrate listening behavior and model the same at home. • Parents or peers talk about particular subjects, then allow the student to give a summary of what has been said. • Newspaper reporter discusses the importance of being a listener and asking questions. • Parents should listen to the student discuss an area of interest, then ask appropriate questions based on the content.
2. Identify positive outcomes of listening and responding appropriately.	• Students observe videotapes of effective communication. • Students conduct activities in which they model a particular behavior from stories and observations. • Students discuss and list on chalkboard the effects listening and responding have in school.	• Parents should help the student identify adult models who display interpersonal skills. • Parents demonstrate interpersonal skills. • Parents discuss the benefits listening and responding have in their lives (e.g., on the job, with spouse, etc.).
3. Identify negative aspects of listening and responding inappropriately.	• Students list on chalkboard consequences of inappropriate listening (e.g., missing instructions, rejection, frustration, poor grades, nonverbal cues). • Students role-play situations depicting consequences of inappropriate listening.	• Parents model appropriate listening behaviors. • Parents praise appropriate listening behaviors of the student.

PERSONAL-SOCIAL SKILLS

Domain: Personal–Social Skills
Competency: 13. Maintaining Good Interpersonal Skills
Subcompetency: 57. Establish and Maintain Close Relationships

Objectives	Activities/Strategies	Adult/Peer Roles
1. Identify qualities of an individual who would be desirable as a dating partner.	• Students list on chalkboard desirable qualities in a dating partner and in a marriage partner, and then compare the two lists. • Students construct an ideal person who contains the desirable attributes for a date (i.e., sincere, honest, compassionate, physically attractive, independent, etc.). • Students discuss the differences between the ideal and the reality, so that they can be realistic when seeking potential dating partners. • Students list on chalkboard the cultural expectations for men and women and how they figure into dating choices. • Class completes interest rating scale in order to demonstrate similar interests for males and females.	• Parents assist the student in identifying qualities most appropriate in dating partners. • Parents discuss desirable qualities of spouse.
2. Identify and demonstrate appropriate procedures for making a date.	• Students role-play situations depicting appropriate and inappropriate procedures for making a date. • Students identify the appropriate and inappropriate procedures depicted in the role-playing. • Class discusses and lists on chalkboard appropriate and inappropriate procedures for making a date.	• Older brothers and sisters, if applicable, discuss and model appropriate procedures for making a date. • Parents provide guidelines for dating procedures.
3. List activities that are appropriate for a date.	• Students list on chalkboard activities that can be jointly experienced (e.g., parties, walks, picnics, studying, etc.). • Class constructs a bulletin board showing couples involved in a variety of activities. • Students contact the local YMCA and libraries regarding community activities. • Students identify community resources for entertainment, recreation, and other dating activities.	• Member of entertainment or recreation section of a local newspaper describes sources of information. • Counselors discuss selecting activities that fit the interests of both people.
4. Identify characteristics of close relationships.	• Students view videotape of close interpersonal relationship in which students review the experience, voice tone/facial expression, concern for their feelings, sincerity, etc. • Students view photographs of people interacting and devise a story to go with the pictures. • Students role-play various components of close relationships (e.g., empathy, respect, trust, acceptance, tolerance, etc.). • Students compose stories depicting several characters in close relationships. • Students discuss the fact that similarity of interests is often the starting point for a close relationship.	• Married couples discuss what they feel are the outstanding characteristics of their close relationship. • Parents discuss what they see as the characteristics of a close relationship. • Peers discuss trust of one another. • Workers discuss how they have developed close relationships through their work association.

PERSONAL-SOCIAL SKILLS

Objectives	Activities/Strategies	Adult/Peer Roles
5. List different types of close relationships.	• Students list on chalkboard close relationships in their own lives. • Students list on chalkboard qualities of the different types of close relationships. • Students discuss the value of having close relationships. • Class constructs a bulletin board of pictures of parents with children, of elderly couples, of grandparents with grandchildren, etc.	• Parents discuss family relationships with the student, emphasizing the positive points of having a close family. • Grandparents discuss that they have had relationships with the student's parents similar to those the student is now experiencing. • Peers discuss the advantages of having each other for friends.
6. Recognize and respond to intimate feelings of others.	• Students listen to audiotapes of persons responding to the feelings of another. • Students view a videotape of an emotional exchange between two persons, so the student can imitate the responding model. • Students practice verbal following and reflective techniques that indicate concern and awareness when listening to another person. • Students discuss the necessity of giving and accepting support and criticism in a close relationship. • Students demonstrate physical ways of expressing feelings toward another (e.g., handshake, hugs, etc.).	• Parents identify instances in which they have responded to the student's feelings. • Parents identify feeling responses in real life or on television. • Foreman/supervisor discusses the importance of being able to respond to the feelings of people in a job situation.
7. Identify persons with whom one could establish a close relationship.	• Students list on chalkboard people whom they seek out for assistance and counseling when necessary. • School psychologist/counselor discusses the importance of talking about problems and describes his or her own role in the school setting. • Students role-play the appropriate way of approaching a person, to discuss a personal matter.	• Social worker discusses elements of the personal contacts developed at work. • Student relates to "best friend" in emotionally intimate manner (mutual exchange). • Persons who have sought assistance (through psychiatry or from friends) discuss the benefits of talking about problems with an understanding person. • Representatives of mental health, counseling center, clergy, etc., discuss facilities.

PERSONAL-SOCIAL SKILLS

Domain: Personal–Social Skills
Competency: 13. Maintaining Good Interpersonal Skills
Subcompetency: 58. Make and Maintain Friendships

PERSONAL-SOCIAL SKILLS

Objectives	Activities/Strategies	Adult/Peer Roles
1. Identify necessary components of a friendship.	• Students describe their interpretation of friendship. • Students role-play persons demonstrating friendship. • Students discuss the behavioral aspects of a friendship. • Students list on chalkboard the behavioral/attitudinal characteristics involved in friendship (e.g., openness, sincerity, understanding, love, friendly behavior, etc.). • Class creates a display on the bulletin board illustrating people engaged in friendly activities.	• Parents identify the similar aspects of friendships and family memberships. • Parents assist the student in identifying essential components of a friendship and assist the student in developing them. • Youth workers discuss the need for friendship in people's lives.
2. List personal considerations in choosing a friend.	• Students conduct values clarification exercises on expectations for a friend. • Students identify and describe their friends at various times in their life. • Students conduct shared interests-values clarification exercise in which they are combined in pairs with similar interests. • Class discusses the equality of friends so that no person is superior in the relationship. • Students discuss choosing friends based on a person's personal qualities.	• Parents assist in identifying interests that could be shared with a friend. • Parents discuss their choice of friends. • Two people who have been friends for long periods of time discuss their relationship with the class.
3. List rights and responsibilities important in personal friendships.	• Students role-play problem situations in which they must respond to a friend's dilemma. • Students discuss the responsibilities of friendship. • Students list on chalkboard the privileges of friendship.	• Parents assist the student in deciding the limitations in helping friends. • Parents emphasize the shared rights and responsibilities of friendships and family life.
4. List activities that can be shared with friends.	• Students discuss what they share with friends (sports, social events, study, etc.). • Class creates a bulletin board illustrating activities that people share. • Students discuss the value of having a variety of friends (e.g., broadens the base of experience, allows for less reliance on one particular person, etc.).	• Parents encourage the student to engage in peer activities (e.g., recreational, study, hobby, etc.). • Recreation personnel discuss the effects of shared experiences on friendships and community facilities and programs.

Domain: Personal–Social Skills
Competency: 14. Achieving Independence
Subcompetency: 59. Strive Toward Self-Actualization

Objectives	Activities/Strategies	Adult/Peer Roles
1. Identify important characteristics for personal growth.	• Class views role-play or videotape of students who are demonstrating good work/study habits, positive attitudes toward self, etc. • Class discusses characteristics which hinder personal growth. • Teacher reads characteristics of a student involved in a task and the class discusses whether the student is proceeding in the appropriate manner. • Students discuss the role one's outlook on life can have on one's ability to grow.	• Counselors or supervisors discuss the importance of developing adequate social/work habits for use in the adult world. • Parents identify ways in which the student can increase growth possibilities (e.g., by practicing tolerance of younger siblings). • Peers discuss reactions to persons with positive and negative outlooks, in terms of their effects on the moods of those around them.
2. List elements necessary for a satisfactory personal life.	• Students conduct a values clarification exercise on identifying personal/material needs. • Students discuss their concept of what determines personal happiness. • Students discuss realistic goals, personal happiness, economic security, and social stability. • Teacher reads stories of persons pursuing different modes of satisfaction (e.g., establishing a family, working two jobs for more money to purchase items, doing volunteer work, etc.), and the class discusses the merits of each mode.	• Former students or peers discuss what they find satisfying in their lives. • Parents discuss their feelings about happiness. • Elderly persons discuss early life goals and how they did or did not achieve them in later life.
3. Identify sources for continued educational/psychological growth.	• Students discuss opportunities in the community for education beyond high school (e.g., night school, trade skill classes, arts and crafts classes, etc.). • Students discuss ways to expand one's awareness utilizing community resources (e.g., parent education classes, social clubs, community organizations, etc.). • Students explore hobbies, special interests, and activities that provide a creative outlet.	• Representatives of community facilities present their programs and discuss ways to expand knowledge through continued education in various fields. • Parents assist the student in identifying avenues of continued growth beyond regular schooling.

PERSONAL-SOCIAL SKILLS

Domain: Personal–Social Skills
Competency: 14. Achieving Independence
Subcompetency: 60. Demonstrate Self-Organization

Objectives	Activities/Strategies	Adult/Peer Roles
1. Develop plan of daily activities.	• Students construct time/activities "budget" showing what they do, when they do it, and how much time they appropriate for each activity. • Students baseline or record how they spend their day for 3 consecutive days (e.g., free time activity, household requirements, etc.). • Students discuss their baselining. • Teacher assigns hypothetical activity which students attempt to integrate into present activity/time commitments. • Students identify priorities in terms of organizing schedules.	• Parents assist the student in establishing a time/activity schedule for household activities. • Parents discuss with student how they plan their days and weekly activities. • Parents discuss priorities in their own activities. • Former students discuss their need for personal organization in order to meet the requirements of family, job, recreation, etc.
2. Identify areas of responsibility in personal life.	• Students identify and list on chalkboard areas of personal responsibility (e.g., personal appearance, behavior, school attendance, punctuality, household chores, etc.). • Students discuss reasons that certain responsibilities are assigned to people. • Teacher devises project in which everyone has a certain responsibility for its success.	• Parents assist the student in compiling areas of responsibility, particularly in home situations. • Parents and student agree on the assignment of certain tasks in the home (to be done on a regular basis) with parents offering feedback on the student's attitude and performance. • Parents discuss their responsibilities as adults.
3. Identify reasons for organizing one's responsibilities/activities.	• Students are presented with hypothetical activities (e.g., work, school, recreational activities) and must organize them in order to be able to participate in all activities. • Students discuss whether things would get done without a plan to organize time. • Students role-play situations illustrating organized and disorganized persons. • Students discuss the need for setting aside specific times for each task.	• Secretaries discuss reasons for organization of an employer's work day. • Parents discuss the organization of the household in terms of routine assignment of tasks, scheduled activities, etc. • Parents discuss what occurs when they do not organize and plan out their day.
4. Develop ways in which personal organization relates to greater independence.	• Students list on chalkboard how an individual feels when he or she is able to organize his or her own time and activities (e.g., competent, in control, independent from assistance from others, etc.). • Students discuss others' perceptions of a student who is able to organize and complete responsibilities. • Students read about different types of behaviors and then evaluate them on a dependent/independent continuum.	• Business person discusses the effects of organization on business. • Former students discuss how being able to plan and manage their time has increased their sense of independence.

PERSONAL-SOCIAL SKILLS

Domain: Personal–Social Skills
Competency: 14. Achieving Independence
Subcompetency: 61. Demonstrate Awareness of How One's Behavior Affects Others

Objectives	Activities/Strategies	Adult/Peer Roles
1. List ways in which behavior affects others around us.	• Students view a videotape of a variety of interpersonal interactions. • Students role-play cooperative/uncooperative behaviors and friendly/unfriendly behaviors, and then discuss their feelings. • Students discuss their responsibilities in school, work, home, and play situations. • Teacher assigns each student a job in the classroom and evaluates how the students' abilities to meet their responsibilities affect others. • Students establish small groups and discuss how each affects the other as an individual and as a group (requires some basic knowledge of group dynamics). • Students discuss the concept of the consequences of one's actions.	• Peers discuss how they feel when someone's behavior affects their activities (e.g., when one person demands his or her own way). • Parents identify behaviors that tend to have either positive or negative effects on others (e.g., a person yelling and a person giving a compliment). • Parents discuss the need for all family members to exercise some responsibility in the maintenance of the home. • Supervisor discusses workers' responsibilities on a job. • Parents discuss how they feel when the student fulfills responsibility.
2. List appropriate behaviors for a variety of situations.	• Students take field trips into the community to observe critical behavior; students should discuss, write, or list appropriate behaviors observed. • Students role-play a situation depicting behavior appropriate to a given situation. • Students identify situations in which appropriate behavior is critical.	• Parents model appropriate behavior. • Parents identify appropriate behavior models in the community for the student . • Guest speaker stresses appropriate behaviors during an interview and on the job.
3. List different cues elicited by others that behavior is inappropriate.	• Students identify verbal, nonverbal, or physical cues which indicate appropriateness or inappropriateness of behavior. • Students dramatize nonverbal cues and discuss them. • Students use pictures to recognize signs of disapproval or rejection by others.	• Parents pair nonverbal cues with verbal cues to illustrate unacceptable behaviors. • Counselor works with students on an individual basis stressing signs of rejection, criticism, and disapproval.
4. List ways to correct inappropriate behavior.	• Students identify examples of inappropriate behavior. • Students discuss alternative appropriate behaviors. • Teachers use behavior management strategies to reinforce self-correction of inappropriate behavior.	• Parents use behavior management techniques at home. • A policeman describes the consequences of inappropriate behavior in the community.

PERSONAL-SOCIAL SKILLS

Domain: Personal–Social Skills
Competency: 15. Making Adequate Decisions
Subcompetency: 62. Locate and Utilize Sources of Assistance

Objectives	Activities/Strategies	Adult/Peer Roles
1. Identify situations in which one would need advice.	• Students brainstorm for possible situations that would necessitate outside assistance or advice (e.g., vocational decision, personal problem, insurance coverage, major purchases, etc.). • Students make a game out of obtaining advice in getting from one location to another. • Students discuss seeking assistance at any point in the decision-making process. • Students role-play a decision-making situation concluding with the decision to seek additional assistance (e.g., buying an automobile).	• Parents discuss the appropriateness of seeking assistance or advice when the student feels it is necessary. • Peers brainstorm for situations in and out of school life where they would seek assistance or advice. • Former students discuss their experiences in seeking advice.
2. List available resources for resolving problems.	• Students list on chalkboard problems they have had and resources used in solving their problems. • Students survey index of community organizations or agencies listing the types of assistance that are available for specific difficulties. • Students take field trips to medical and mental health clinics, social services, vocational rehabilitation offices, etc. • Students list on chalkboard persons who offer advice or assistance without fees (e.g., clergy, friends, teachers, coworkers, etc.). • Students list on chalkboard persons who offer assistance for fees (e.g., doctors, lawyers, psychologists, etc.). • Students list on chalkboard agencies that offer services on a sliding scale (e.g., Family Counseling, Planned Parenthood, Legal Aid/Public Defenders Office, etc.). • Class discusses problems involved in seeking assistance (e.g., fear of exposure, pride, lack of information about the nature of services offered, etc.).	• Representative from a community referral agency discusses the nature of the referral service and the way students could take advantage of its services. • Parents identify whom they call on for advice or assistance when necessary. • Staff members from community mental health and Legal Aid Society discuss the specific nature of the services offered by their facilities.
3. Given particular situations, describe the procedures for contacting persons for assistance.	• Class takes a field trip to a service referral agency or the location where phones are in contact with a referral switchboard or crisis center. • Class lists on chalkboard areas where assistance services may be needed. • Students practice using phone book to find appropriate services. • Students role-play phoning clinics for appointments. • Students discuss ways they have sought assistance for difficulties and the results of that assistance.	• Parents or peers observe the student role-playing phone contacts with assisting agencies. • Parents or peers role-play a problem situation in which the student with a problem is advised to seek further assistance.

PERSONAL-SOCIAL SKILLS

Objectives	Activities/Strategies	Adult/Peer Roles
4. List potential outcomes of seeking advice.	• Students read letters and advice from the "Dear Abby" columns of the newspaper and discuss possible outcomes. • Students discuss the consequences of failing to seek advice or assistance when it is warranted (e.g., purchasing a car, home, etc.). • Students hear advice given for particular situations, then discuss ways the recipient could incorporate that advice into problem-solving decisions. • Students discuss obtaining advice and developing a negative attitude towards advice giver if the result is unfavorable.	• People who have sought assistance for problems discuss how they have felt after outside intervention. • Parents discuss the importance of accepting wise counsel from respected persons, while still evaluating the practicality of that advice for their particular situations. • Parents discuss their feelings about obtaining advice from others when the consequences of the advice are unfavorable.

Domain: Personal–Social Skills
Competency: 15. Making Adequate Decisions
Subcompetency: 63. Anticipate Consequences

Objectives	Activities/Strategies	Adult/Peer Roles
1. Describe consequences or outcomes of decision making.	• Students discuss basic cause-effect relationships, using physical examples (e.g., bouncing Ping Pong ball, shooting marbles, a pinball machine, and a tuning fork). • Students read or hear stories about, and identify consequences of, characters' behaviors. • Students discuss consequences in terms of risks involved in particular actions (e.g., breaking the law). • Students discuss the need to weigh risks with regard to the value of the desired goals.	• Parents or peers discuss the consequences of violating the law. • Peers discuss with parents the kinds of risks they incur in the nonschool setting.
2. List and demonstrate knowledge of ways in which personal behavior produces consequences.	• Students role-play behaviors that provoke reactions (positive and negative) in the other participants. • Students discuss emotional reactions as consequences, and how they produce consequences that color the reactor's perception, feelings, and behavior. • Students conduct interviews with friends, parents, and relatives to discover their reactions to students' behaviors.	• Parents or peers discuss their feelings surrounding the student's behavior. • Judge discusses the legal system in terms of administering consequences for law-breaking. • Foreman, supervisor, or personnel director discusses consequences of behavior in a work setting.

PERSONAL-SOCIAL SKILLS

Objectives	Activities/Strategies	Adult/Peer Roles
3. Describe the concept of maximum gain for minimum risk.	• Students role-play "television game show" in which they are rewarded for responding with correct answers. • Students discuss the evaluation of taking risks in terms of a person's value system (i.e., is there consistency between what the person is willing to risk and the intensity of the value in question?). • Students make selections of risk-taking behaviors for hypothetical situations and explain the reasons for their choices.	• Parents or peers practice self-assertiveness with the student for specific situations (e.g., asking for information on the telephone and in person). • Parents tell the student about risks they have taken in their lives (e.g., physical, emotional, financial). • Successful business person discusses risks involved in owning and managing a business.

PERSONAL-SOCIAL SKILLS

Domain: Personal–Social Skills
Competency: 15. Making Adequate Decisions
Subcompetency: 64. Develop and Evaluate Alternatives

Objectives	Activities/Strategies	Adult/Peer Roles
1. Define the meaning of alternatives.	• Students read or hear stories about people who have encountered difficulties in achieving goals, then offer suggestions as to how the person can change the situation. • Students discuss the concept of alternatives, particularly with regard to the continuation of an individual's growth. • Students list on chalkboard goals and all possible alternative means for reaching their goals. • Students discuss the benefits of considering alternatives in meeting goals.	• Parents discuss the need for establishing alternatives in achieving goals. • Parents discuss obtained goals and alternatives taken to reach their goals. • Former student who has experienced frustrations of a desired goal discusses the alternatives he pursued.
2. List possible alternatives with respect to a personal goal.	• Students choose a hypothetical goal and analyze it in terms of alternatives to it. • Students determine the shortest and longest route to reaching the hypothetical goal. • Students examine resource material to explore alternatives. • Students implement an alternative goal and assess the success or failure of the selection process.	• Parents assist the student in selecting alternatives to situations that occur in the home (e.g., different ways of introducing younger siblings to others).

Objectives	Activities/Strategies	Adult/Peer Roles
3. Describe a compromise with respect to a personal goal.	• Students role-play positions in opposition and then devise a plan that allows them to free themselves from the deadlock. • Students discuss compromise as a basic form of alternative, in that each person must give a little in order to proceed in the task. • Students list on chalkboard compromises they must make with classmates. • Students discuss compromises they have made in their families.	• Parents identify compromises that settle family disagreements. • Parents discuss with student compromises they have made at work and at home. • Peers discuss ways in which they reach a consensus in the selection of where to go on a date.
4. List resourses for information that develops alternatives.	• Students are given a hypothetical situation in which goals are frustrated; they must devise alternative plans of action that would produce a satisfactory solution. • Students list on chalkboard resources available in establishing alternatives (e.g., the library, community directories, people who have faced similar situations, people who have accomplished the goal, etc.). • Students discuss how an alternative to a particular goal can become a new goal and consider the realistic possibility, desirability, and practicality of a goal. • Students role-play step-by-step procedures of checking resources for each alternative.	• Vocational or employment counselor discusses how to identify alternatives in job, social, and personal situations. • Parents or peers identify resources that help them select alternatives.

PERSONAL-SOCIAL SKILLS

Domain: Personal–Social Skills
Competency: 15. Making Adequate Decisions
Subcompetency: 65. Recognize Nature of a Problem

Objectives	Activities/Strategies	Adult/Peer Roles
1. Given a list of situations with positive/negative aspects of personal ideas, examine each as a positive or negative.	• Teacher reads a particular situation and students respond with their perceptions of whether a particular behavior is appropriate. • Class discusses the need to evaluate one's own ideas and actions from both positive and negative perspectives to determine whether they are practical. • Class role-plays everyday situations and discusses the positive and negative aspects of the situations.	• Parents identify pros and cons of the decisions students make. • Employment counselor discusses pros and cons in thinking about future jobs.

Objectives	Activities/Strategies	Adult/Peer Roles
2. Identify why ideas, values, and plans have both potentially positive and negative implications.	• Teacher tells a story of two people who have the same goal but different life situations, and the students discuss the positive and negative effects of the goal for each of the two persons. • Students discuss situations which could have resulted in either positive or negative consequences. • Students attempt a consensus on right/wrong and beneficial/detrimental aspects of a particular situation.	• Parents discuss the idea that what might be good for one situation is not necessarily good for another situation. • Parents discuss situations which could have resulted in either positive or negative consequences.
3. Identify a situation which requires examination of positive/negative aspects.	• Class provides examples of situations containing both positive and negative aspects (e.g., lying, cheating, stealing, volunteering time, etc.). • Students use values clarification strategy to identify positive and negative aspects of situations, and the class reaches a consensus on what is the best way to proceed in a given situation.	• Parents share their values with the student by examining positive and negative aspects of a situation. • Principal comes into classroom to examine school-related situations.

Domain: Personal–Social Skills
Competency: 15. Making Adequate Decisions
Subcompetency: 66. Develop Goal-Seeking Behavior

Objectives	Activities/Strategies	Adult/Peer Roles
1. Identify ways that goals affect one's life.	• Class discusses the concept of goal setting and its elements (e.g., self-assessment, reality testing, motivation, perseverance, etc.). • Students read a story about people who are actively pursuing self-established goals and discuss the positive effects of goals (e.g., give direction, structure, and meaning to life, etc.). • Students identify and role-play the accomplishment of personal goals. • Students express feelings about themselves during the process of accomplishment of hypothesized goals.	• Parents discuss danger of drifting through life without regard to what it does to a person's self-concept. • Parents discuss how achieved goals have affected them (e.g., raising a family, learning a trade, etc.).

Objectives	Activities/Strategies	Adult/Peer Roles
2. List outcomes to be considered in goal setting.	• Students discuss how particular goal attainment fits an individual's values. • Students discuss measurable outcomes of particular goals (e.g., salaries, security, amount of free time, etc.). • Students interview persons whom they feel have met their goals, and ask whether the original expectations were met. • Students discuss the result of goals with regard to personal satisfaction (e.g., will this goal allow the student to work with other persons? will it allow students to work with tools and machines? etc.).	• Parents discuss what they feel are the key elements of the goal outcome (e.g., will the person be satisfied with the goal, given his life needs and values?).
3. List examples of individuals who have set and attained their goals.	• Students interview persons they perceive as successful in attaining their goals. • Students read stories of famous people and the reasons they set particular goals, and what reaching those goals did for their lives. • Students list on chalkboard short- and long-range goals for hypothetical students and improvise strategies for goal attainment.	• Parents explain short- and long-range goals they have for their families.
4. Set one goal for school, home, recreation.	• Students discuss their perceptions of goals. • Students differentiate between a goal and an immediate activity (e.g., wanting to be a gardener is different from wanting to go on a picnic). • Students list on chalkboard differences between immediate and long-range goals. • Students discuss setting goals as a personal decision (cannot be someone else's idea).	• Parents discuss their own goals when they were the student's age and their present adult goals. • Peers discuss what goals seem available to them and how they find out more information about particular goals.
5. Set short-term and long-term personal goals.	• Students collectively determine criteria for short- and long-range goals. • Students list on chalkboard all possible personal goals and divide them into short- and long-range goals. • Students investigate, by interview or research, the prerequisites for their potential goals. • Students construct displays on bulletin board depicting people in jobs considered appealing by students.	• Parents discuss their short- and long-range goals. • Parents identify resource persons who could supply prerequisite information about employment goals for the student.

PERSONAL-SOCIAL SKILLS

Objectives	Activities/Strategies	Adult/Peer Roles
6. Identify characteristics of realistic goals.	• Students take a field trip to a community college or vocational technical school to discuss career goals with a vocational evaluator, vocational resource educator, vocational evaluation specialist, vocational counselor, or other related professional. • Students choose a preferred goal and weigh prerequisite skills with their own abilities and limitations. • Students discuss acceptance of responsibility and motivation as key factors in making a realistic decision. • Students discuss that values must be consistent with the desired goal (e.g., a person must feel that helping others is valuable if he or she considers being a nurses' aid or child care attendant, etc.).	• Employment counselors discuss their jobs and goals. • Employment counselor discusses the importance of consistency and a "good fit" between one's ability and one's goals.
7. Identify appropriate persons for obtaining assistance with setting and achieving goals.	• Students take a field trip to an employment office for a discussion with an employment counselor. • Counselor or teacher conducts values clarification exercises on decision-making skills in regard to goal selection. • Teacher discusses student's assets and liabilities in regard to goal-setting (private interview).	• Members of the clergy or a mental health/counseling center discuss personal factors involved in setting goals. • Parents serve as resources for the student in selecting directions.
8. Identify potential barriers to goals.	• Students take a field trip to a facility serving individuals with disabilities. • Students discuss such barriers as poor planning, a lack of persistence, physical limitations, and outside pressures (peers, parents). • Students discuss guarding against the possibility of letting a handicap prevent the student from obtaining a goal. • Teacher or class reads the story of a person with a handicap who is faltering in pursuit of a goal, and class suggests strategies for achieving the goal.	• Former students discuss the problems they have encountered in achieving goals. • Persons with handicaps discuss problems they have faced in attaining goals and how they overcame them. • Persons who have altered goals because of an unrealistic choice discuss factors that forced them to change directions.
9. Set model personal goals.	• Students devise individualized projects that require planning time, gathering resources, etc. • Students evaluate and set a goal in terms of how realistic it is in light of their own interests, abilities, resources, etc.	• Parents discuss their own model goals. • Parents assist the student in establishing a workable goal that can be accomplished in the home setting. • Peers discuss goals each student is working on and how success in achieving the goal will affect the student. • Former students discuss their goals with students.

PERSONAL-SOCIAL SKILLS

Domain: Personal–Social Skills
Competency: 16. Communicating with Others
Subcompetency: 67. Recognize and Respond to Emergency Situations

Objectives	Activities/Strategies	Adult/Peer Roles
1. Identify sights and sounds of emergency situations.	• Teacher plays a tape-recording of various emergency sounds (sirens, fire alarms, tornado alerts, air raid), and students identify the sounds and discuss the necessary steps to take with each. • Class constructs a display on a bulletin board depicting emergency situations (fire, downed power line, gas line break, etc.) and appropriate actions. • Students list on chalkboard the possible meanings of flashing red lights on vehicles. • Students role-play emergency situations and accompanying sights and sounds in reacting to each emergency.	• Civil Defense representative discusses emergency warning systems and how to respond to them. • Parents or peers instruct students in emergency warnings in own locality. • Parents and students role-play actions to take in case of emergencies.
2. Identify appropriate authorities to contact in emergency situations.	• Class takes a field trip to a police station, fire station, or hospital, and observes real or mock emergency calls. • Students list on chalkboard emergency situations and discuss the appropriate persons to contact. • Students role-play calls for different emergencies with other class members, evaluating their effectiveness. • Students demonstrate the ability to contact a telephone operator and explain an emergency situation. • Students discuss their responsibility to self and society to report accidents, emergencies, and crisis situations to the appropriate authorities.	• Parents identify emergency actions taken on television medical programs. • Members of police, fire department, emergency squad, or ambulance service demonstrate proper way of reporting an accident or emergency. • Parents or peers simulate emergency calling techniques with the student. • Manager of a local movie theater discusses the appropriate way of alerting the staff to an emergency. • Parents/peers role-play emergency communications with the student, acting as both the reporter and the person who responds to the report.
3. Describe personal communication indicating emergency situations.	• Students hear tape-recordings of mock situations in which persons are experiencing emergencies and discuss content, voice tone, and rapidity of speech. • Students discuss the types of statements that suggest emergencies. • Students role-play nonverbal communications indicating emergencies (e.g., gasping for breath, holding one's neck, hand over heart or on abdomen, pained look on one's face, etc.). • Students list on chalkboard questions to ask a person in an emergency situation. • Students role-play verbal and nonverbal communications in identifying emergencies.	• Parents mention to student statements suggestive of home emergencies (e.g., "quick, call the doctor," etc.). • Switchboard operator for police, fire, or hospital discusses communications relative to emergencies. • Fire fighter, doctor, or hospital attendant discusses necessary actions for particular types of emergencies.

PERSONAL-SOCIAL SKILLS

Objectives	Activities/Strategies	Adult/Peer Roles
4. List personal responsibilities in emergency situations.	• Students identify personal capabilities in responding to an emergency situation. • Students identify ways in which they could be of assistance in emergencies. • Students role-play ways to respond to an emergency situation. • Students discuss appropriate nonaction in an emergency situation (e.g., staying away from a fire or accident scene when professionals are in charge of the situation).	• Parents encourage the student to accept responsibility in emergency situations. • Guest speaker and film from the Fire Department, Highway Department, Police Department, etc. are presented.

Domain: Personal–Social Skills
Competency: 16. Communicating with Others
Subcompetency: 68. Communicate with Understanding

Objectives	Activities/Strategies	Adult/Peer Roles
1. Demonstrate a variety of verbal expressions related to communication.	• Students listen to tapes and films modeling different forms of verbal expression (e.g., expressing emotions, asking and giving directions, expressing ideas, speaking voice, intonation, etc.). • Students discuss different situations and the types of communication appropriate to the specific situation (e.g., loud talking in group with competing noise, whispering during a musical performance, etc.). • Students are given particular situations and role-play appropriate responses (e.g., you have just walked into a surprise party being given for you—what would you say?).	• Parents and student role-play verbal responses in different settings. • Parents accompany the student to movies, plays, and community meetings and identify various types of verbal expression. • Performers in a local theater company discuss the range of verbal expressions.
2. Identify and demonstrate methods of speaking appropriately in a social conversation.	• Students observe a videotape conversation and discuss important elements in the communication (e.g., inquiry, response, conclusion, etc.). • Teacher presents students with a social situation and students discuss the verbal development of the situation. • Students list conversational skills on chalkboard. • Students practice courtesies such as speaking in turn, using appropriate language, using proper tone, etc. • Class participates in its own version of a television talk show. • Students practice discussion skills in small groups and identify similarities and differences between speaking to several persons and one person.	• Parents or peers engage in conversations with the student on topics and offer feedback on effective and ineffective techniques used by the student. • Parents discuss different types of conversations and amenities based upon the particular situation. • Television or radio interviewer discusses conducting conversations with interviewees. • Parents or peers watch a television talk show with the student and identify various elements of the discussion.

PERSONAL-SOCIAL SKILLS

Objectives	Activities/Strategies	Adult/Peer Roles
3. Demonstrate proper use of telephone.	• Students list on chalkboard common expressions used in answering the telephone. • Students discuss telephone answering voice and attitude when answering the telephone. • Students take turns role-playing telephone conversation as the caller and as the party called. • Students practice listening for key words (e.g., name, number, reason for call). • Students role-play a telephone conversation in which students record a message.	• Parents role-play how to conduct a conversation on the telephone. • Parents demonstrate how to write down messages. • When parents are out of the home, they call in and leave a message or number where they can be reached.
4. Demonstrate appropriate volume and intensity in conversation.	• Students tape-record voices to hear themselves. • Students demonstrate control in volume-intensity of voice. • Students describe emotional attitudes identified by voice volume and intensity. • Students listen to auditory modeling exercises for voice inflection, then imitate the model. • Students list on chalkboard places in which soft and loud voices can be used.	• Parents role-play voice volume and intensity based upon content of conversation. • Television or radio personality discusses the use of the voice in communicating ideas.

PERSONAL-SOCIAL SKILLS

Domain: Personal–Social Skills
Competency: 16. Communicating with Others
Subcompetency: 69. Know Subtleties of Communication

Objectives	Activities/Strategies	Adult/Peer Roles
1. Identify nonverbal elements of communication.	• Students play charades and guess what is being acted out. • Students view videotapes of people using nonverbal communication techniques. • Students watch television with the volume off and attempt to identify the story line from nonverbal communication. • Students make up their own television story and attempt to express the moods of the story nonverbally.	• Members of a theater company demonstrate nonverbal techniques. • Mime gives class performance. • Parents or peers play charades with the students. • Parents or peers identify nonverbal behavior in other people.

PERSONAL-SOCIAL SKILLS

Objectives	Activities/Strategies	Adult/Peer Roles
2. Identify verbal expressions that correspond to feelings.	• Students list on chalkboard verbal statements that reflect their feelings. • Teacher gives students statements and asks them to collectively identify the feelings of the statements. • Teacher gives students feelings and asks them to collectively come up with corresponding statements.	• Parents role-play statements and ask student to identify appropriate feelings. • Parents pantomime feelings and ask student to guess possible statements to accompany those feelings.
3. Identify verbal expressions that are inconsistent with feelings.	• Students list on chalkboard verbal statements and role-play feelings that conflict with statements (e.g., "I am so angry"— said while smiling, etc.). • Students discuss statements which may produce a variety of feelings. • Students discuss verbal expressions and role-play feelings inconsistent with the expressions. • Students identify a popular personality who has expressed views different from their own.	• Parents or peers assist the student in identifying people whose ideas are opposing each other (on television or radio) and note their verbal and emotional interaction. • Parents role-play feelings inconsistent with their behaviors.
4. Demonstrate verbal and nonverbal elements of communication.	• Class presents a play in which everyone has a speaking part, allowing students to integrate verbal and nonverbal expressions. • Students observe television, movies, and drama to identify combined verbal and nonverbal responses. • Students hear a tape and express the nonverbal component of the communication. • Students discuss communication as a verbal and behavioral act.	• Parents view television, movies, and drama with the student and identify actions combining verbal and nonverbal communication. • Actor(s) from a local repertory company present class performance.

OCCUPATIONAL GUIDANCE AND PREPARATION

Domain: Occupational Guidance and Preparation
Competency: 17. Knowing and Exploring Occupational Possibilities
Subcompetency: 70. Identify Remunerative Aspects of Work

Objectives	*Activities/Strategies*	*Adult/Peer Roles*
1. Identify why people are paid for working.	• Students look at pictures of people performing different jobs. • Students are given a worksheet to complete, telling the reasons for going to school, and the type of job and income they hope to obtain from attending school. • Students list on chalkboard the kinds of goods and services different jobs provide for the community. • Students discuss community needs for certain goods and services. • Students discuss their own experiences with paid employment. • Students choose two jobs and verbally explain the reasons why a person would be paid for performing each job (e.g., services performed, time spent on job, education and/or training required to perform the job, etc.). • Students discuss other forms of remuneration.	• Parents or peers discuss what their jobs are and why they are getting paid. • Workers from different jobs discuss their job responsibilities and types of remuneration.
2. Identify why some jobs pay better than others.	• Students look at pictures of people performing jobs and explain the differences between jobs regarding education, training, and time spent on the job. • Students identify general categories of jobs along with training, education, and rate of pay. • Students research jobs that they are interested in, identifying the level of training and education needed. • Students take field trips to job sites to discuss requirements for employment at those sites. • Students discuss the salary they expect to be paid, based on their training and experience. • Students discuss why some jobs pay by the hour while others are salaried.	• Parents discuss requirements for their jobs and the rate of pay. • Workers or peers discuss the relationship of requirements and demands for their jobs to salary.

OCCUPATIONAL GUIDANCE AND PREPARATION

LESSON PLAN 13   17.70.5A:13

LCCE Objective 17.70.5. Given a paycheck stub, calculate deduction information.

Lesson Objective: Student will define types of deductions.

Instructional Resources: Worksheet **Important Vocabulary.**

Lesson Introduction: A number of terms appear on a paycheck stub. You need to be familiar with the meaning of each term.

School Activity: **Time: 1 session**

Task:

1. Discuss the concept of deductions, for example, large yearly payments for insurance or taxes divided into smaller amounts that are subtracted from each monthly check by your employer. Explain that the amount of money a person earns is not the same as the amount available to spend. Total earnings are referred to as gross pay; net pay represents the amount left after certain deductions.

2. Describe each of the following deductions:
    *   FICA - deduction for Social Security benefits paid at retirement or illness.
    *   Federal income tax - payment withheld for federal income taxes.
    *   State tax - payment withheld for state income taxes.
    *   City tax - payment withheld for city income tax.
    *   Pension - deduction for a retirement program.
    *   Union dues - deduction for monthly dues to union or professional organization.
    *   Voluntary savings - savings deductions, e.g., U.S. savings bonds.
    *   Health, life, and/or disability insurance - deductions for insurance payments.

3. Students complete Worksheet, **Important Vocabulary** in pairs and review definitions in class.

Lesson Plan Evaluation:

  Activity: Students will complete the worksheet.

  Criteria: Student will correctly define 8 out of 10 terms.

Career Role: Employee
Career Stage: Awareness

Objectives	Activities/Strategies	Adult/Peer Roles
3. Discuss personal needs that are met through wages.	• Students discuss 10 personal needs. • Students discuss what needs they hope to meet with their salaries. • Students list on chalkboard necessary payments which must be deducted from one's salary (e.g., rent , food, etc.). • Students discuss fringe benefits of a work situation (e.g., retirement, education, planning for the future, medical, security, etc.) and how these satisfy personal needs.	• Peers or parents discuss budgeting their income. • Peers or parents discuss needs that are directly or indirectly met by wages (e.g. necessities, luxuries, recreation, etc.).
4. Discuss positive and negative aspects of different kinds of wages.	• Students discuss differences of wage earnings. • Students compute salaries based on various rates of pay. • Students discuss purchasing ability based upon wages calculated.	• Parents discuss their own wages with students. • Recent graduates receiving various kinds of wages discuss positive and negative aspects of their experiences. • Personnel officer explains different wages paid in his or her setting.
5. Given a paycheck stub, calculate deduction information.	• Teacher provides students with several paycheck stubs and reviews on chalkboard deduction information. • Students calculate balance of initial income given, from a list of prescribed taxable deductions.	• Parents review check stubs with student concerning deduction information.

Domain: Occupational Guidance and Preparation
Competency: 17. Knowing and Exploring Occupational Possibilities
Subcompetency: 71. Locate Sources of Occupational and Training Information

Objectives	Activities/Strategies	Adult/Peer Roles
1. List sources of occupational information.	• A career counselor presents program identifying sources of occupational information available (e.g., State Employment Offices, Department of Labor Office, The Division of Vocational Rehabilitation Offices, *Dictionary of Occupational Titles, Occupational Outlook Handbook*, etc.). • Students collect examples of the kind of information provided by each source and display them on posterboard. • Students take a field trip to a State Employment Office. • Students discuss which resources they are most likely to utilize. • An employment counselor discusses resources found in the community and school.	• Parents or peers help the student identify community sources of occupational information. • Peers accompany the student on trips to these sources. • Employment service counselor identifies occupational information resources in the community.

OCCUPATIONAL GUIDANCE AND PREPARATION

Objectives	Activities/Strategies	Adult/Peer Roles
2. List information provided by the sources from Objective 4.	• Counselor discusses specific resources and the kind of information he or she can provide. • Students take field trips to these various resources. • Students construct a display on bulletin board identifying the major services available at each source. • Students select a potential future occupation and present to the class facts about the occupation they learned from the different sources in Objective 1.	• Rehabilitation, employment, or vocational counselor describes the kinds of information provided by these agencies. • Parents or peers accompany the student on field trips to various sources. • Parents or peers discuss the major purpose of each of these agencies.
3. Use occupational information sources to demonstrate how to obtain information specific to a job.	• Students are inserviced as to the use of the reference sources in Objective 1. • Students are assigned a specific job or occupation and asked to obtain information about the occupation. • Students identify and list on chalkboard jobs or occupations in their vocational area which have the best outlook.	• Representatives from various sources demonstrate how to utilize their facilities. • Parents or peers help the student use sources to obtain information on specific jobs.
4. Locate sources of training information.	• Students contact agencies such as The Division of Vocational Rehabilitation, State Employment Offices, and local community colleges, to obtain sources of training information. • Students take a field trip to recommended training sites for work sample testing and job simulation experience. • Students discuss those experiences which appeared to be particularly insightful or beneficial.	• Parents or peers help the student identify sources of training information. • Parents accompany student on trips to agency or institutional offices.
5. Identify one kind of information provided by training information.	• Students select one kind of information provided by training resources and share the information with the class.	• Parents discuss with student one kind of information provided by training information.

Domain: Occupational Guidance and Preparation
Competency: 17. Knowing and Exploring Occupational Possibilities
Subcompetency: 72. Identify Personal Values Met Through Work

Objectives	Activities/Strategies	Adult/Peer Roles
1. List economic reasons for working at a job.	• Students list on chalkboard 15 activities they like to participate in, and what effort or cost is involved in each activity. • Students list on chalkboard 10 necessities of living and discuss whether the necessities are economically dependent upon someone working at a job. • Students list on chalkboard 5 activities and/or necessities that do not depend upon financial resources.	• Parents or peers discuss their first job and experiences with becoming economically independent.

OCCUPATIONAL GUIDANCE AND PREPARATION

Objectives	Activities/Strategies	Adult/Peer Roles
2. Identify how a job affects building personal and social relationships.	• Students discuss being employed as a sense of belonging. • Students discuss the way in which a job allows one to form new friendships and social relationships. • Students discuss ways in which a work situation is similar to and different from other social situations. • Students list on chalkboard social activities in which coworkers engage outside the job.	• Parents or peers discuss their own experiences of making friends on the job. • Parents or peers discuss social activities they have shared with coworkers away from the job.
3. Identify personal needs that can be met through work.	• Students list on chalkboard the personal needs they feel work meets (e.g., fulfillment, satisfaction, self-esteem, self-respect, accomplishment, independence, security, socialization, etc.). • Students bring in pictures of workers who appear to be meeting their personal needs, and display them on posterboard. • Students rank these needs met through work. • Students parallel school experiences with possible work experiences which meet personal needs.	• Parents discuss the concept of personal needs. • A working student explains how work meets his or her personal needs. • Guest speakers from the community discuss how their work helps them meet their personal needs.
4. Describe how work relates to one's self-esteem.	• Students define and discuss what self-esteem means to them. • Students bring in pictures of workers which appear to represent defined and discussed characteristics of self-esteem, and display them on posterboard. • Students discuss the reasons why being employed allows one to value oneself. • Guidance counselor discusses the relationship of self-esteem to being gainfully employed. • Students interview workers in the community to gain their feelings about work.	• Parents define and discuss what self-esteem means to them. • A working student is invited to talk to the class and explain how work meets his or her self-esteem needs. • Guest speakers from the community discuss how their work helps them meet their self-esteem needs.

OCCUPATIONAL GUIDANCE AND PREPARATION

Domain: Occupational Guidance and Preparation
Competency: 17. Knowing and Exploring Occupational Possibilities
Subcompetency: 73. Identify Societal Values Met Through Work

Objectives	Activities/Strategies	Adult/Peer Roles
1. Identify ways in which individual workers help society.	• Students identify workers who affect their daily lives. • Students exchange magazine pictures of workers and discuss their beliefs about how each worker in the picture contributes to society. • Teachers discuss their beliefs about how teaching contributes to society. • Students discuss the probable consequences of members of certain occupations not working. • Students list on chalkboard the roles of workers from different occupations. • Students discuss ways that workers contribute to society (e.g., purchasing goods and services, paying taxes).	• Parents or peers discuss their beliefs regarding the contribution of their jobs to society. • Parents or peers discuss how workers help maintain the standard of living in the community. • Members of unions, industries, or agencies present ways in which workers are important to the community.
2. Identify ways in which members of a specific occupation contribute to society.	• Students list on chalkboard specific services provided by major occupations. • Class takes field trips to observe members of different occupations at work. • Students are assigned a specific occupation to investigate. • Students create a display on the bulletin board which lists specific occupations and their major contributions. • Students role-play members of different occupations and discuss the importance of their jobs.	• Parents or peers discuss their jobs and contributions to the community. • Member of the Chamber of Commerce identifies major local industries and jobs, and discusses contributions to the community. • Representatives from local industries identify contributions to the community.
3. Identify ways in which workers on different jobs are interdependent.	• A qualified person in the community gives a presentation covering major occupations involved in meeting our daily needs. • Students discuss what would be different if one of the major occupations mentioned did not exist, and what other occupations would be affected as a result of the absence. • Students identify relationships between jobs in different communities.	• Parents or peers discuss the interdependence of their jobs. • Government official discusses the interdependence of business, industry, farming, and government. • Workers from a specific occupation discuss their dependence on members of other occupations.
4. Describe ways society rewards different occupations.	• Students discuss fringe benefits which society considers rewards based on the job (e.g., sick leave, vacation time, working conditions, etc.). • Students discuss the benefits which are considered rewards by society. • Given a list of occupations available locally, students identify occupations that provide high income. • Given the same list of occupations, students identify occupations that provide high esteem. • Given the same list, students identify occupations that provide both high income and high esteem.	• Parents or peers identify the aspects of their jobs for which society rewards them. • Guest speakers from various occupations discuss societal rewards.

OCCUPATIONAL GUIDANCE AND PREPARATION

Domain: Occupational Guidance and Preparation
Competency: 17. Knowing and Exploring Occupational Possibilities
Subcompetency: 74. Classify Jobs into Occupational Categories

Objectives	Activities/Strategies	Adult/Peer Roles
1. Locate jobs using Yellow Pages and want ads.	• Students in class review, with the teacher, the format and contents of the Yellow Pages and local newspaper. • Students list on chalkboard 10 household items which could need repairing and locate the companies in the Yellow Pages that repair those items. • Students locate 10 occupations they are familiar with and find their corresponding job positions in the want ads of the local newspaper.	• Parents or peers review the Yellow Pages and local want ads with the student. • Parents ask students to identify items in the home which could break down and state where to go to repair them. • Parents request students to find a listing of those occupations in the want ads and the Yellow Pages.
2. Locate occupational categories and sort jobs into different occupational categories.	• Students clip pictures from magazines, of people performing jobs from different classifications (e.g., skilled, unskilled, professional, etc.). • Students discuss the different pictures and as a group decide upon the classification of the jobs. • Students review the *Guide for Occupational Exploration, Dictionary of Occupational Titles*, and *The Classification of Jobs* books with the teacher. • Students are given a list of occupations and are asked to identify them by categories using any of the three books. • Students are given a list of jobs and are asked to sort the jobs into different categories using any of the three books.	• Parents or peers assist the student in identifying and categorizing several selected occupations. • Employment counselor, rehabilitation counselor, or vocational evaluator discusses job classifications and demonstrates the use of the three books.
3. Locate information about job classifications.	• Students take field trip with parents to local State Employment Office to discuss classification of jobs. • Student and teacher review the use of the three books used in Objective 1. • Students are given a list of jobs by the teacher and are asked to locate, as quickly as possible, using *The Classification of Jobs* book, the job classification of each job.	• Parents or peers discuss classification of jobs (e.g., skilled, unskilled, professional, etc.). • Representative of employment agency discusses classification of jobs.

OCCUPATIONAL GUIDANCE AND PREPARATION

Objectives	Activities/Strategies	Adult/Peer Roles
4. List major categories of jobs related to interest.	• Students check want ads and employment services for opportunities. • Students discuss jobs which seem most interesting to them. • Students take paper-and-pencil interest inventory test (i.e., Strong-Campbell Interest Inventory, machine-scored). • Students discuss major classification criteria used with these jobs. • Counselor demonstrates how to use relevant literature. • Students use these sources to obtain information about specific jobs. • Students list on chalkboard what they are looking for in a job. • Students simulate a "Career Day."	• Parents or peers discuss what is interesting about their jobs. • Employment service counselor explains major job categories and identifies information relevant to each. • Workers from different occupations come to school for a "Career Day."
5. List general job categories.	• Students discuss the way jobs are classified (e.g., type of work, salary, level of training or education, white vs. blue collar, skilled vs. unskilled, etc.). • Counselor identifies various sources of occupational information and the kinds of information each provides. • Students identify specific information they would like to have about a prospective job. • Students create a display on a bulletin board which lists major classification systems with representative jobs.	• Employment service counselor identifies major criteria used in different occupational classification systems. • Job placement specialist discusses the kinds of occupations available locally.
6. Locate training requirements and wages for common job classifications.	• Students discuss how and where to locate information about occupational classification (e.g., *Guide for Occupational Exploration, Dictionary of Occupational Titles, The Classification of Jobs*). • Students practice utilizing these resources to obtain specific information (e.g., training, wages, etc.). • Students identify job families or related jobs a person with specific kinds of skills might perform. • Students take a field trip to a vocational evaluation site. • Counselor explains the concept of job and occupational clusters. • Students design job samples.	• Employment service counselor demonstrates how to use the occupational classification systems to obtain specific information. • Workers from a specific occupation discuss other jobs they would be able to perform with their level of skill and training. • Vocational evaluators discuss their duties and functions as evaluators, and their tools for assessment.

OCCUPATIONAL GUIDANCE AND PREPARATION

Domain: Occupational Guidance and Preparation
Competency: 17. Knowing and Exploring Occupational Possibilities
Subcompetency: 75. Investigate Local Occupational and Training Opportunities

Objectives	Activities/Strategies	Adult/Peer Roles
1. Select an occupational area and find local employers in the Yellow Pages.	• Students use the newspaper help wanted ads to identify occupations that are of interest. • Students create a display on the bulletin board illustrating school and community sources of occupational information. • Students select an occupation, review the Yellow Pages under the occupational title or job required, review listing of employers, and select local employers.	• Parents or peers help the student identify local sources of occupational information. • Representatives from each source discuss the kind of information they provide. • Business person discusses local occupational opportunities and industrial opportunities. • Employment service representative discusses job opportunities available locally and why these jobs are found in this location.
2. Collect and read help wanted ads in the occupational areas selected in Objective 1.	• Students clip help wanted ads from the newspaper regarding the local occupational areas selected, and bring them to class.	• Parent and student review help wanted ads regarding occupations in local areas.
3. Utilize sources of employment information.	• A local employer gives a demonstration on how to utilize each resource (e.g., who to talk to, what questions to ask, etc.). • Students discuss how they would acquire specific kinds of information. • Students identify the pros and cons of each source. • Students practice using sources to obtain specific information.	• Employment service or rehabilitation counselor demonstrates how to obtain specific information from these agencies.
4. Locate sources of employment information.	• Students take a field trip to various sources of information. • Students record, in an occupational notebook, the kind of information available at each resource. • Students construct a display on a bulletin board identifying the kind of information available at each source.	• Parents or peers help student locate various sources. • Peers accompany the student on trips to the various sources. • Employment service counselor discusses local sources of information on job opportunities. • Rehabilitation counselor discusses opportunities for training and employment.

OCCUPATIONAL GUIDANCE AND PREPARATION

Domain: Occupational Guidance and Preparation
Competency: 18. Selecting and Planning Occupational Choices
Subcompetency: 76. Make Realistic Occupational Choices

Objectives	Activities/Strategies	Adult/Peer Roles
1. Identify jobs of interest.	• Students collect newspapers, want ads, and other literature containing a list of jobs available in the community. • Students brainstorm and list on chalkboard jobs which are available in their community. • Students construct a display on a bulletin board listing all potential jobs by occupational grouping. • Students identify and list characteristics of jobs they would like to perform. • Students choose one or more jobs they might like to perform.	• Parents or peers help the student construct a list of potential jobs in the community. • Parents discuss characteristics about their employment which they enjoy. • Representative of the State Employment Service helps the student construct a list of jobs in the community. • Member of the Chamber of Commerce discusses employment opportunities in the community.
2. Obtain specific information about jobs of interest.	• Students identify available resources for obtaining information about jobs. • Counselor demonstrates ways to research a job as well as obtain information about resources available in the community. • Students take a field trip to the Job Service government agency to learn about jobs of interest. • Students list on chalkboard desirable jobs, and obtain specific information about each. • Students interview workers, supervisors, and employment personnel to obtain information about employment.	• Parents or peers help the student utilize various job information resources in the community. • Parents or peers help the student research jobs in which the student has expressed interest. • Placement specialist or vocational counselor presents information about specific jobs. • Peers who have done a particular job talk to the student about that job experience.
3. Obtain observational information about jobs of interest through participation (e.g., on-site visits, work samples, job tryouts).	• Students obtain information about a prospective job through observation, training, job tryout, summer employment, etc. • Students discuss what they like or dislike about jobs, based on their experiences. • Students edit their list of prospective jobs on the basis of their experiences and discussion. • Students keep a notebook of experiences on the job.	• Parents arrange for the student to have job-related experiences. • Parents or peers discuss with the student what kind of self-knowledge they have acquired through their experiences. • Parents or peers help the student revise occupational goals on the basis of experience and discussions. • Former students discuss similar experiences with the student.
4. Identify a job of intererest that is commensurate with interests and abilities.	• Students identify jobs of interest and the abilities needed to be successful on the job. • Students identify what they believe to be their skills and abilities. • Students work with a counselor to identify jobs which are available in the community, and are appropriate, in terms of the student's level of education, training, work experience, expressed interests, etc. • Students discuss aspects of their vocational choices. • Each student lists on chalkboard potential jobs along with relevent information. • Students discuss pros and cons of each job.	• Parents help the student identify his or her strengths, abilities, and weaknesses in relation to obtaining and keeping a job. • Parents help the student identify potential jobs related to his or her level of training and experience. • Parents or peers talk with the student on how jobs are related to experience. • Former students discuss changes in their goals due to positive or negative job experiences.

OCCUPATIONAL GUIDANCE AND PREPARATION

Domain: Occupational Guidance and Preparation
Competency: 18. Selecting and Planning Occupational Choices
Subcompetency: 77. Identify Requirements of Appropriate and Available Jobs

Objectives	Activities/Strategies	Adult/Peer Roles
1. Identify the availability and location of jobs.	• Students clip job listings from the local newspaper and put listings and location of jobs on a bulletin board. • Students are presented with job listings and are asked to find location and telephone numbers of jobs in the telephone directory. • Students telephone companies and inquire about the availability of jobs. • Students take a field trip to the local Job Service Agency to learn about local employment. • Lectures or demonstrations are given on how aptitudes are measured (e.g., job samples, performance tests, etc.).	• Parents and student look through the local newspaper want ads for job listings and locations. • Parents and student visit local Job Service.
2. List specific job-related requirements.	• Students investigate the kinds of skills, abilities, education, and level of training or experience required to enter a specific job. • Students discuss the match between requirements for a specific job and their skills, abilities, etc. • Students construct a notebook listing desirable jobs and the requirements for each. • Students talk with workers about the jobs they are investigating. • Students discuss union membership needed for specific jobs and the advantages and benefits of labor unions.	• Parents discuss the kinds of jobs the student may find desirable. • Parents help the student obtain information about specific requirements for each job. • Parents help the student eliminate from the list jobs in the community that are either inappropriate or unavailable.
3. Identify an alternative for each occupation for which personal qualifications are not commensurate with identified requirements.	• Students discuss what is meant by the demands of a job. • Students investigate demands involved in a particular job (e.g., being on one's feet all day, being able to get along with coworkers, being able to work around noise, etc.). • Students talk with workers about the jobs they are investigating. • Students list on chalkboard specific jobs and the kinds of demands involved in each job, and then do an analysis comparing those demands with their own abilities. • A local employer gives a presentation on employment available in the community. • Students discuss specific jobs which they find either undesirable or unrealistic in terms of their ability, training, and experience. • Students discuss why they find certain jobs more appealing and realistic than others.	• Parents discuss with the student desirable and undesirable jobs. • Parents help the student obtain information about the demands of each of these jobs. • Parents help the student identify the kinds of demands he or she may be unable to meet. • Parents help the student identify alternative, desirable, and realistic employment available in the community.

OCCUPATIONAL GUIDANCE AND PREPARATION

Domain: Occupational Guidance and Preparation
Competency: 18. Selecting and Planning Occupational Choices
Subcompetency: 78. Identify Occupational Aptitudes

Objectives	Activities/Strategies	Adult/Peer Roles
1. Identify different aptitudes necessary in the performance of various jobs.	• A career expert gives a lecture on how aptitudes relate to ability to perform a job. • Students discuss how aptitudes (abilities) are related to occupational choice. • Students take a field trip to local vocational assessment office to learn about aptitudes.	• Parents explain to the student how aptitudes (abilities) are related to performance on a job. • Parents discuss with the student how knowledge of one's aptitudes relates to occupational choice. • Parents discuss their aptitudes as relating to employment. • Vocational evaluator discusses different methods for obtaining knowledge about one's aptitudes.
2. Identify personal aptitudes.	• Students are tested in different modalities. • Students are observed in different settings (e.g., performing work samples and being given objective feedback about their performances). • Each student lists on chalkboard potential jobs related to his or her own aptitudes. • Each student lists on chalkboard his or her own strong and weak points.	• Parents or peers discuss with the student what appear to be his or her strengths and weaknesses.
3. Identify activities that could improve personal aptitude necessary for a preferred job.	• Students use the *Dictionary of Occupational Titles* to identify aptitudes. • Students design on posterboard a realistic program or plan for personally improving aptitudes. • Students discuss aptitudes and what to do to improve them. • Language arts teachers provide individual programs to improve reading and writing. • Vocational education teachers prescribe individual programs to improve eye-hand coordination, dexterity, and speed and accuracy.	• Parents or peers engage in activities with the student in order to improve aptitudes. • Parents follow up an individualized program at home. • Tutor, adult, or peer assists the student in remedial activities.

OCCUPATIONAL GUIDANCE AND PREPARATION

Domain: Occupational Guidance and Preparation
Competency: 18. Selecting and Planning Occupational Choices
Subcompetency: 79. Identify Major Occupational Interests

Objectives	Activities/Strategies	Adult/Peer Roles
1. Identify occupational categories of interest.	• A career counselor gives a presentation on the types of jobs and training available in the community. • Students discuss which jobs seem most appealing or interesting. • Students construct a notebook of potential jobs with information about each job. • Students visit job sites which are of interest to them. • Students take the Strong-Campbell Vocational Interest Inventory (S-C II) and the Career Occupational Preference System Interest Inventory (COPS) tests and discuss the tests results. • Students list on chalkboard the occupational categories that interest them, derived from S-C II and COPS. • Students discuss their expectations of themselves working in those occupational categories.	• Parent helps the student identify the types of employment available in the community. • Parent asks the student to describe an ideal job. • Parent and student discuss the ideal job and types of employment available in the community in terms of occupational categories. • Members of various occupations discuss their jobs with students on a "Career Day."
2. Rank areas of personal interest in order of importance in finding an occupation.	• Student lists on chalkboard his or her own personal interests. • Counselor discusses and identifies student's interests relating to employment. • Student rank orders his or her interests. • Students list, on chalkboard or newsprint, aspects of different jobs (e.g., salary, types of work, location, work setting, etc.). • Students discuss which aspects of the job are most and least important to them. • Students rank order their personal interests from least to most important in finding an occupation. • Students discuss their beliefs about which of their interests a job is expected to satisfy.	• Parents discuss what they find appealing about their jobs. • Parents or peers discuss what they look for in a job and why that characteristic of their job is appealing.
3. Identify how interests relate to jobs.	• Students identify their interests. • Students list on chalkboard jobs which they believe meet their interests. • Students construct a notebook of potential jobs with information about each job. • Employment counselor gives presentation to students regarding jobs. • Students visit job sites they believe meet their interests. • Students discuss and share experiences and beliefs regarding job sites.	• Parents ask the student to describe an ideal job. • Parents or peers discuss how their jobs relate to their interests. • Parents and student visit job sites that reflect their interests. • Representatives from various employment sources present information on how interests relate to jobs.

OCCUPATIONAL GUIDANCE AND PREPARATION

Objectives	Activities/Strategies	Adult/Peer Roles
4. Describe ways the chosen job of interest relates to future personal goals.	• Counselor leads class discussion about occupational progress toward long-range goals. • Students construct a life chart bulletin board illustrating steps in achieving a long-range goal (e.g., completing the job, doing a certain type of work, working with others, getting paid, etc.). • Students list, on chalkboard or newsprint, their interests, and which of those interests they expect to meet through their jobs.	• Parents describe the steps they took to reach their current occupational situation. • Rehabilitation counselor discusses decision-making process in making a career choice

Domain: Occupational Guidance and Preparation
Competency: 18. Selecting and Planning Occupational Choices
Subcompetency: 80. Identify Major Occupational Needs

Objectives	Activities/Strategies	Adult/Peer Roles
1. Identify needs that can be met through one's occupation and rank them in order of personal preference.	• Students identify their needs and select an occupation of interest they believe will meet many of their needs. • Students take a field trip to selected occupational environments and observe and discuss what workers do in these environments. • Students determine what needs are met by their working environments and rank them by personal preference. • Students rank needs.	• Parents discuss with students needs which are met by their jobs and rank their needs. • Rehabilitation counselor identifies major needs one may realistically meet through work. • Workers from different occupational environments discuss or demonstrate what it is like to work in that environment.
2. Identify personal-social needs met through work.	• Students identify needs met through the working environment. • Students identify personal-social needs from needs met through the working environment. • Students discuss and define personal-social needs from other needs (e.g., social interaction, committee work, etc.).	• Parents or peers discuss and define personal-social needs met through work.
3. Name status needs met through work.	• Students discuss and define status needs as opposed to other needs (e.g., prestige, money, respect, power). • Students identify and list on chalkboard or newsprint status needs met through work.	• Parents or peers discuss and define status needs met through work.
4. Identify factors that the student needs in a personal occupational environment.	• Students discuss and define occupational environments which are personal in character (e.g., social services, human services, recreational therapy). • Students role-play those occupations to identify skills, characteristics, and job requirements for those personal occupations.	• Parents or peers discuss and define occupational environments which are personal in character.

OCCUPATIONAL GUIDANCE AND PREPARATION

Objectives	Activities/Strategies	Adult/Peer Roles
5. Identify the most personally satisfying aspects and the least satisfying aspects about a given specific job.	• Students take field trips to various selected work settings where workers discuss or demonstrate what job duties they perform. • Student performs specific tasks or jobs in school. • Students discuss what is most and least satisfying about specific jobs.	• Vocational counselor discusses the responsibilities involved in various occupations. • Parents or peers discuss the most important needs they meet through their jobs.
6. Identify criteria one would use in selecting an occupation.	• Students brainstorm reasons why people work. • Students construct on posterboard a hierarchy of major personality characteristics (e.g., likes, dislikes, need for structure, etc.) one would attempt to meet in selecting an occupation. • Group discussion on counseling allows the student to identify his or her own personality characteristics.	• Workers from different occupations discuss their reasons for choosing that occupation. • Rehabilitation counselor identifies major needs one may realistically meet through work. • Parents or peers discuss why they chose their occupations.

Domain: Occupational Guidance and Preparation
Competency: 19. Exhibiting Appropriate Work Habits and Behaviors
Subcompetency: 81. Follow Directions and Observe Regulations

Objectives	Activities/Strategies	Adult/Peer Roles
1. Perform a series of tasks in response to verbal instructions.	• Teacher demonstrates a sequence of steps to complete a job and students perform these under teacher supervision. • Students participate in games in which players are required to follow verbal instructions.	• Peers play games with the student in which players are expected to follow a series of instructions . • Parents or peers practice giving the student different kinds of verbal instructions and observing his or her performance. • Parents make a game out of linking directions together.
2. Perform a series of tasks in response to written instructions.	• Students complete activities which require them to follow a set of written instructions. • Each student is asked to explain a set of written instructions to another student or to the teacher. • Students are asked to prepare a dish or meal by following a recipe or construct a model from written directions. • Students collect samples of written instructions (e.g., auto repair, model assembly, tax return, etc.). • Students participate in a treasure hunt by following written instructions. • Students write a short list of directions from school to a specific destination.	• Parents engage the student in activities around the home which involve following a set of written instructions (e.g., doing chores, going to the store, house-cleaning, etc.).

OCCUPATIONAL GUIDANCE AND PREPARATION

Domain: Occupational Guidance and Preparation
Competency: 19. Exhibiting Appropriate Work Habits and Behaviors
Subcompetency: 82. Recognize Importance of Attendance and Punctuality

Objectives	Activities/Strategies	Adult/Peer Roles
1. Identify reasons for good attendance and punctuality.	• An employment counselor gives a presentation on why attendance and punctuality are important. • Students discuss benefits of good attendance and punctuality. • Students create a display on the bulletin board which lists reasons for good attendance and punctuality.	• Parents explain the importance of being punctual. • Parents discuss attitudes toward people who are late. • Parents or peers discuss how tardiness and absenteeism may have caused problems for them. • Employer discusses why tardiness and absenteeism are problems for him or her.
2. Identify acceptable and unacceptable reasons for tardiness and absenteeism.	• A local employer gives a presentation of the various causes of tardiness and absenteeism (e.g., illness, missing a bus, getting up late, etc.). • Students discuss the difference between a legitimate vs. an illegitimate reason for tardiness or absenteeism. • Students role-play supervisor and employee, and class votes on acceptability of given reasons for tardiness. • Students construct a bulletin board which lists legitimate vs. illegitimate excuses for missing work. • Students discuss what may happen if one is chronically late or absent from work.	• Parents help the student identify reasons why he or she might be late or absent from work, and which of these reasons are legitimate. • Parents or peers discuss experiences they have had with absenteeism and tardiness, and how this affected their work. • Employer discusses how to deal with problems of tardiness or absenteeism.
3. Identify appropriate action to take if late or absent from work.	• Students discuss what to do in case of absence or tardiness on a job. • Students role-play what to do in each case (e.g., call in, talk with the foreman, notify supervisor, etc.).	• Parents or peers describe the level of action they take when they are late or absent from work. • Employer discusses appropriate action to take when one expects to be late or absent from work.

Domain: Occupational Guidance and Preparation
Competency: 19. Exhibiting Appropriate Work Habits and Behaviors
Subcompetency: 83. Recognize Importance of Supervision

Objectives	Activities/Strategies	Adult/Peer Roles
1. List roles and responsibilities of supervision.	• A supervisor gives a presentation on the role of supervision (e.g., responsibilities, duties, etc.). • Students discuss and list on chalkboard roles and responsibilities of supervisors in specific situations (e.g., camp director and camp counselor, foreman and employee, principal and teacher, etc.). • Students observe a situation involving a supervisor and supervisee, and discuss their reactions. • Students role-play situations involving a supervisor and supervisee, and alternate roles.	• Parents or peers discuss their reactions to being supervised and/or supervising. • Former students discuss their experiences with supervisors. • Foreman discusses roles and responsibilities with factory workers.
2. Identify the appropriate response to a supervisory instruction.	• Students role-play responding to various supervisory instructions (e.g., acceptance, defiance, etc.). • Vocational education teacher observes student's responses to instructions and discusses these with the class.	• Supervisors from business or industry present a discussion of good and bad responses to their instructions and suggest types of responses they would like to receive. • Parents discuss their feelings and reponses to supervisory instruction.
3. Complete a job following supervisor's instructions.	• Student completes specific activities while under direct supervision (e.g., playing a game, cooking a meal, sports, etc.). • A student role-plays a supervisor and gets other students to complete an assigned task. • Students discuss their reactions to a supervisor and being supervised. • Students discuss their ability to cooperate. • Students participate in activities while under indirect supervision (e.g., landscaping, painting, home repair, etc.)	• Parents assign the student various tasks around the home and evaluate performance. • Employees discuss the need for supervision on the job and how to respond to it.

Domain: Occupational Guidance and Preparation
Competency: 19. Exhibiting Appropriate Work Habits and Behaviors
Subcompetency: 84. Demonstrate Knowledge of Occupational Safety

Objectives	Activities/Strategies	Adult/Peer Roles
1. Identify potential safety hazards on the job.	• A demonstration is given of typical safety hazards to be found in specific job groups. • Students take a field trip to job sites and discuss safety with foreman, shop stewards, and plant operations personnel. • Students discuss how to eliminate or minimize these hazards. • Students role-play what action to take when confronted with a specific hazard. • Vocational teacher describes how to identify a potential safety hazard.	• Parents describe safety hazards that may be found on the job. • Parents take student to job sites and discuss hazards with plant operations personnel. • Occupational safety specialist describes how to identify and deal with potential safety hazards.
2. Identify jobs that require safety equipment and identify the equipment.	• Students list on chalkboard jobs which require protective uniforms and discuss the reasons for them. • Students describe typical safety precautions used in industrial jobs. • Students describe special instruction required when working on certain jobs (e.g., wear rubber gloves, protective goggles, protective shoes, etc.). • Students role-play specific sets of safety precautions.	• Parents and student discuss jobs which are dangerous and require special safety precautions. • Parents or peers or workers discuss safety precautions they must take on the job, and the importance of these precautions.
3. Identify main reasons for practicing safety on the job.	• Students discuss safety standards required on jobs. • Students role-play situations in which safety precautions are not observed and discuss dangers involved. • Students create a display on a bulletin board which lists reasons for practicing safety on the job. • Students take field trips to local industries or businesses to point out safety signs posted and to discuss meanings and reasons for these.	• Parents discuss the safety precautions that are observed on their jobs. • Workers from different jobs discuss the kinds of safety precautions they must observe. • Disabled workers discuss the necessity of safety on the job. • Representative from State Employment Services discusses number of worker hours and money lost on jobs because of failure to observe safety precautions.
4. Follow safety instructions on the job (e.g., wear rubber gloves, safety goggles).	• Students describe typical safety precautions used in industrial jobs. • Students describe special instruction required when working on certain jobs (e.g., wear rubber gloves, protective goggles, protective shoes, etc.). • Students role-play specific sets of safety precautions.	• Parents or peers or workers discuss safety precautions they must take on the job.

Domain: Occupational Guidance and Preparation
Competency: 19. Exhibiting Appropriate Work Habits and Behaviors
Subcompetency: 85. Work with Others

Objectives	Activities/Strategies	Adult/Peer Roles
1. Identify reasons for working with others.	• Students identify and list on chalkboard activities for which more than one person is required. • Students engage in activities for which more than one person is required. • Students discuss their feelings about working with others. • Students identify and list on chalkboard the benefits of working with others. • Students identify situations in which there is cooperation and shared responsibility. • Students engage in team games or sports.	• Parents or peers help the student identify activities in day-to-day life which require more than one person. • Peers work with the student on tasks requiring more than one person. • Parents or peers discuss reasons for cooperation and shared responsibilities (e.g., household chores, etc.).
2. Identify the importance of individual components of a cooperative effort.	• Students demonstrate the dependence of the group on individuals by participating in a simulated activity in which one member leaves or doesn't cooperate. • Students take a field trip to an industry to observe assembly work. • A coach discusses the importance of cooperation in athletics.	• Parents demonstrate the role of individuals in household tasks. • Parents discuss how their job success involves a team effort. • Student athletes discuss how they learned cooperation on the playing field. • Workers from the community discuss aspects of cooperation in their jobs.
3. Complete a task working with other persons.	• Students are assigned to work in pairs on various tasks. • Students discuss what they like or dislike about working with others. • Students participate in games in which cooperation is required to reach a goal. • Students are presented with a task that requires two or more people to perform.	• Parents or peers work with the student to complete various household tasks. • Parents or peers discuss with the student what role each will assume in completing a task. • Peers engage in games or sports with the student.

Domain: Occupational Guidance and Preparation
Competency: 19. Exhibiting Appropriate Work Habits and Behaviors
Subcompetency: 86. Meet Demands for Quality Work

Objectives	Activities/Strategies	Adult/Peer Roles
1. Identify minimum quality standards for various jobs.	• Class discusses reasons for quality standards when producing products. • Vocational counselor leads a class discussion of various quality standards both in general and for local business and industry. • Class takes field trips to industries to observe quality control.	• Industry representatives present discussions of their quality standards. • Parents discuss quality standards required on their own jobs. • Parents discuss with student the dangers of producing inferior products.

OCCUPATIONAL GUIDANCE AND PREPARATION

Objectives	Activities/Strategies	Adult/Peer Roles
2. Identify reasons for quality standards.	• A local employer gives a presentation of the meaning of minimum quality standards on specific tasks or jobs. • Students discuss reasons for minimum quality standards in employment. • Students discuss possible results of failure to maintain quality standards in specific jobs (e.g., shoddy clothing, spoiled food, etc.). • Students list on chalkboard criteria for evaluating the quality of a specific job or task.	• Workers discuss major reasons for minimum quality standards on the job. • Quality control expert explains his or her job and why it is important. • Parents or peers discuss standards which must be met on their jobs. • Consumer expert discusses quality control and its importance to the consumer.
3. Perform simulated work tasks which have minimum quality standards.	• Students relate minimum quality standards to earning academic letter grades. • Students identify and list on chalkboard minimum quality standards in a specific task, activity, or job. • Students observe a task or job being performed according to minimum quality standards. • Students perform a task or job according to minimum quality standards. • Students participate in regular vocational training or work study to get practice in meeting and maintaining minimum quality standards. • Students perform jobs in the classroom in which the class sets standards and evaluates each other's performances (e.g., routine classroom housekeeping chores or a simulation, etc.).	• Employment service counselor discusses the relationship of ability to meet minimum quality standards and employment. • Parents or peers give the student feedback on performance, with suggestions for improvement.

Domain: Occupational Guidance and Preparation
Competency: 19. Exhibiting Appropriate Work Habits and Behaviors
Subcompetency: 87. Work at a Satisfactory Rate

Objectives	Activities/Strategies	Adult/Peer Roles
1. Identify the need for performing jobs at a satisfactory rate.	• Students take a field trip to different job sites to observe workers. • Students record the time it takes workers to complete a particular task. • Students discuss the average time for completing work activities and the need to work at a particular rate of speed. • Students replicate a job (work activities). • Students establish a particular rate of speed at which to complete the work and then attempt to complete the job at that rate of speed. • Students discuss each other's performances. • Class discusses "piecework" as a production rate incentive. • Students discuss advantages and disadvantages of working at a specific rate of speed.	• Parents discuss the need to perform their own jobs at a specific rate of speed and how others depend upon their performance to complete their jobs. • Parents and student discuss "time lines" for completing household chores.

OCCUPATIONAL GUIDANCE AND PREPARATION

Objectives	Activities/Strategies	Adult/Peer Roles
2. Identify satisfactory rates required for specific jobs.	• A local employer gives a demonstration of job performance in the classroom or workshop. • Students are asked to perform a specific job within a time frame. • Students receive feedback on the quality of performance from other students, teacher, or evaluator. • Students take field trip and observe workers performing specific jobs. • Students discuss duties entailed in a specific job and skills required to complete those duties. • Students time average rate of speed in completing tasks. • Students simulate a specific job and attempt to complete it at the computed average rate. • Class discusses the actual rate of speed as compared with the computed average rate.	• Parents or peers discuss the kinds of duties their jobs entail. • Workers from different jobs meet with the student to discuss rates on their jobs.
3. List reasons why a job must be performed at a certain rate of speed.	• Students discuss employer expectations. • Students investigate why some workers are paid by the hour, some receive a salary, and some are paid according to their production. • Each student is asked to obtain specific information about jobs in which he or she is interested. • Students create a display on a bulletin board illustrating examples of rate per different jobs. • Students take field trips to jobs with different performance rates (e.g., assembly plants, kitchens, etc.).	• Parents or peers discuss the kinds of responsibilities entailed in their jobs. • Student accompanies parents/peers to the job (when possible) and observes their performance.
4. Perform a job at a satisfactory rate.	• Students identify and compute average time rates for jobs which involve sorting, collating, and assembling. • Students participate in activities which give the teacher a chance to assess skills (e.g., sorting, collating, assembling).	• Parents receive a checklist of skills that can be assessed through activities in the home. • Parent make a game out of completing household chores within specified time limits. • Parents or peers discuss the rate of speed expected in their jobs. • Employment counselor meets with the student to discuss performance rates.

OCCUPATIONAL GUIDANCE AND PREPARATION

Domain: Occupational Guidance and Preparation
Competency: 20. Seeking, Securing, and Maintaining Employment
Subcompetency: 88. Search for a Job

Objectives	Activities/Strategies	Adult/Peer Roles
1. Identify the steps involved in searching for a job.	• A career counselor gives a demonstration of a logical step-by-step method of searching for a job. • A career counselor gives a presentation on sources of information about prospective jobs (e.g., want ads, employment service, friends, etc.). • Students create a display on a bulletin board illustrating step-by-step procedures and sources. • Class role-plays step-by-step procedures in job search. • Students tour State Employment Service. • Students engage in job search exercises. • Students keep a continuous display on a bulletin board containing the latest job leads from newspaper, employment agencies, etc.	• Parents discuss sources of information about prospective jobs. • Parents help the student develop a logical procedure to use in searching for a job. • An employment specialist gives a presentation on how to search for a job. • Representative from the State Employment Service discusses preliminary job search procedures.
2. Identify a potential job through employment resources.	• Students take a field trip to an employment service to acquaint themselves with services and procedures. • Class lists on chalkboard common resources used in locating job opportunities (e.g., newspapers, Job Service, etc.). • Class reads newspaper ads to identify appropriate jobs. • Class lists jobs on the bulletin board. • Students discuss the advantages and disadvantages of various job information resources.	• Parents assist the student in reading newspaper ads on a regular basis. • Vocational rehabilitation counselor presents discussion of services through that agency.
3. Arrange a real or simulated job interview.	• Class outlines steps in securing a job interview. • Students practice mock telephone calls to arrange an interview, and are observed to evaluate whether they give and ask for necessary information. • Students call a personnel interviewer in business or industry to arrange an interview for a job advertised in the newspaper. • Students take a field trip to a personnel office to discuss procedures to follow in securing a job interview.	• Parents role-play telephone calls to arrange interviews with the student. • Parents observe while the student arranges real interviews.

OCCUPATIONAL GUIDANCE AND PREPARATION

Domain: Occupational Guidance and Preparation
Competency: 20. Seeking, Securing, and Maintaining Employment
Subcompetency: 89. Apply for a Job

Objectives	Activities/Strategies	Adult/Peer Roles
1. Identify appropriate job application procedures.	• A career counselor gives a presentation on the steps involved in applying for a job. • Students role-play steps involved in applying for a job. • Students create a display on a bulletin board illustrating steps in the procedure. • Students add information to occupational information scrapbook.	• Parents or peers help the student identify steps involved in the job application process. • Employment specialist gives presentation on how to apply for a job.
2. Collect a personal data sheet to be used for job application.	• Class prepares outlines of data generally required on job applications. • Class reviews job application forms from various businesses. • Class takes a field trip to a local community college to discuss personal data sheet with job placement counselor, vocational resource educator, or other counselors providing that service. • Class reviews completed outlines. • Class prepares individual resumés. • Students complete actual procedures for obtaining Social Security cards (if they are not already registered).	• Parents assist the student with completion of the data required in the outlines prepared in class. • Personnel officers or interviewers discuss the critical points of a personal data sheet to be used for job application.
3. Complete a real or simulated job application with spelling assistance.	• A career counselor demonstrates the procedures for completion of a job application. • Students discuss the kind of information needed to fill out a job application. • Students create a display on a bulletin board which contains several examples of application forms. • Students complete a card they can carry that contains personal data (e.g., social security number, birth date, address, etc.). • Students practice filling out different job applications.	• Parents explain the basic information needed for job applications. • Parents or peers demonstrate how to fill out a job application. • Parents or peers allow the student to complete an application and correct mistakes.
4. Apply for a real or simulated job in person or by telephone.	• A career counselor gives a presentation on the appropriate dress, behavior, and conversation when applying for a job. • Students role-play the entire application process (e.g., finding a job, dressing appropriately, obtaining transportation, and holding conversation, etc.). • Students construct a display on a bulletin board depicting the do's and don'ts of applying for a job.	• Parents explain that neat appearance and manners are important in applying for a job. • Parents allow the student to identify a desirable job and go through the entire job application process. • Representatives from various companies discuss their expectations relative to appearance and application.

OCCUPATIONAL GUIDANCE
AND PREPARATION

Domain: Occupational Guidance and Preparation
Competency: 20. Seeking, Securing, and Maintaining Employment
Subcompetency: 90. Interview for a Job

Objectives	Activities/Strategies	Adult/Peer Roles
1. Obtain an interview or carry out a mock interview.	• A career counselor gives a presentation on ways to obtain an interview (e.g., telephone, letter, in person, etc.). • Students discuss how and when to use each method. • Students role-play what to say and do when applying by phone or in person. • Students create a display on a bulletin board showing the do's and don'ts of obtaining a job interview. • Students add information to their occupational information scrapbooks.	• Parents discuss different ways to obtain a job interview. • Parents discuss what is involved in each method. • Parents or peers role-play obtaining an interview. • A job placement specialist gives a presentation on the do's and don'ts of obtaining a job interview.
2. Identify interview behaviors.	• Students construct a display on a bulletin board illustrating the various stages of an interview and the types of behavior required. • Guidance counselor presents a discussion of proper interview behavior. • Class views videotaped interviews and identifies appropriate and inappropriate behaviors.	• Parents role-play or practice interviews with the student. • Personnel officers or interviewers discuss good and bad interview behaviors.
3. Complete a real or simulated job interview.	• Students role-play and/or videotape job interviews and then discuss their performances. • Students complete mock interviews with community personnel and receive their critiques. • Students complete interviews in potential employment situations.	• Parents discuss with the student how to behave in a job interview. • Parents or peers role-play a job interview with the student. • Parents or peers help the student correct any inappropriate behavior he or she displays in the role-play. • Employers discuss their expectations for interviews. • Former students, peers, and young adults discuss their experiences with the entire procedure from job search to employment.
4. Obtain transportation to and from the interview.	• Students discuss means of transportation available to them. • Students identify an interview site and list on chalkboard the means of getting there. • Students practice identifying different locations and discussing which means of transportation to use in getting to each. • Students discuss the importance of punctuality to the interview.	• Parents help the student identify all available means of transportation. • Employment personnel discusses punctuality for the interview and on the job.

OCCUPATIONAL GUIDANCE AND PREPARATION

Domain: Occupational Guidance and Preparation
Competency: 20. Seeking, Securing, and Maintaining Employment
Subcompetency: 91. Know How to Maintain Post-School Occupational Adjustment

Objectives	Activities/Strategies	Adult/Peer Roles
1. Identify potential problems encountered on the job.	• An employer gives a presentation on the kinds of problems one typically encounters on a job. • Students discuss how one might deal with these problems. • Students role-play problem situations. • School counselor talks about the kinds of problems typically encountered in adjusting to any new situation (e.g., making friends, adjusting to new routines, etc.).	• Parents or peers discuss kinds of problems they encounter or have seen others encounter while adjusting to a new job. • Employers discuss their most frequent employee problems. • Employees discuss their most frequent employment problems.
2. For potential problems, identify potential solutions.	• Students role-play different problems encountered on the job (e.g., poor quality work, absenteeism, tardiness, etc.); students discuss and identify causes of problems depicted in role-play; students discuss possible methods for dealing with the problems. • Students list on chalkboard specific job or job-related problems and at least one method for dealing with each. • Students keep notebooks listing specific methods for dealing with problems. • Students design a display on a bulletin board depicting typical job adjustment problems. • Students role-play problem resolution, with each student playing the role of the supervisor.	• Parents and student list potential employment problems. • Parents or peers discuss the methods they or their employed friends use in dealing with problems. • Supervisor, foreman, or counselor discusses ways to deal with adjustment problems. • Former students discuss their experiences in work adjustment.
3. Identify resources for assistance if problems cannot be personally resolved.	• Students discuss their problems with other students and how they resolved them. • Students discuss whom the student can see outside of work if he or she is having a work problem. • Students identify conflicts at work, and list on chalkboard resources for conflict resolution. • Students discuss what might be done at work to minimize these problems • Students add resource information to occupational information scrapbooks.	• Parents help students identify resources from whom they may receive help for a job-related problem. • Peers discuss their experiences with similar types of problems. • Various professionals (e.g., school counselor, rehabilitation counselor, employment counselor, psychologist) give presentations of the kind of assistance they can provide.

Domain: Occupational Guidance and Preparation
Competency: 20. Seeking, Securing, and Maintaining Employment
Subcompetency: 92. Demonstrate Knowledge of Competitive Standards

Objectives	Activities/Strategies	Adult/Peer Roles
1. Determine the minimum level of skill and performance required for a specific job.	• Students discuss minimum standards required for a specific job. • Students discuss standards based upon the job being completed. • Class makes on-site visits to a job location. • Class selects an appropriate job sample of a job observed and attempts to meet the performance requirements.	• Parents or peers take the student on trips to observe workers in action. • Workers discuss performance requirements and demonstrate job skills.
2. Identify potential remedial activities which might be required by an occupation.	• Class discusses ways in which speed and accuracy can be improved (e.g., practice exercises, similar task exercises, etc.). • Physical education instructor demonstrates ways to improve eye-hand coordination (e.g., use of VALPAR equipment, computer games, etc.). • Class takes field trips to factories and discusses remediation with appropriate personnel (e.g., foreman, personnel officer, trainers, etc.).	• Parents devise tasks at home in which speed and accuracy can be improved through practice. • Supervisors from industry present their production standards and demonstrate ways they help employees adjust to these standards.
3. Determine the level of personal abilities required for a specific occupation.	• Students prepare a written analysis of requirements of specific jobs and their own individual aptitudes. • Students take a field trip to observe workers performing. • Students discuss the responsibilities entailed in the jobs they find desirable. • Students construct notebooks listing desirable jobs and requirements and responsibilities of each. • Students create a display on a bulletin board which contains illustrations of jobs. • Students take a field trip to a local community college and discuss, with a vocational evaluator or appropriate counselor, personal abilities required on jobs.	• Parents help the student identify major responsibilities of several potential jobs. • Representatives of several occupations discuss responsibilities that exist in all jobs.

Domain: Occupational Guidance and Preparation
Competency: 20. Seeking, Securing, and Maintaining Employment
Subcompetency: 93. Know How to Adjust to Changes in Employment

Objectives	Activities/Strategies	Adult/Peer Roles
1. Identify factors that determine successful employment adjustment.	• Students discuss factors which determine successful and unsuccessful employment adjustment (e.g., social relationships, positive work attitude, on-time task completion, etc.). • Students take a field trip to job sites and discuss successful employment adjustment with employers and employees. • Students role-play successful employment adjustment.	• Parents or peers discuss with students their concepts of successful employment adjustment. • Employment counselor, human resource director, or other employment person presents information on successful employment adjustment.
2. Identify factors that determine unsuccessful employment adjustment.	• Students discuss and list on chalkboard factors which determine unsuccessful employment adjustment (e.g., poor performance, poor work attitude, difficulty getting along with others, etc.). • Students role-play employee and supervisor utilizing unsuccessful employment characteristics.	• Adults or peers discuss what they consider to be unsuccessful adjustments to employment. • Parents relate experiences with fellow workers who have been fired or forced to resign.
3. Identify potential employment variations within a specific occupation.	• Students discuss and list on chalkboard minimum standards required for specific jobs. • Students make on-site visits to job locations. • Students obtain written job specifications from employers for particular jobs which designate levels of employment for those positions. • Students discuss significant differences between levels of the same position.	• Parents or peers discuss significant differences between employees possessing jobs with the same title. • Parents help the student identify major responsibilities of several potential jobs. • Representatives of several occupations discuss responsibilities that exist in all jobs.
4. Identify factors that lead to termination of employment.	• Students list on chalkboard classroom behaviors which cause problems for them and then relate these behaviors to work settings. • Students list on chalkboard behaviors they believe would lead to termination of their employment.	• Representatives from various companies discuss their employee expectations and their process of termination.
5. Identify factors that lead to promotion at place of employment.	• Students discuss minimum standards required for specific jobs. • Students make on-site visits to job locations to discuss, with employers and employees, factors which have resulted in employee promotions. • Students discuss what is gained from job promotions. • Students role-play situation involving promotion decision making.	• Parent or peers discuss, with student, factors or reasons for their promotions. • Company representative presents to class factors leading to employment promotions.

OCCUPATIONAL GUIDANCE AND PREPARATION

Domain: Occupational Guidance and Preparation
Competency: 21. Exhibiting Sufficient Physical–Manual Skills
Subcompetency: 94. Demonstrate Stamina and Endurance

Objectives	Activities/Strategies	Adult/Peer Roles
1. Identify the need for stamina on the job.	• Teacher defines stamina or endurance. • Students list on chalkboard reasons for certain levels of endurance (e.g., safety, productivity, etc.). • Students create a display on the bulletin board illustrating different types of physical activities required in work situations.	• Parents discuss with the student the endurance requirements of their routine activities. • School nurse explains bodily reactions to physical activities.
2. Perform at the 80% level of age-normed simulated work task.	• Students are assigned simulated tasks in the school setting which require stamina. • Students determine the average performance rate for their age group in completing the tasks. • Students attempt to complete the tasks at an 80% performance level. • Students chart their own times for specific tasks requiring stamina. • Physical education teachers test students' endurance and design programs to improve or maintain physical conditioning.	• Parents observe the student's performance on physical tasks and assign routine home duties requiring stamina. • A work evaluator helps design simulated tasks with expected performance levels.
3. Identify jobs in which endurance and strength are critical.	• Students pair off and list on chalkboard jobs requiring endurance and strength. • Students create a display on a bulletin board illustrating jobs requiring physical stamina and strength. • Students visit job sites in the community that require high levels of endurance.	• Parents discuss with the student the physical demands of their jobs. • Personnel officer from a factory presents information regarding endurance requirements of specific jobs.

OCCUPATIONAL GUIDANCE AND PREPARATION

Domain: Occupational Guidance and Preparation
Competency: 21. Exhibiting Sufficient Physical–Manual Skills
Subcompetency: 95. Demonstrate Satisfactory Balance and Coordination

Objectives	*Activities/Strategies*	*Adult/Peer Roles*
1. Demonstrate satisfactory balance and coordination on non-work tasks.	• Students participate in activities requiring various degrees of balance and coordination (e.g., baseball, tennis, etc.). • Physical education instructor suggests activities for improving individual student's balance and coordination. • Students maintain a record of their performance in activities.	• Parents receive, from school, a list of activities which will develop the student's balance and coordination. • Parents or peers serve as participant observers in these activities with the student. • Parents or peers help the student identify areas of participation. • Parents or peers create game activities at home which require balance and coordination (e.g., relay game balancing hard-boiled egg on spoon, etc.). • Physical and occupational therapists explain activities for remediating specific problems in balance and coordination.
2. Demonstrate satisfactory balance and coordination on simulated work tasks.	• Students list on chalkboard simulated work tasks requiring balance and coordination that they can perform at school. • Students participate in specific tasks designed to measure balance and coordination. • Students create a display on a bulletin board illustrating people performing tasks requiring balance and coordination.	• Parents or peers encourage the students to engage in job-related activities around the home. • Parents or peers provide the student with feedback on performance. • Occupational therapist suggests remedial activities for improving balance and coordination.
3. Describe the relationship between balance and coordination and job performance.	• Teacher defines balance and coordination and discusses their relationship to job performance. • Physical education instructor demonstrates balance and coordination skills. • Students identify and list on chalkboard activities which require balance and coordination.	• Parents or peers identify balance and coordination in daily functioning. • Peers help the student participate in sports and games to improve balance and coordination. • Physical therapist discusses the reasons people have problems in balance and coordination.

OCCUPATIONAL GUIDANCE AND PREPARATION

Domain: Occupational Guidance and Preparation
Competency: 21. Exhibiting Sufficient Physical–Manual Skills
Subcompetency: 96. Demonstrate Manual Dexterity

Objectives	Activities/Strategies	Adult/Peer Roles
1. State three different kinds of physical–manual dexterity.	• Students list on chalkboard tasks requiring physical-manual dexterity. • Students differentiate between the types of physical-manual dexterity required to perform the tasks listed (e.g., watch repairman—fine motor, use of scissors, placing pegs in pegboard; surgeon—gross and fine motor, etc.).	• Parents or peers relate the physical-manual dexterity skills utilized during current and past employments. • Parents and student discuss household chores and the physical-manual dexterity skills needed to perform them.
2. Demonstrate personal level of dexterity in both work and non-work tasks.	• Counselor administers dexterity tests (e.g., Purdue Pegboard, GATB, Talent Assessment Program, VALPAR, etc.). • Students chart their own dexterity skills and abilities.	• Parents and student make competitive games out of tasks requiring dexterity skills. • Parents observe and report the student's dexterity in household activities and recreation. • Vocational assessment counselor talks with class about dexterity skills and evaluates sample of students.
3. Demonstrate adequate dexterity on work tasks appropriate to an identified occupation.	• Students pair off and collectively identify 35 occupations and the levels of dexterity required on the jobs—using Dictionary of Occupational Titles (DOT). • Students combine their lists and compare their own personal levels of dexterity with levels required by the DOT. • Students observe others demonstrating satisfactory dexterity on specific jobs. • Students perform these specific jobs. • Students discuss jobs in which they have difficulty. • Students practice improving their dexterity.	• Workers from different occupations demonstrate jobs involving varying degrees of dexterity. • Parents assist the student in carrying out practice exercises in improving dexterity. • Vocational assessment counselor or vocational evaluator discusses dexterity skills and occupations with the student.
4. Identify reasons for dexterity.	• Teacher defines and illustrates dexterity. • Students list on chalkboard situations in which manual dexterity is important. • Teacher or counselor identifies jobs requiring different levels of manual dexterity (unskilled to highly skilled).	• Workers discuss or demonstrate dexterity in their jobs. • Parents or peers discuss or demonstrate jobs around the home requiring varying degrees of dexterity.
5. Name two occupations commensurate with determined dexterity.	• Vocational counselor or teacher helps students identify occupations they might enter, based on their levels of dexterity. • Students take field trips to observe workers performing these occupations. • Students discuss which of these occupations seem most appropriate for their future. • Students compile a notebook of potential jobs.	• Employment service counselor helps the student identify occupations. • Vocational or rehabilitation counselor discusses services the student might receive to improve dexterity.

Domain: Occupational Guidance and Preparation
Competency: 21. Exhibiting Sufficient Physical–Manual Skills
Subcompetency: 97. Demonstrate Sensory Discrimination

Objectives	Activities/Strategies	Adult/Peer Roles
1. Describe five kinds of sensory discrimination.	• Students use their bodies to refer to five types of sensory discrimination. • Students name and list on chalkboard the senses used in identifying different stimuli and completing tasks. • Teacher and students design games to identify objects through the use of the five senses (e.g., students are blindfolded and asked to identify foods through sense of smell, etc.).	• Parents and student make games out of the use of the five senses.
2. Demonstrate size and shape discrimination.	• Students design their own tasks using different-sized objects to evaluate discrimination. • Teacher or counselor uses work samples to evaluate size and shape discrimination (selected components of the Talent Resources Program). Other commercially available tests include Great Shapes (Teaching Resources Corporation) and Revised Minnesota Paper Form Board Test (Psychological Corporation).	• Parents allow the student to use objects such as measuring devices (cups, rulers) to demonstrate and practice size and shape discrimination. • Vocational evaluator from a rehabilitation facility discusses and demonstrates evaluation techniques and remediation procedures.
3. Demonstrate color discrimination.	• Teacher, counselor, or nurse administers established color vision/discrimination tests. Other color discrimination tests include Small Parquetry with Pattern Cards (Teaching Resources Corporation), and Farnsworth-Munsell 100 Hue Test for Color Discrimination (Psychological Corporation). • Teacher arranges own test using everyday objects such as colored posterboards, crayons, etc.	• Parents quiz the student about color of household objects, as well as other objects when away from home.
4. State the need for sensory discrimination on an identified job.	• Students list on chalkboard jobs that require sensory discrimination. • Teacher arranges a field trip to a job site where workers demonstrate the sensory discrimination required.	• Parents discuss, with students, sensory requirements of routine household duties. • Working parents describe sensory discrimination requirements of their jobs. • Graduates discuss the need for sensory discrimination.
5. Demonstrate auditory discrimination.	• Although definitive auditory evaluations require specially trained personnel, the teacher can arrange classroom situations in which students identify spoken words while a record player provides background interference. Practical evaluation devices for use in the classroom with younger students are Sound Boxes (J.A. Preston Corporation).	• Parents attend to the student's auditory behavior at home and note strengths and weaknesses; deficit identification should be brought to the attention of medical personnel and school personnel. • Public health service worker provides audiologist to evaluate student's auditory discrimination.

4. Student Competency Assessment

Evaluation of student competency has experienced a number of innovative approaches since the advent of psychological testing in the early part of this century. Originally, the level of student achievement was determined in a fairly subjective manner. Teachers decided what was failing, satisfactory, or excellent. Visiting examiners administered oral examinations. In 1845 the Boston public schools substituted written examinations for oral testing. Standardized educational achievement testing in the United States had begun. Rapid advancement in testing occurred as a result of Binet's and Terman's work with intelligence testing. The advantage of objective group testing was demonstrated by Otis in his work with the Army during World War I. Differential aptitude testing was a logical consequence as educators and psychometricians recognized the usefulness of testing for vocational counseling. Much sophistication has been achieved in psychometrics, but the current state of the art is less precise and satisfactory than desirable.

Misuse of tests and recent discoveries regarding the appropriateness of some tests in certain situations, coupled with the humanistic movement in counseling, psychology, and education, have led to a general distrust of test results. Some states have legislated against administering certain tests in the public schools. (Many test items are biased against culturally different students and students with disabilities. Efforts toward differential interpretation of results have not proven to be a satisfactory solution to the problem.) In some cases, test designers have been prompted to revise tests or design new ones for these special groups, but with limited success.

Today, one can choose from thousands of available tests purporting to measure almost everything. But exactly what a test does measure and how well it does its job are being critically examined by concerned educators. The results are not encouraging. In fact the traditional grades subjectively assigned in high school are generally as good a predictor of college achievement as any sophisticated instrument. Although such judgments are undeniably based on some objective data, the human decision-making element remains. Such a component may be more accurate and reliable than psychometric theory would imply.

Tests designed to evaluate intelligence and psychomotor skills are generally based on comparisons between people in general. Performance below the average means only that testing reveals what a person cannot do compared with others. For an educator dealing with many students with special needs, such testing provides only an initial evaluation, and a fairly nonspecific one at that. Although demonstrable changes in IQ scores have been achieved with certain interventions, most students will probably not perform significantly better on IQ tests over time. With the advent of career education, educators have turned their attention more to goals and interventions that cannot be measured by traditional evaluation instruments. Increased competence in caring for one's daily needs will probably not be reflected in an IQ score or in the results of achievement batteries. Neither will a greater understanding of the world of work or awareness of one's occupational interests. Therefore, an educator dealing with the career education of a student is faced first with establishing goals and then with determining the extent to which these goals have been attained.

The 22 life-centered competencies relate directly to the concept of career education. The behavioral objectives for the competency units represent tasks the student should be able to perform in order to demonstrate competence. This approach provides the educator with a relatively comprehensive set of goals for career education. The task remains to determine an appropriate evaluation system to measure student attainment and progress. Examination of the behavioral objectives presented in Chapter 3 will lead even persons sophisticated in the use of tests to conclude that there is probably no existing instrument or system sufficient to evaluate these objectives. Although many objectives can be evaluated by commercially available tests, it is doubtful that any test or battery of tests will adequately evaluate all objectives.

Because traditional psychometric techniques have limited usefulness in evaluating student achievement, particularly in areas related to career education, alternative approaches are required. A proposed alternative is to directly observe student performance on relevant tasks in a systematic, standardized manner. In a competency-based curriculum, learning can be measured best by comparing students to themselves as opposed to comparing them to other students. This is especially important in evaluating students with disabilities, since their progress may not reflect gains typically sought with other youngsters. Small improvements may represent major accomplishments. A method of evaluation is needed in which students can demonstrate progress in many areas. A philosophical position recognizing the importance of independent living skills and the value of small increments in improvement is also required.

THE COMPETENCY RATING SCALE (CRS)

The Competency Rating Scale (CRS), presented in Figure 4–1, has been developed as a systematic approach to organizing and standardizing the assessment of students in the Life Centered Career Education Curriculum. The Manual, presented in Appendix A, presents a detailed explanation of the CRS and necessary procedures for using this system. The CRS Manual may be copied for separate use.

The CRS is a rating scale built around the 22 life-centered competencies. The 22 competencies have been further delineated into 97 subcompetencies. These subcompetencies serve as the actual CRS items. The Manual presents several behavioral criteria to use in judging student mastery of a subcompetency. These criteria are identical to the behavioral objectives of the life-centered competency units

presented in Chapter 3. Students are rated by the person most knowledgeable about their performance in a specific area, usually a teacher.

The use of specific behavioral criteria and precise definition of rating values is intended to enhance the reliability and validity of the ratings. Original criteria were reviewed and rank ordered by five national education experts to determine the appropriateness of the criteria to a given subcompetency. The criteria (behavioral objectives) presented for each subcompetency in the CRS represent a revision of the original criteria using the rankings and suggestions of the expert reviewers. The CRS Manual includes descriptions of the types of information regarding performance needed to rate students, who should do the rating, when rating should be done, criteria for rating, a rating key defining numerical rating values, and CRS Record Forms for recording and summarizing ratings as well as recording demographic data. The CRS Record Forms are divided into the three career education domains (Daily Living Skills, Personal-Social Skills, and Occupational Guidance and Preparation Skills) for convenience.

CRS users are encouraged to perform an initial rating to be followed by at least annual readministrations. The rater can assign ratings of the degree of mastery (0 = Not Competent, 1 = Partially Competent, 2 = Competent) for each subcompetency using the suggested behavioral criteria. Ratings are recorded and summarized on the appropriate CRS Record Forms. Results of CRS ratings can be used to develop individualized curricula. Following implementation of individualized curricula, the CRS can be used to evaluate program effectiveness.

THE LCCE COMPETENCY ASSESSMENT BATTERIES

Many users of the LCCE Curriculum and the Competency Rating Scale (CRS) have strongly suggested a more objective method of assessing the LCCE compentencies. Thus, project staff have now developed both knowledge and performance batteries. Each of these is described below.

LCCE Knowledge Battery

The Knowledge Battery is a standardized criterion-referenced instrument. It uses objective questions to assess students' knowledge in critical areas. It has been developed for special education teachers to use with 7th- through 12th-grade students with mild intellectual or specific learning disabilities .

The Knowledge Battery consists of 200 multiple-choice questions, which are broken down into three LCCE domains: Daily Living, Personal-Social, and Occupational Skills. There are 20 questions for each of the 20 competencies assessed by the Battery. Competencies #21 and #22 are not assessed with the Knowledge Battery because they involve the exhibition of manual skills and the development of skills in a specific occupation and cannot be evaluated with a knowledge test. Each domain's section requires 1 to 2 hours to administer, depending on the ability level of the examinees.

Instructional objectives of the LCCE Curriculum were used as guidelines for the development of Knowledge Battery test items. The instructional objectives define the important content areas of the Curriculum and provide a basis for the development of test items to ensure comprehensive treatment of each subcompetency area. The instructional objectives that deal strictly with knowledge were covered only on the Knowledge Battery. Questions for each competency were divided among the subcompetencies comprising that competency. The items selected for each subcompetency were spread among the objectives comprising that skill.

The Knowledge Battery is designed for small-group administration. The optimal group size is six to eight students. If larger groups are tested—even using proctors—the performance of examinees, especially students with mild intellectual disabilities, will be a lower and less accurate assessment of their true skills. Items should be presented to examinees both verbally by the examiner and in written form in the test booklet. Verbal presentation is recommended because the reading skills of examinees may vary above and below the fourth-grade reading level, the level at which the Battery was written.

LCCE Performance Battery

The Performance Battery consists of 21 competency tests covering all but Competency #22, "Obtaining a Specific Occupational Skill," which varies according to the skill being taught. Since it would be extremely time consuming to require students to actually perform/demonstrate every competency area in the multitude of situations and settings that will be needed, a worksheet approach to ascertaining competency mastery was used in many areas. One class period per test can be used for 14 of the 21 performance tests. These performance tests use a worksheet that generally contains five questions worth two points each. There are seven competency tests that require the student to fill out applications and blank forms of various types, figure a budget, manipulate small objects, cook a meal, store food, and so forth. The administration time for these operations usually will not exceed one or two class periods. The total time estimated for the Battery is approximately 35+ hours.

As with the Knowledge Battery, the instructional objectives of the Curriculum Guide were used as guidelines to develop the Performance Battery test items. Because of the short nature of the Battery, not all objectives could be addressed; thus, those that were most important to the deter-

mination of competency acquisition and were readily able to be assessed were chosen.

The Performance Battery should be administered to small groups of six to eight students so the examiner can attend to the student's questions regarding items. Items should be presented verbally to the students as they read along on the worksheets. Similar procedures to those outlined in the Knowledge Battery Manual for "Preparation for Test Administration" should be followed.

Each competency test specifies the materials needed for giving the tests, some general instructions to the examiner, and the instructions to give to the students. It is permissible to explain certain words that students do not understand, as long as the examiner does not give away the answers. The number of materials the examiner will have to secure to administer the various tests has been minimized. However, in some instances, there are several items that must be available.

The LCCE Competency Batteries are unique in that they offer comprehensive, curriculum-based assessment (CBA) measures of career development competence. There are few comprehensive measures of this nature relating directly to a specific curriculum. Thus, we believe educators will find this to be a very useful tool in their efforts to provide more extensive career development for their students. Although the Assessment Batteries focus on students with mild intellectual disabilities and students with severe learning disabilities, they should help provide a framework for offering career education services to other disability groups as well.

A more extensive description of the LCCE Competency Assessment Batteries and their use, as well as the actual test batteries, are available from CEC.

INDIVIDUALIZED EDUCATION PROGRAM

The Education for All Handicapped Children Act of 1975 (Public Law 94-142) mandated the establishment of an individualized education program (IEP) for every student with a disability. In 1990, Public Law 101-476 gave this Act a new title, The Individuals with Disabilities Education Act (IDEA). One of the most important provisions was a mandate that every eligible student have transition services incorporated into his or her IEP no later than age 16 and, when appropriate, beginning at age 14 or younger. It may be appropriate to include a statement of the interagency responsibilities or linkages in the IEP before the student leaves the school setting.

In an attempt to assist educators in fulfilling this requirement, a suggested IEP structure and form for including transition services are presented in this chapter. This form is to serve as an illustration of how the LCCE approach can be integrated into an IEP or ITP format. State and local educational agencies will have their own forms and requirements.

The LCCE IEP form consists of the following sections:

Section   I: Present Level of Educational Performance
Section   II: Annual Goals
Section   III: Specific Educational Services
Section   IV: Short-Term Individual Objectives
Section   V: Dates and Length of Time Relative to Specific Educational Services
Section   VI: Extent to Which Student Will Participate in Regular Education Program
Section   VII: Justification for Type of Educational Placement
Section   VIII: Individuals Responsible for Implementing the IEP and Transitional Services
Section   IX: Objective Criteria, Evaluation Procedures, and Schedule for Assessing Short-Term Objectives
Section   X: Date, Location, and Time for Next IEP Committee Review Conference

A sample IEP form for a hypothetical student is presented in Figure 4–2. A blank form has been included in Appendix B and may be duplicated.

The Competency Rating Scale can be used in both the development and evaluation of the IEP. For example, the level of educational performance for Section I can be partly determined by the initial administration of the CRS (Figure 4–1, first rating column). The cumulative average score resulting from a complete CRS rating can be used as one general index of educational performance. In addition, the use of the two competency assessment batteries described earlier, the LCCE Knowledge Battery and the LCCE Performance Battery, is recommended. Academic levels can be assessed using achievement tests.

The annual functional/transition goals for Section II can be chosen from the 22 competencies (Part B) and other transitional/support services (Part C). The extent of the impact of instruction in each competency area can later be determined using the CRS (Figure 4–1, second rating column) and posttesting results on the Knowledge Battery and/or the respective performance tests. The specific educational services in Section III can be developed from the competency units as well as from other sources. The short-term objectives for Section IV can be selected from the 97 subcompetencies as well as other sources. The CRS (Figure 4–1, second rating column) can be used to evaluate the degree of mastery of these short-term objectives since the CRS items are identical to the subcompetencies.

Section V is used to establish timelines for the use of special services. Section VI is used to determine the percentage of regular class time which would be used to achieve the annual goals. Section VII requires a justification of educational placement. The results of an initial CRS evaluation could provide at least part of this justification.

Section VIII requires the names of persons and the roles and responsibilities each will assume in the educational program. Section IX can be completed using CRS behavioral criteria for objective criteria. The CRS, Knowledge Battery, and Performance Battery are appropriate evaluation procedures. A scheduling of the next LCCE assessments can at least partially complete the assessment schedule requirement for transition services. Section X requires a scheduled time for the next IEP committee review conference.

Thus, an IEP with functional skills and transition components can be constructed from the LCCE competencies and competency units and can be evaluated at least in part by the three LCCE assessment instruments. The educator can establish goals, criteria for success, and a method of recording the necessary individualized plans and can then evaluate the outcomes of those plans. Although these components are designed so they can be used separately, the combination of an LCCE IEP competency unit, the CRS, and Knowledge and Performance assessments can be considered a complete planning, instructional, and evaluation package. In addition, the LCCE Self-Determination Scale (SDS) can add further information about the student's self-determination skills.

Figures 4–1 and 4–2 illustrate the use of the Competency Rating Scale Record Forms and the Student Individualized Education Program Form in a hypothetical situation. The IEP in Figure 4–2 represents a program developed from the results of a learner's initial CRS rating (see first column, Figure 4–1). The second column in Figure 4–1 presents the end-of-year CRS rating. Items that relate to the IEP goals and objectives are indicated by asterisks. Annual evaluation should include all CRS items, not just the items specified in the IEP. Although use of the CRS to evaluate fewer goals and objectives is feasible, the user is encouraged to rate all items and then examine those items which relate to specific goals and objectives.

This description of student evaluation and curriculum planning simply represents a suggested approach. Every educator must determine for himself or herself whether or not this approach is appropriate in a given setting. However, the LCCE IEP form could be used as the transition component and attached to the regular IEP form used by the school district.

FIGURE 4–1

LIFE CENTERED CAREER EDUCATION

Competency Rating Scale

Record Form

DAILY LIVING SKILLS

Student Name _____ Susan _____ Date of Birth _____ 1-10 _____ Sex ___ F ___

School _____ Progressive _____ City ___ Columbia _____ State ___ MO ___

Directions: Please rate the student according to his/her mastery of each item using the rating key below. Indicate the ratings in the column below the date for the rating period. Use the NR rating for items which cannot be rated. For subcompetencies rated 0 or 1 at the time of the final rating, place a check (✔) in the appropriate space in the *yes* or *no* column to indicate his or her ability to perform the subcompetency with assistance from the community. Please refer to the CRS manual for explanation of the rating key, description of the behavioral criteria for each subcompetency, and explanation of the *yes* or *no* column.

Rating Key: 0 = Not Competent   1 = Partially Competent   2 = Competent   NR = Not Rated

To what extent has the student mastered the following subcompetencies?

Subcompetencies	*Rater(s)*	JR	JR							Yes	No
	Grade Level	7	8								
	Date(s)	5/25/96	5/6/97								
DAILY LIVING SKILLS											
1. Managing Personal Finances											
1. Identify Money and Make Correct Change		2	2	__	__	__	__	__	__	__	__
2. Make Responsible Expenditures		1	1	__	__	__	__	__	__	__	__
3. Keep Basic Financial Records		0	*1	__	__	__	__	__	__	__	__
4. Calculate and Pay Taxes		0	0	__	__	__	__	__	__	__	__
5. Use Credit Responsibly		0	*1	__	__	__	__	__	__	__	__
6. Use Banking Services		0	*2	__	__	__	__	__	__	__	__
2. Selecting and Managing a Household											
7. Maintain Home Exterior/Interior		1	1	__	__	__	__	__	__	__	__
8. Use Basic Appliances and Tools		1	1	__	__	__	__	__	__	__	__
9. Select Adequate Housing		0	1	__	__	__	__	__	__	__	__
10. Set Up Household		0	1	__	__	__	__	__	__	__	__
11. Maintain Home Grounds		1	1	__	__	__	__	__	__	__	__
3. Caring for Personal Needs											
12. Demonstrate Knowledge of Physical Fitness, Nutrition, and Weight		1	1	__	__	__	__	__	__	__	__
13. Exhibit Proper Grooming and Hygiene		1	2	__	__	__	__	__	__	__	__
14. Dress Appropriately		1	2	__	__	__	__	__	__	__	__
15. Demonstrate Knowledge of Common Illness, Prevention, and Treatment		0	0	__	__	__	__	__	__	__	__
16. Practice Personal Safety		0	1	__	__	__	__	__	__	__	__

FIGURE 4–1 (continued)

Subcompetencies	Rater(s)	JR	JR						Yes	No
	Grade Level	7	8							
	Date(s)	5/25/96	5/6/97							
4. *Raising Children and Meeting Marriage Responsibilities*										
17. Demonstrate Physical Care for Raising Children		0	*2	—	—	—	—	—	—	—
18. Know Psychological Aspects of Raising Children		0	*1	—	—	—	—	—	—	—
19. Demonstrate Marriage Responsibilities		0	0	—	—	—	—	—	—	—
5. *Buying, Preparing, and Consuming Food*										
20. Purchase Food		1	1	—	—	—	—	—	—	—
21. Clean Food Preparation Areas		1	1	—	—	—	—	—	—	—
22. Store Food		1	1	—	—	—	—	—	—	—
23. Prepare Meals		0	1	—	—	—	—	—	—	—
24. Demonstrate Appropriate Eating Habits		1	1	—	—	—	—	—	—	—
25. Plan and Eat Balanced Meals		0	1	—	—	—	—	—	—	—
6. *Buying and Caring for Clothing*										
26. Wash/Clean Clothing		1	1	—	—	—	—	—	—	—
27. Purchase Clothing		1	1	—	—	—	—	—	—	—
28. Iron, Mend, and Store Clothing		1	1	—	—	—	—	—	—	—
7. *Exhibiting Responsible Citizenship*										
29. Demonstrate Knowledge of Civil Rights and Responsibilities		1	1	—	—	—	—	—	—	—
30. Know Nature of Local, State, and Federal Governments		1	1	—	—	—	—	—	—	—
31. Demonstrate Knowledge of the Law and Ability to Follow the Law		0	1	—	—	—	—	—	—	—
32. Demonstrate Knowledge of Citizen Rights and Responsibilities		0	1	—	—	—	—	—	—	—
8. *Utilizing Recreational Facilities and Engaging in Leisure*										
33. Demonstrate Knowledge of Available Community Resources		1	1	—	—	—	—	—	—	—
34. Choose and Plan Activities		1	1	—	—	—	—	—	—	—
35. Demonstrate Knowledge of the Value of Recreation		1	2	—	—	—	—	—	—	—
36. Engage in Group and Individual Activities		0	2	—	—	—	—	—	—	—
37. Plan Vacation Time		0	1	—	—	—	—	—	—	—
9. *Getting Around the Community*										
38. Demonstrate Knowledge of Traffic Rules and Safety		1	1	—	—	—	—	—	—	—
39. Demonstrate Knowledge and Use of Various Means of Transportation		1	1	—	—	—	—	—	—	—
40. Find Way Around the Community		1	1	—	—	—	—	—	—	—
41. Drive a Car		0	0	—	—	—	—	—	—	—

Total Possible Score (TPS) = N x 2 __82__	Total Actual Score (TAS)	24	44	—	—	—	—	—
	Average Score (AS) = TAS/N	.59	1.07	—	—	—	—	—

Comments: <u>There was significant improvement in this domain during the year although more emphasis on the subcompetencies is needed next year.</u>

*Denotes skill areas of instruction noted in the student's IEP for the year. Refer to the CRS manual for calculation and interpretation.

FIGURE 4–1 (continued)
LIFE CENTERED CAREER EDUCATION
Competency Rating Scale
Record Form

PERSONAL-SOCIAL SKILLS

Student Name _____Susan_____ Date of Birth _____1-10_____ Sex ___F___

School _____Progressive_____ City ___Columbia_____ State ___MO___

Directions: Please rate the student according to his/her mastery of each item using the rating key below. Indicate the ratings in the column below the date for the rating period. Use the NR rating for items which cannot be rated. For subcompetencies rated 0 or 1 at the time of the final rating, place a check (✔) in the appropriate space in the *yes* or *no* column to indicate his or her ability to perform the subcompetency with assistance from the community. Please refer to the CRS manual for explanation of the rating key, description of the behavioral criteria for each subcompetency, and explanation of the *yes* or *no* column.

Rating Key: 0 = Not Competent   1 = Partially Competent   2 = Competent   NR = Not Rated

To what extent has the student mastered the following subcompetencies?

Subcompetencies	*Rater(s)*	JR	JR						Yes	No
	Grade Level	7	8							
	Date(s)	5/25/96	5/6/97							
PERSONAL-SOCIAL SKILLS										
10. Achieving Self-Awareness										
42. Identify Physical and Psychological Needs		0	0	—	—	—	—	—	—	—
43. Identify Interests and Abilities		1	1	—	—	—	—	—	—	—
44. Identify Emotions		1	1	—	—	—	—	—	—	—
45. Demonstrate Knowledge of Physical Self		1	1	—	—	—	—	—	—	—
11. Acquiring Self-Confidence										
46. Express Feelings of Self-Worth		1	1	—	—	—	—	—	—	—
47. Describe Others' Perception of Self		1	1	—	—	—	—	—	—	—
48. Accept and Give Praise		1	1	—	—	—	—	—	—	—
49. Accept and Give Criticism		1	1	—	—	—	—	—	—	—
50. Develop Confidence in Oneself		0	1	—	—	—	—	—	—	—
12. Achieving Socially Responsible Behavior										
51. Demonstrate Respect for the Rights and Properties of Others		1	1	—	—	—	—	—	—	—
52. Recognize Authority and Follow Instructions		1	1	—	—	—	—	—	—	—
53. Demonstrate Appropriate Behavior in Public Places		1	1	—	—	—	—	—	—	—
54. Know Important Character Traits		1	1	—	—	—	—	—	—	—
55. Recognize Personal Roles		0	1	—	—	—	—	—	—	—

FIGURE 4–1 (continued)

Subcompetencies	Rater(s)	JR	JR							
	Grade Level	7	8							
	Date(s)	5/25/96	5/6/97						Yes	No
13. *Maintaining Good Interpersonal Skills*										
56. Demonstrate Listening and Responding Skills		1	1	—	—	—	—	—	—	—
57. Establish and Maintain Close Relationships		0	1	—	—	—	—	—	—	—
58. Make and Maintain Friendships		0	1	—	—	—	—	—	—	—
14. *Achieving Independence*										
59. Strive Toward Self-Actualization		0	0	—	—	—	—	—	—	—
60. Demonstrate Self-Organization		0	0	—	—	—	—	—	—	—
61. Demonstrate Awareness of How One's Behavior Affects Others		0	1	—	—	—	—	—	—	—
15. *Making Adequate Decisions*										
62. Locate and Utilize Sources of Assistance		1	1	—	—	—	—	—	—	—
63. Anticipate Consequences		1	1	—	—	—	—	—	—	—
64. Develop and Evaluate Alternatives		0	0	—	—	—	—	—	—	—
65. Recognize Nature of a Problem		1	1	—	—	—	—	—	—	—
66. Develop Goal-Seeking Behavior		0	1	—	—	—	—	—	—	—
16. *Communicating with Others*										
67. Recognize and Respond to Emergency Situations		1	1	—	—	—	—	—	—	—
68. Communicate with Understanding		1	*2	—	—	—	—	—	—	—
69. Know Subtleties of Communication		0	*2	—	—	—	—	—	—	—

Total Possible Score (TPS) = N x 2 __56__

Total Actual Score (TAS)	17	26	—	—	—	—	—
Average Score (AS) = TAS/N	.61	.93	—	—	—	—	—

Comments: Some improvement in this area but there should be considerably more emphasis next year.

*Denotes skill areas of instruction noted in the student's IEP for the year. Refer to the CRS manual for calculation and interpretation.

FIGURE 4–1 (continued)
LIFE CENTERED CAREER EDUCATION
Competency Rating Scale
Record Form

OCCUPATIONAL GUIDANCE AND PREPARATION

Student Name _____Susan_____ Date of Birth ___1-10___ Sex ___F___

School ___Progressive___ City ___Columbia___ State ___MO___

Directions: Please rate the student according to his/her mastery of each item using the rating key below. Indicate the ratings in the column below the date for the rating period. Use the NR rating for items which cannot be rated. For subcompetencies rated 0 or 1 at the time of the final rating, place a check (✔) in the appropriate space in the *yes* or *no* column to indicate his or her ability to perform the subcompetency with assistance from the community. Please refer to the CRS manual for explanation of the rating key, description of the behavioral criteria for each subcompetency, and explanation of the *yes* or *no* column.

Rating Key: 0 = Not Competent   1 = Partially Competent   2 = Competent   NR = Not Rated

To what extent has the student mastered the following subcompetencies?

Subcompetencies	Rater(s)	JR	JR						Yes	No
	Grade Level	7	8							
	Date(s)	5/25/96	5/6/97							
OCCUPATIONAL GUIDANCE AND PREPARATION										
17. Knowing and Exploring Occupational Possibilities										
70. Identify Remunerative Aspects of Work		1	2	—	—	—	—	—	—	—
71. Locate Sources of Occupational and Training Information		0	*2	—	—	—	—	—	—	—
72. Identify Personal Values Met Through Work		0	*2	—	—	—	—	—	—	—
73. Identify Societal Values Met Through Work		0	*1	—	—	—	—	—	—	—
74. Classify Jobs into Occupational Categories		0	0	—	—	—	—	—	—	—
75. Investigate Local Occupational and Training Opportunities		0	0	—	—	—	—	—	—	—
18. Selecting and Planning Occupational Choices										
76. Make Realistic Occupational Choices		0	0	—	—	—	—	—	—	—
77. Identify Requirements of Appropriate and Available Jobs		0	1	—	—	—	—	—	—	—
78. Identify Occupational Aptitudes		0	1	—	—	—	—	—	—	—
79. Identify Major Occupational Interests		0	1	—	—	—	—	—	—	—
80. Identify Major Occupational Needs		0	1	—	—	—	—	—	—	—
19. Exhibiting Appropriate Work Habits and Behaviors										
81. Follow Directions and Observe Regulations		0	0	—	—	—	—	—	—	—
82. Recognize Importance of Attendance and Punctuality		1	1	—	—	—	—	—	—	—
83. Recognize Importance of Supervision		1	1	—	—	—	—	—	—	—
84. Demonstrate Knowledge of Occupational Safety		0	0	—	—	—	—	—	—	—
85. Work with Others		1	1	—	—	—	—	—	—	—
86. Meet Demands for Quality Work		1	1	—	—	—	—	—	—	—
87. Work at a Satisfactory Rate		0	0	—	—	—	—	—	—	—

FIGURE 4–1 (continued)

Subcompetencies	Rater(s)	JR	JR							
	Grade Level	7	8							
	Date(s)	5/25/96	5/6/97							
									Yes	No
20. Seeking, Securing, and Maintaining Employment										
88. Search for a Job		—	2	—	—	—	—	—	—	—
89. Apply for a Job		—	1	—	—	—	—	—	—	—
90. Interview for a Job		0	1	—	—	—	—	—	—	—
91. Know How to Maintain Post-School Occupational Adjustment		0	0	—	—	—	—	—	—	—
92. Demonstrate Knowledge of Competitive Standards		0	0	—	—	—	—	—	—	—
93. Know How to Adjust to Changes in Employment		0	0	—	—	—	—	—	—	—
21. Exhibiting Sufficient Physical–Manual Skills										
94. Demonstrate Stamina and Endurance		0	1	—	—	—	—	—	—	—
95. Demonstrate Satisfactory Balance and Coordination		0	1	—	—	—	—	—	—	—
96. Demonstrate Manual Dexterity		0	1	—	—	—	—	—	—	—
97. Demonstrate Sensory Discrimination		0	0	—	—	—	—	—	—	—
22. Obtaining Specific Occupational Skills										
a. _____		NR	NR	—	—	—	—	—	—	—
b. _____		—	—	—	—	—	—	—	—	—
c. _____		—	—	—	—	—	—	—	—	—
d. _____		—	—	—	—	—	—	—	—	—
e. _____		—	—	—	—	—	—	—	—	—

Total Possible Score (TPS) = N x 2 __56__

Total Actual Score (TAS) __6__ __22__ — — — — —

Average Score (AS) = TAS/N __.21__ __.79__ — — — — —

Cumulative TPS: 194

Cumulative TAS __47__ __92__ — — — — —

Cumulative AS __.47__ __.93__ — — — — —

Comments: __This LCCE domain needs strong emphasis the last 3 years of the student's program.__ _____

*Denotes skill areas of instruction noted in the student's IEP for the year. Refer to the CRS manual for calculation and interpretation.

FIGURE 4–2
LIFE CENTERED CAREER EDUCATION
INDIVIDUALIZED EDUCATION PROGRAM FORM
(Use attachments as needed for each student)

Student Name: ___Susan___ School: ___Progressive___ Grade: _8_ Date: ___6/3/96___

SECTION I: Present Level of Educational Performance

Reading Level:	3.3 (CAT)	Math Level:	2.0 (CAT)
CRS Scores:	DLS (.59) PSS (.61)	OGP (.21)	(Maximum = 2.0)
KB Scores:	DLS (40%) PSS (43%)	OGP (25%)	TOT (38%)
PB Scores:	Mastery (Comp. 8)	No Mastery (Comps. 3, 5, 18, 21)	

SECTION II: Annual Goals

A. Academic Goals (see attachment)

B. LCCE Functional Skills for Transition Preparation (check those that apply)

This student will progress toward acquiring functional behaviors in the following competency areas. (Check the appropriate annual goals.)

_x_	1. Managing Personal Finances	____	12. Achieving Socially Responsible Behavior
____	2. Selecting and Managing a Household	____	13. Maintaining Good Interpersonal Skills
____	3. Caring for Personal Needs	____	14. Achieving Independence
_x_	4. Raising Children and Meeting Marriage Responsibilities	____	15. Making Adequate Decisions
____	5. Buying, Preparing, and Consuming Food	_x_	16. Communicating with Others
____	6. Buying and Caring for Clothing	_x_	17. Knowing and Exploring Occupational Possibilities
____	7. Exhibiting Responsible Citizenship	____	18. Selecting and Planning Occupational Choices
____	8. Utilizing Recreational Facilities and Engaging in Leisure	____	19. Exhibiting Appropriate Work Habits and Behaviors
____	9. Getting Around the Community	____	20. Seeking, Securing, and Maintaining Employment
____	10. Achieving Self-Awareness	____	21. Exhibiting Sufficient Physical–Manual Skills
____	11. Acquiring Self-Confidence	____	22. Obtaining Specific Occupational Skills

C. Other Transitional/Support Services Goals (check those that apply)

____	1. Financial Assistance/Income Support	____	5. Transporation
____	2. Advocacy Legal Services	____	6. Other _____
____	3. Medical	____	7. Other _____
____	4. Insurance	____	8. Other _____

SECTION III: Specific Educational Services Needed

Goal & Subcomp. Numbers	Special Services Needed	Special Media/Materials and Equipment	Individual Implementors
A	(See attachment)		
B 1 (3, 5, 6)	Job shadowing experience (banks, credit agencies), simulated business activities, speakers, home assignments	Credit banking & other forms, LCCE lesson plans, materials for setting up a model bank & store, transportation	Special education/math/business ed. teachers, bank & credit company employees, parents, peers
B 4 (17, 18)	Visits to public health department and day care centers, student role-play activities, community input	Various health charts, thermometers, tub for bathing, medicine bottles, transportation	Special education/health teachers, school nurse, parents, public health nurse, nursery school personnel, child guidance center staff
B 16 (68, 69)	Group activities, role-playing (e.g., TV show)	Videotapes & films, telephones, audio recorders	Special education/speech/language arts teachers, parents, peers, TV or radio interviewer
B 17 (71, 72, 73)	Field trips, role-play activities/simulations, community input, home assignments	Bulletin boards, occupational literature, magazines, newspapers	Special education/work-study teachers, career counselors, employers, Chamber of Commerce, VR counselor

FIGURE 4–2 (continued)
LIFE CENTERED CAREER EDUCATION
INDIVIDUALIZED EDUCATION PROGRAM FORM

SECTION IV: Short-Term Individual Objectives

A. Academic Goals (see attachment)

B. LCCE Functional Skills for Transition Preparation (check those that apply)

____ 1. Identify Money and Make Correct Change (1)	____ 39. Demonstrate Knowledge and Use of Various Means of Transportation (9)
____ 2. Make Responsible Expenditures (1)	____ 40. Find Way Around the Community (9)
_x_ 3. Keep Basic Financial Records (1)	____ 41. Drive a Car (9)
____ 4. Calculate and Pay Taxes (1)	____ 42. Identify Physical and Psychological Needs (10)
_x_ 5. Use Credit Responsibly (1)	____ 43. Identify Interests and Abilities (10)
_x_ 6. Use Banking Services (1)	____ 44. Identify Emotions (10)
____ 7. Maintain Home Exterior/Interior (2)	____ 45. Demonstrate Knowledge of Physical Self (10)
____ 8. Use Basic Appliances and Tools (2)	____ 46. Express Feelings of Self-Worth (11)
____ 9. Select Adequate Housing (2)	____ 47. Describe Others' Perception of Self (11)
____ 10. Set Up Household (2)	____ 48. Accept and Give Praise (11)
____ 11. Maintain Home Grounds (2)	____ 49. Accept and Give Criticism (11)
____ 12. Demonstrate Knowledge of Physical Fitness, Nutrition, and Weight (3)	____ 50. Develop Confidence in Oneself (11)
____ 13. Exhibit Proper Grooming and Hygiene (3)	____ 51. Demonstrate Respect for the Rights and Properties of Others (12)
____ 14. Dress Appropriately (3)	____ 52. Recognize Authority and Follow Instructions (12)
____ 15. Demonstrate Knowledge of Common Illness, Prevention, and Treatment (3)	____ 53. Demonstrate Appropriate Behavior in Public Places (12)
____ 16. Practice Personal Safety (3)	____ 54. Know Important Character Traits (12)
_x_ 17. Demonstrate Physical Care for Raising Children (4)	____ 55. Recognize Personal Roles (12)
_x_ 18. Know Psychological Aspects of Raising Children (4)	____ 56. Demonstrate Listening and Responding Skills (13)
____ 19. Demonstrate Marriage Responsibilities (4)	____ 57. Establish and Maintain Close Relationships (13)
____ 20. Purchase Food (5)	____ 58. Make and Maintain Friendships (13)
____ 21. Clean Food Preparation Areas (5)	____ 59. Strive Toward Self-Actualization (14)
____ 22. Store Food (5)	____ 60. Demonstrate Self-Organization (14)
____ 23. Prepare Meals (5)	____ 61. Demonstrate Awareness of How One's Behavior Affects Others (14)
____ 24. Demonstrate Appropriate Eating Habits (5)	____ 62. Locate and Utilize Sources of Assistance (15)
____ 25. Plan and Eat Balanced Meals (5)	____ 63. Anticipate Consequences (15)
____ 26. Wash/Clean Clothing (6)	____ 64. Develop and Evaluate Alternatives (15)
____ 27. Purchase Clothing (6)	____ 65. Recognize Nature of a Problem (15)
____ 28. Iron, Mend, and Store Clothing (6)	____ 66. Develop Goal-Seeking Behavior (15)
____ 29. Demonstrate Knowledge of Civil Rights and Responsibilities (7)	____ 67. Recognize and Respond to Emergency Situations (16)
____ 30. Know Nature of Local, State, and Federal Governments (7)	_x_ 68. Communicate with Understanding (16)
____ 31. Demonstrate Knowledge of the Law and Ability to Follow the Law (7)	_x_ 69. Know Subtleties of Communication (16)
____ 32. Demonstrate Knowledge of Citizen Rights and Responsibilities (7)	____ 70. Identify Remunerative Aspects of Work (17)
____ 33. Demonstrate Knowledge of Available Community Resources (8)	_x_ 71. Locate Sources of Occupational and Training Information (17)
____ 34. Choose and Plan Activities (8)	_x_ 72. Identify Personal Values Met Through Work (17)
____ 35. Demonstrate Knowledge of the Value of Recreation (8)	_x_ 73. Identify Societal Values Met Through Work (17)
____ 36. Engage in Group and Individual Activities (8)	____ 74. Classify Jobs into Occupational Categories (17)
____ 37. Plan Vacation Time (8)	____ 75. Investigate Local Occupational and Training Opportunities (17)
____ 38. Demonstrate Knowledge of Traffic Rules and Safety (9)	____ 76. Make Realistic Occupational Choices (18)
	____ 77. Identify Requirements of Appropriate and Available Jobs (18)

FIGURE 4–2 (continued)
LIFE CENTERED CAREER EDUCATION
INDIVIDUALIZED EDUCATION PROGRAM FORM

____ 78. Identify Occupational Aptitudes (18)	____ 89. Apply for a Job (20)
____ 79. Identify Major Occupational Interests (18)	____ 90. Interview for a Job (20)
____ 80. Identify Major Occupational Needs (18)	____ 91. Know How to Maintain Post-School Occupational Adjustment (20)
____ 81. Follow Directions and Observe Regulations (19)	
____ 82. Recognize Importance of Attendance and Punctuality (19)	____ 92. Demonstrate Knowledge of Competitive Standards (20)
____ 83. Recognize Importance of Supervision (19)	____ 93. Know How to Adjust to Changes in Employment (20)
____ 84. Demonstrate Knowledge of Occupational Safety (19)	____ 94. Demonstrate Stamina and Endurance (21)
____ 85. Work with Others (19)	____ 95. Demonstrate Satisfactory Balance and Coordination (21)
____ 86. Meet Demands for Quality Work (19)	
____ 87. Work at a Satisfactory Rate (19)	____ 96. Demonstrate Manual Dexterity (21)
____ 88. Search for a Job (20)	____ 97. Demonstrate Sensory Discrimination (21)

C. Other Transitional/Support Services Objectives (see attachment)

SECTION V: Date and Length of Time relative to specific educational services needed for this student

Goal Number	Beginning Date	Ending Date	Goal Number	Beginning Date	Ending Date
B 1 (3, 5, 6)	9-1-96	12-15-96			
B 4 (17, 18)	9-1-96	12-15-96			
B 16 (68, 69)	1-10-97	5-20-97			
B 17 (71, 72, 73)	1-10-97	5-20-97			

SECTION VI: Description of Extent to which this student will participate in the regular educational program

	Percentage of Time	Narrative Description/Reaction
Language arts	15 %	Build greater communication skills
Math	10 %	Use practical, everyday situations and materials
Science	____ %	
Social science	____ %	
Vocational (Bus.) & Work Study	15 %	Limited typing & clerical skills—resource room needed
Physical education	5 %	No physical limitation
(other) Health	10 %	Provide supports and some coteaching lessons
(other) Speech	5 %	Has problems expressing self; shy

FIGURE 4–2 (continued)
LIFE CENTERED CAREER EDUCATION
INDIVIDUALIZED EDUCATION PROGRAM FORM

SECTION VII: Justification for type of educational placement of this student

Narrative Description/Reaction

LCCE SCAR/KB/PB measures indicate these as primary needs and relate to student's interests and preferences at this time. Not enough instruction has been provided in these areas and it is felt she can benefit from this focus.

SECTION VIII: Individual Responsible for implementing the individualized education program and transitional services

Name	*Role/Responsibility*
Special education, vocational education, math, health, work-study, and language arts teachers	Participating in assisting Susan to learn the subcompetencies noted in Section IV B
Bank, credit company, nursery school, TV & radio interviewers, career counselors, Chamber of Commerce personnel, vocational rehabilitation, guidance center, & public health workers	
Parents/families, peers	

SECTION IX: Objective Criteria, Evaluation Procedures, and Schedule for assessing short-term objectives

Objective Criteria can be found in the LCCE Competency Rating Scale (CRS), the LCCE Knowledge Battery (KB), and the LCCE Performance Battery (PB). Criteria listed reflect the short-term individual objectives checked in Section IV, Part B, of this form.

Evaluation Procedures can be determined by the IEP Committee reviewing the manuals for the Competency Rating Scale, Knowledge Battery, and Performance Battery.

Schedule for Assessment should include time, date, frequency, place, etc.

PB pretests to be administered prior to instruction and posttests upon completion. KB to be readministered in 1 year.

SECTION X: Estimated Date, Location, and Time for next IEP Committee Review Conference

11/1/97   10:00 a.m.   Junior High School   Room 100

Appendix A
Competency
Rating Scale Manual

COMPETENCY RATING SCALE MANUAL

The life-centered approach to career education bases its curriculum on 22 competencies that have been identified as necessary for personal independence in the community and on the job (Brolin, 1974). These 22 competencies have been further delineated into subcompetencies in its revised edition. If this curriculum is to be used, a uniform method of evaluating student performance and progress in career education is needed. Although there are numerous educational and psychological devices and systems in existence for evaluating student performance in a variety of areas, none appears to be sufficiently specific or comprehensive for the criteria that define the subcompetencies. The Competency Rating Scale (CRS) is an initial attempt to meet this need by providing educators with a systematic means of assessing student mastery of the subcompetencies. The purpose of this manual is to furnish the user with a guide for rating student performance for each subcompetency, as well as a comprehensive explanation of each subcompetency.

The CRS is a rating scale that the user completes by judging a student's mastery of the subcompetencies using the criteria presented in Chapter 3 of this manual. Like any assessment device or system, the CRS requires a certain degree of training of the rater before actual use with students. Since the CRS requires judgments regarding student performance and behavior, it is necessary that all raters employ the same criteria when making judgments. This is critical if the user intends to compare students to one another or to evaluate changes in individual performance or behavior over time.

The manual is divided into four sections. Section I describes the rating key and how to rate student performance and behavior. Section II explains the use of the CRS Record Form. Section III presents explanations and behavioral criteria for the subcompetencies. Section IV describes interpretation of CRS results.

The task of assessing student performance in any subject area is a difficult one. This task becomes increasingly difficult for the educator dealing with the career education of students with disabilities.

SECTION I—RATING STUDENT PERFORMANCE

The Rating Key

The CRS provides four alternative ratings for student performance on each subcompetency. There are three sources from which the user can draw information to establish the rating for a given subcompetency. The most valid source of information is the rater's immediate personal observation of student performance and behavior. The rater's personal records or notes regarding student performance and behavior are probably less valid, but acceptable. Finally, written or verbal reports from other personnel are the least valid source of information, but they may be necessary.

When sufficient information exists to rate a subcompetency, one of the following ratings should be selected.

0 = *Not Competent.* The student is unable to perform any of the behavioral criteria for the subcompetency. This rating should be used for students who, in

the judgment of the rater, cannot be expected to perform this subcompetency satisfactorily for independent living. Such a student will require special help to master the subcompetency or, if not scheduled for further formal education, will require assistance from public or private individuals or agencies to accomplish the behavioral criteria.

1 = *Partially Competent*. The student is able to perform at least one but not all of the behavioral criteria for the subcompetency. This rating should be used for students who, in the judgment of the rater, can be expected to perform this subcompetency satisfactorily for independent living following normal teaching intervention during formal education. Such a student might require assistance from public or private individuals or agencies if he or she is not scheduled for further formal education.

2 = *Competent*. The student is able to perform all the behavioral criteria for the subcompetency. This rating should be used only for those students who, in the judgment of the rater, are able to perform the behavioral criteria satisfactorily for independent living without assistance or further formal education.

NR = *Not Rated*. The rater should use this rating for subcompetencies he or she is unable to rate due to absence of sufficient information or other logistical difficulty such as insufficient time.

If, at the time a student is scheduled to discontinue formal education, that student is not capable of independently performing the behavioral criteria for a subcompetency, the rater should determine whether or not the student could accomplish the subcompetency with assistance from others normally available in the student's environment. This is a *yes* or *no* decision and is further explained in Section II.

The Rater

Optimally, the same individual should rate a student's performance and behavior for all of the subcompetencies. However, logistical difficulties may preclude this. For this reason, the subcompetencies are separated into the three Life Centered Career Education domains: Daily Living Skills, Personal–Social Skills, and Occupational Guidance and Preparation (Section III). The CRS Record Form (Section II) is also separated into these three domains. It is highly desirable that the same individual rate all subcompetencies in a particular domain. If this type of procedure is not possible, one individual should be designated to coordinate the ratings of more than one rater within a domain. If more than one rater is employed, the coordinator should take care to ensure that these raters strictly adhere to the behavioral criteria for the subcompetencies. It is particular-

ly important that ratings be as precise and consistent as possible since CRS results may be used to develop and evaluate individualized education programs.

Rating Intervals

Space is provided on the CRS Record Form (Section II) for seven ratings. It is suggested that the CRS be administered at the beginning of grade 7 and at the end of grades 7, 8, 9, 10, 11, and 12 to establish initial functioning and to monitor changes in performance and behavior. (The CRS could be used at the elementary grade level too, if desired.) If the rater is unfamiliar with a student entering grade 7, rating should be postponed until adequate observation has taken place to ensure accurate ratings. If the CRS is employed after a student has completed any of the intermediate or secondary years, it is recommended that an initial rating be administered followed by yearly ratings. The user is free to administer the CRS as frequently as is deemed advisable. However, caution should be taken not to "teach for the test." In other words, ratings should not take place immediately after the student has been taught a subcompetency, unless the user intends to do further ratings. A single rating following instruction will provide little information regarding long-term mastery of the subcompetency.

SECTION II—USING THE CRS RECORD FORM

The CRS Record Form is separated into three sections corresponding to the three domains: Daily Living Skills, Personal–Social Skills, and Occupational Guidance and Preparation. Each part can be administered independently. As noted in Section I of the manual, it is desirable that one individual rate all subcompetencies in a particular domain. This is a matter that each user must determine depending on his or her particular situation. A blank CRS Record Form is presented in Appendix B and may be used as a master for duplication. Figure A–1 at the end of the CRS Manual presents a completed Record Form for a hypothetical student. An initial rating at the beginning of grade 7 and annual ratings at the end of grades 7, 8, 9, 10, 11, and 12 are illustrated.

Identifying Information

The CRS Record Form provides space to record the student's name, date of birth, and sex. Space is also provided for the name and address of the student's school.

Directions

The directions for the CRS Record Form indicate that the user should choose one of the four possible ratings for each subcompetency. The numerical ratings should be recorded in the space to the right of the subcompetency. The NR rating should be assigned to items that are not rated. The subcompetencies are listed on the left side of the CRS Record Form and are grouped under the competencies. Space is provided at the head of each rating column to record the rater's name(s), the student's grade level, and the date(s) of the rating period. If the ratings are completed in a single day, only that date need be recorded. However, if the ratings require more than one day, the user should record both the beginning and ending dates. It is recommended that ratings be completed as quickly as possible (e.g., one day to one week).

A *yes/no* rating is possible in the final column on the right side of the CRS Record Form. This space is provided for the rater to indicate whether or not a student who is finishing formal education can perform unmastered subcompetencies with the assistance of individuals normally present in his or her environment. This column needs to be completed only for subcompetencies assigned a final rating of 0 or 1. Place a check (✔) in the *yes* or *no* space if needed.

The user will note that Competency 22 in the Occupational Guidance and Preparation Domain has no subcompetencies. Space is provided following Competency 22 to list specific occupational skill training the student is receiving during the six intermediate and secondary years. The rater should rate this training in the same manner as the other subcompetencies by treating the skill training as a subcompetency. However, only the training during the final year of education is rated, although training received every year should be recorded. Consequently, a numerical rating only for item *e* (training received during the final year of education) should be recorded in the seventh rating column. A similar *yes* or *no* rating can also be determined for this training if it is not complete at the end of the formal education.

Space is provided following the listing of the subcompetencies for the total possible score if a student were assigned the highest rating for each subcompetency in a domain. This value is determined by omitting Competency 22 from the calculations, except for ratings in the last year of formal education. The total possible score can be calculated by counting the number of rated items (N) and multiplying by the highest possible rating (2). Thus, total possible score (TPS) = N x 2. To the right of the total possible score, space is provided to record the student's total actual score (TAS), which is the sum of the ratings for all rated items. Space is provided below the TAS to record the average score per item (AS). The AS is calculated by dividing the TAS by N (thus, AS = TAS ÷ N). Space is provided at the end of the Occupational Guidance and Preparation section for a cumulative total possible score, a cumulative total actual score, and a cumulative average score. The cumulative TPS can be calculated by adding the TPSs for the three domains. Note: The TPS and the cumulative TPS must be calculated for *each* administration since the number of rated items may vary with each administration. The cumulative TAS can be calculated by adding the TASs from the three domains. The cumulative AS can be calculated by adding the ASs from the three domains and dividing by 3. Thus, the user can evaluate performance and behavior for each domain as well as the three domains combined. There is space provided for comments at the end of each Record Form.

SECTION III—BEHAVIORAL CRITERIA FOR RATING SUBCOMPETENCIES

A list of the 97 subcompetencies grouped into the three career education domains follows. Each subcompetency is conceptually described and further defined by behavioral criteria. A rank ordering of the criteria for each subcompetency in order of importance for the subcompetency was performed by five national education experts. Further revision of the original criteria considered clarity and specificity. As discussed in Section I, the rater should compare student performance to the behavioral criteria for each subcompetency to determine the degree of mastery. The ratings from the rating key can then be assigned to each subcompetency (item) based on the number of criteria that the student is able to perform for each subcompetency.

DAILY LIVING SKILLS

1. **Managing Personal Finances**
   1. *Identify Money and Make Correct Change*
      1. Identify coins and bills less than or equal to $100 in value.
      2. Count money in coin and bill denominations with sums less than or equal to $20.
      3. Make correct change from both bills and coins for amounts less than or equal to $50.
   2. *Make Responsible Expenditures*
      1. Identify prices on labels and tags of merchandise.
      2. Choose most economical buy among like items of a similar quality.
      3. Identify purchases as necessities or luxuries in the area of food, clothing, housing, and transportation.
      4. Determine amount of money saved by buying sale items.
      5. Compare prices of an item in three stores.
   3. *Keep Basic Financial Records*
      1. Construct a monthly personal budget for your present income.
      2. Identify financial information and financial records which should be retained.
      3. Record personal major income and expenses for one month.
      4. Calculate balances of major debts
      5. List basic terms used in keeping financial records.
   4. *Calculate and Pay Taxes*
      1. Know types of taxes normally assessed in the geographic area.
      2. Know penalties and deadlines for the payment of taxes.
      3. Know sources of assistance for the filing of taxes.
      4. Complete a 1040 tax form.

5. *Use Credit Responsibly*
   1. Identify resources for obtaining a loan.
   2. Name advantages and disadvantages of using credit cards.
   3. Complete a loan application.
6. *Use Banking Services*
   1. Open a checking account.
   2. Open a savings account.
   3. Write checks, make deposits, and record checking transactions.
   4. Make deposits and withdrawals, and record savings transactions.

2. Selecting and Managing a Household

7. *Maintain Home Exterior/Interior*
   1. Identify basic tools used in exterior maintenance.
   2. List routine cleaning and maintenance activities.
   3. Outline a weekly housekeeping routine.
   4. Identify the uses of common household cleaning products and equipment.
8. *Use Basic Appliances and Tools*
   1. Name common appliances and tools found in the home and tell how each is used.
   2. Demonstrate appropriate use of basic appliances and tools.
   3. Name safety procedures when using appliances and tools.
   4. Perform basic home care tasks.
9. *Select Adequate Housing*
   1. List personal or family housing requirements, including space, location, and yard.
   2. Identify different types of housing available in the community.
   3. Identify advantages and disadvantages of different types of housing.
   4. Identify procedures for renting a house or apartment.
   5. Identify procedures for buying a house.
10. *Set Up Household*
    1. Describe procedures for connecting utility services.
    2. Acquire or ensure presence of basic household items.
    3. Acquire or ensure presence of furniture and major appliances.
11. *Maintain Home Grounds*
    1. Perform common home maintenance and repairs (e.g., grass cutting, painting, bush trimming, etc.).

3. Caring for Personal Needs

12. *Demonstrate Knowledge of Physical Fitness, Nutrition, and Weight*
    1. Know ways nutrition relates to health.
    2. Know a meal balanced for nutritional and caloric content.
    3. Know ways in which exercise relates to health.
    4. Identify and demonstrate correct ways of performing common physical exercises.
13. *Exhibit Proper Grooming and Hygiene*
    1. Demonstrate basic aspects of proper hygiene.
    2. Identify proper grooming.
    3. Identify proper products for hygiene and where to obtain them.
    4. Identify proper products for grooming and where to obtain them.

14. *Dress Appropriately*
    1. List clothing appropriate for different weather conditions.
    2. List clothing appropriate for different activities.
    3. Given an occasion, choose the appropriate clothing to be worn.
15. *Demonstrate Knowledge of Common Illness, Prevention, and Treatment*
    1. Identify major symptoms of common illnesses.
    2. State how cleanliness is related to health.
    3. Locate sources of assistance with medical problems.
    4. Identify dosage information from a medicine bottle label.
    5. List common medicines found in the home and their uses.
    6. Demonstrate basic first aid techniques.
16. *Practice Personal Safety*
    1. Identify ways to secure home from intruders.
    2. Identify things to do to avoid personal assault.
    3. Identify and demonstrate self-protection or self-defense behaviors and techniques.
    4. List precautions to follow when dealing with strangers.
    5. Identify potential hazards in the home.
    6. List and demonstrate actions to take in the event of an emergency.

4. Raising Children and Meeting Marriage Responsibilities

17. *Demonstrate Physical Care for Raising Children*
    1. List physical responsibilities involved in child care.
    2. Given a hypothetical situation, demonstrate basic safety measures for a child who has ingested poison or is cut severely.
    3. Identify common childhood illnesses and a symptom and treatment for each.
    4. Identify basic stages of child development and a characteristic of each.
    5. Identify potential dangers to children outside the home.
    6. Demonstrate procedures for care of child's physical health.
18. *Know Psychological Aspects of Raising Children*
    1. Identify changes when a child enters the family.
    2. Name psychological needs of the child and tell how these can be provided.
    3. Name parental responsibilities involved in the psychological care of the child.
    4. Identify common family problems and a way of dealing with each of the problems.
19. *Demonstrate Marriage Responsibilities*
    1. Identify reasons for marriage.
    2. Describe a personal responsibility in marriage.
    3. Identify joint responsibility in marriage.

5. Buying, Preparing, and Consuming Food

20. *Purchase Food*
    1. Construct a weekly shopping list within a budget.
    2. List characteristics of perishable foods.
    3. Identify the following types and cuts of meat, fish, and poultry.
    4. Identify how to use newspaper ads to take advantage of sales.

21. *Clean Food Preparation Areas*
    1. Identify importance of personal hygiene in food preparation areas.
    2. List reasons for cleaning work area and materials after food preparation.
    3. Identify and demonstrate appropriate cleaning procedures.
    4. Identify and demonstrate appropriate waste disposal procedures.
22. *Store Food*
    1. Identify the need for proper food storage.
    2. Identify appropriate food storage techniques.
    3. Identify appearance of foods when they have spoiled.
    4. Identify and demonstrate food storage procedures.
23. *Prepare Meals*
    1. Identify food preparation procedures.
    2. Identify and demonstrate the use of basic appliances and tools.
    3. List basic recipe abbreviations and cooking terms.
    4. Practice kitchen safety procedures.
    5. Prepare a full-course meal for one or more people.
24. *Demonstrate Appropriate Eating Habits*
    1. Identify the need for proper manners and eating behavior.
    2. Identify and demonstrate proper manners and eating behavior at a meal.
    3. Identify and demonstrate the proper way to set table and serve food.
    4. Identify and demonstrate proper manners and eating behavior at a public place.
25. *Plan and Eat Balanced Meals*
    1. List the basic food groups required in each meal.
    2. Identify appropriate foods eaten at typical daily meals.
    3. Plan a day's meals within a given budget.

6. Buying and Caring for Clothing

26. *Wash/Clean Clothing*
    1. Identify the following laundry products and their uses: bleaches, detergents, and fabric softeners.
    2. Identify and demonstrate appropriate laundering procedures for different types of clothing.
    3. Demonstrate use of laundry facilities at a laundromat.
27. *Purchase Clothing*
    1. List basic articles of clothing.
    2. Identify personal body measurements and clothing sizes.
    3. List major clothing categories by dress, work, casual, sports, school.
    4. Given a hypothetical budget, select a school wardrobe.
    5. State the importance of matching colors and fabrics.
28. *Iron, Mend, and Store Clothing*
    1. Identify and demonstrate proper ironing procedures for common fabric.
    2. Demonstrate appropriate safety precautions for using ironing equipment.
    3. Identify when, how, and where to store clothing.
    4. Identify and demonstrate procedures for mending clothing.

7. Exhibiting Responsible Citizenship

29. *Demonstrate Knowledge of Civil Rights and Responsibilities*
    1. Identify basic civil rights when being questioned by law enforcement officials.
    2. Locate resources where one can acquire legal aid.
    3. Identify actions to take when a crime has been witnessed.
    4. List basic civil rights.
    5. Identify who must register with the selective service.
    6. Identify when eligible individuals must register.
    7. Locate the address of the selective service or recruitment office nearest the student's home.
30. *Know Nature of Local, State, and Federal Governments*
    1. Identify the purpose of government.
    2. Define democracy and representative government.
    3. Identify the branches of government, their functions, and one major official of each branch of government.
    4. Identify one way states might be different without a federal government.
    5. Identify one duty of each level of government.
31. *Demonstrate Knowledge of the Law and Ability to Follow the Law*
    1. List types of local law.
    2. Identify possible consequences of violating laws.
    3. List basic reasons for government and laws.
    4. Explain and demonstrate the basic court system and its procedures.
32. *Demonstrate Knowledge of Citizen Rights and Responsibilities*
    1. Locate community services available to citizens.
    2. List major responsibilities of citizens.
    3. Identify voting requirements and demonstrate procedures.
    4. Identify why it is important to be an informed voter.
    5. List the dates for primary and general elections, and demonstrate procedures for registration.
    6. Identify sources which inform the voter about election issues.

8. Utilizing Recreational Facilities and Engaging in Leisure

33. *Demonstrate Knowledge of Available Community Resources*
    1. List sources of information about specific recreational activities.
    2. List activities appropriate to each season of the year.
    3. Locate recreational facilities and equipment in the community.
    4. Participate in recreational activities outside the home.
34. *Choose and Plan Activities*
    1. List personal leisure activities.
    2. List costs, times, locations, and physical requirements of activities.
    3. Develop individual plan of leisure activities.
35. *Demonstrate Knowledge of the Value of Recreation*
    1. List differences between leisure that involves nonpaid work activities and relaxation.
    2. List ways in which recreation affects both physical and mental health.
    3. List personal requirements of leisure time.

36. *Engage in Group and Individual Activities*
  1. Identify reasons for participating in group activities.
  2. Identify and demonstrate knowledge of rules of group activities.
  3. List qualities of good sportsmanship.
  4. Identify and demonstrate the proper care of sports equipment.
  5. Identify general safety rules of physical activities.
37. *Plan Vacation Time*
  1. Identify financial considerations involved in planning a vacation.
  2. List time considerations involved in planning a vacation.
  3. List possible vacation activities.
  4. Locate resources available for help with making vacation plans.
  5. Construct a proposed vacation plan, including cost, time, transportation, facilities, and activities.

9. Getting Around the Community

38. *Demonstrate Knowledge of Traffic Rules and Safety*
  1. Identify the purpose and demonstrate procedures for pedestrian safety signs.
  2. List reasons for common traffic and safety rules and practices.
  3. Identify vehicle safety signs of the driver's education sign test.
39. *Demonstrate Knowledge and Use of Various Means of Transportation*
  1. Identify types of transportation available in the community.
  2. Identify reasons transportation is needed and the type most appropriate.
  3. Identify and demonstrate procedures to take a train, interstate bus, taxi, airplane.
40. *Find Way Around the Community*
  1. Given a picture of a numbered house, identify numbers of houses on either side.
  2. Given city and state maps, identify directions, symbols, and distance.
  3. Identify basic community resources.
41. *Drive a Car*
  1. Given driving problems related to weather, demonstrate knowledge of appropriate technique.
  2. Describe appropriate procedures to follow after being involved in an accident.
  3. Identify everyday basic driving knowledge.
  4. Demonstrate proficiency on the written portions of the operator's exam.

PERSONAL–SOCIAL SKILLS

10. Achieving Self-Awareness

42. *Identify Physical and Psychological Needs*
  1. List basic physical needs.
  2. List basic psychological needs.
  3. Identify ways to meet the physical needs.
  4. Identify ways to meet the psychological needs.

43. *Identify Interests and Abilities*
  1. List abilities common to most people.
  2. Identify interests common to most people.
  3. Demonstrate goal setting in relation to pursuing an interest or ability and show how goals are attained.
44. *Identify Emotions*
  1. Identify common emotions (fear, love, hate, sadness).
  2. List ways in which one's emotions affect the behavior of self and others.
  3. Identify ways in which one may cope with emotions.
  4. Differentiate particular emotions in self and others.
45. *Demonstrate Knowledge of Physical Self*
  1. Identify major systems of the body.
  2. List personal physical characteristics.
  3. Describe typical physical characteristics and dimensions.
  4. Identify major parts of the body.

11. Acquiring Self-Confidence

46. *Express Feelings of Self-Worth*
  1. List positive physical and psychological attributes.
  2. Express ways in which positive attributes make him/her feel good.
  3. List the characteristics necessary to feel good about oneself.
  4. Describe ways in which the actions of others affect one's feelings of self-worth.
47. *Describe Others' Perception of Self*
  1. List potential reactions of others to oneself.
  2. Construct a personal view of how others see oneself.
  3. Describe the relationship between one's own behaviors and others' reactions.
  4. Demonstrate awareness of individual differences in others.
48. *Accept and Give Praise*
  1. Identify statements of praise in everyday activities.
  2. List appropriate and inappropriate responses to praise.
  3. Respond to praise statements by others.
  4. List the effects of praise on oneself.
49. *Accept and Give Criticism*
  1. Identify critical and/or rejecting types of statements.
  2. List appropriate ways to respond to criticism and/or rejection.
  3. Respond appropriately to critical statements.
  4. List positive and negative effects of criticism.
50. *Develop Confidence in Oneself*
  1. Identify and describe positive characteristics of oneself in a variety of areas.
  2. List appropriate ways to express confidence in oneself.
  3. Make positive statements about oneself.
  4. Identify potential reactions of others to expressions of self-confidence.

12. Achieving Socially Responsible Behavior

51. *Demonstrate Respect for the Rights and Properties of Others*
  1. Identify personal and property rights of others.
  2. Identify a reason for respecting the rights and properties of others.
  3. Demonstrate respect for others and their property.
  4. List appropriate situation and procedures for borrowing the property of others.

52. *Recognize Authority and Follow Instructions*
   1. Identify common authority roles.
   2. Identify aspects of following instructions (e.g., safety, order, convenience).
   3. Identify situation in which the individual has the right to disregard instructions from authorities.

53. *Demonstrate Appropriate Behavior in Public Places*
   1. Identify appropriate behavior in public places.
   2. Identify and demonstrate appropriate behaviors when using transportation facilities.
   3. Identify and demonstrate appropriate behaviors when using eating facilities.
   4. Identify and demonstrate appropriate behaviors when using recreational facilities.

54. *Know Important Character Traits*
   1. Identify own acceptable character traits.
   2. Identify acceptable character traits in others.
   3. List character traits necessary for acceptance in group activities.
   4. List character traits that inhibit acceptance.

55. *Recognize Personal Roles*
   1. Identify current roles.
   2. Identify possible future roles.
   3. List roles of significant others.
   4. Describe the rights and obligations in personal roles as they interact with the roles of others.

13. Maintaining Good Interpersonal Skills

56. *Demonstrate Listening and Responding Skills*
   1. Identify proper listening and responding techniques.
   2. Identify positive outcomes of listening and responding appropriately.
   3. Identify negative aspects of listening and responding inappropriately.

57. *Establish and Maintain Close Relationships*
   1. Identify qualities of an individual who would be desirable as a dating partner.
   2. Identify and demonstrate appropriate procedures for making a date.
   3. List activities that are appropriate for a date.
   4. Identify characteristics of close relationships.
   5. List different types of close relationships.
   6. Recognize and respond to intimate feelings of others.
   7. Identify persons with whom one could establish a close relationship.

58. *Make and Maintain Friendships*
   1. Identify necessary components of a friendship.
   2. List personal considerations in choosing a friend.
   3. List rights and responsibilities important in personal friendships.
   4. List activities that can be shared with friends.

14. Achieving Independence

59. *Strive Toward Self-Actualization*
   1. Identify important characteristics for personal growth.
   2. List elements necessary for a satisfactory personal life.
   3. Identify sources for continued educational/psychological growth.

60. *Demonstrate Self-Organization*
   1. Develop plan of daily activities.
   2. Identify areas of responsibility in personal life.
   3. Identify reasons for organizing one's responsibilities/activities.
   4. Develop ways in which personal organization relates to greater independence.

61. *Demonstrate Awareness of How One's Behavior Affects Others*
   1. List ways in which behavior affects others around us.
   2. List appropriate behaviors for a variety of situations.
   3. List different cues elicited by others that behavior is inappropriate.
   4. List ways to correct inappropriate behavior.

15. Making Adequate Decisions

62. *Locate and Utilize Sources of Assistance*
   1. Identify situations in which one would need advice.
   2. List available resources for resolving problems.
   3. Given particular situations, describe the procedures for contacting persons for assistance.
   4. List potential outcomes of seeking advice.

63. *Anticipate Consequences*
   1. Describe consequences or outcomes of decision making.
   2. List and demonstrate knowledge of ways in which personal behavior produces consequences.
   3. Describe the concept of maximum gain for minimum risk.

64. *Develop and Evaluate Alternatives*
   1. Define the meaning of alternatives.
   2. List possible alternatives with respect to a personal goal.
   3. Describe a compromise with respect to a personal goal.
   4. List resources for information that develops alternatives.

65. *Recognize Nature of a Problem*
   1. Given a list of situations with positive and negative aspects of personal ideas, examine each as positive or negative.
   2. Identify why ideas, values, and plans have both potentially positive and negative implications.
   3. Identify a situation which requires examination of positive or negative aspects.

66. *Develop Goal-Seeking Behavior*
   1. Identify ways that goals affect one's life.
   2. List outcomes to be considered in goal setting.
   3. List examples of individuals who have set and attained their goals.
   4. Set one goal for school, home, recreation.
   5. Set short-term and long-term personal goals.
   6. Identify characteristics of realistic goals.
   7. Identify appropriate persons for obtaining assistance with setting and achieving goals.
   8. Identify potential barriers to goals.
   9. Set model personal goals.

16. Communicating with Others

67. *Recognize and Respond to Emergency Situations*
   1. Identify sights and sounds of emergency situations.
   2. Identify appropriate authorities to contact in emergency situations.
   3. Describe personal communication indicating emergency situations.
   4. List personal responsibilities in emergency situations.

68. *Communicate with Understanding*
    1. Demonstrate a variety of verbal expressions related to communication.
    2. Identify and demonstrate methods of speaking appropriately in a social conversation.
    3. Demonstrate proper use of telephone.
    4. Demonstrate appropriate volume and intensity in conversation.
69. *Know Subtleties of Communication*
    1. Identify nonverbal elements of communication.
    2. Identify verbal expressions that correspond to feelings.
    3. Identify verbal expressions that are inconsistent with feelings.
    4. Demonstrate verbal and nonverbal elements of communication.

OCCUPATIONAL GUIDANCE AND PREPARATION

17. Knowing and Exploring Occupational Possibilities

70. *Identify Remunerative Aspects of Work*
    1. Identify why people are paid for working.
    2. Identify why some jobs pay better then others.
    3. Discuss personal needs that are met through wages.
    4. Discuss positive and negative aspects of different kinds of wages.
    5. Given a paycheck stub, calculate deduction information.
71. *Locate Sources of Occupational and Training Information*
    1. List sources of occupational information.
    2. List information provided by the sources from objective 1.
    3. Use occupational information sources to demonstrate how to obtain information specific to a job.
    4. Locate sources of training information.
    5. Identify one kind of information provided by training information.
72. *Identify Personal Values Met Through Work*
    1. List an economic reason to work at a job.
    2. Identify how a job affects building personal and social relationships.
    3. Identify personal needs that can be met through work.
    4. Describe how work relates to one's self-esteem.
73. *Identify Societal Values Met Through Work*
    1. Identify ways in which individual workers help society.
    2. Identify ways in which members of a specific occupation contribute to society.
    3. Identify ways in which workers on different jobs are interdependent.
    4. Describe ways society rewards different occupations.
74. *Classify Jobs into Occupational Categories*
    1. Locate jobs using yellow pages and want ads.
    2. Locate occupational categories and sort jobs into different occupational categories.
    3. Locate information about job classifications.
    4. List major categories of jobs related to interest.
    5. List general job categories.
    6. Locate training requirements and wages for common job classifications.

75. *Investigate Local Occupational and Training Opportunities*
    1. Select an occupational area and find local employers in the Yellow Pages.
    2. Collect and read help wanted ads in the occupational areas selected in Objective 1.
    3. Utilize sources of employment information.
    4. Locate sources of employment information.

18. Selecting and Planning Occupational Choices

76. *Make Realistic Occupational Choices*
    1. Identify jobs of interest.
    2. Obtain specific information about jobs of interest.
    3. Obtain observational information about the above jobs through participation (e.g., on-site visits, work samples, job tryouts).
    4. Identify a job of interest that is commensurate with interests and abilities.
77. *Identify Requirements of Appropriate and Available Jobs*
    1. Identify the availability and location of jobs.
    2. List specific job-related requirements.
    3. Identify an alternative for each occupation for which personal qualifications are not commensurate with identified requirements.
78. *Identify Occupational Aptitudes*
    1. Identify different aptitudes necessary in the performance of various jobs.
    2. Identify personal aptitudes.
    3. Identify activities which could improve personal aptitude necessary for a perfect job.
79. *Identify Major Occupational Interests*
    1. Identify occupational categories of interest.
    2. Rank areas of personal interest in order of importance in finding occupation.
    3. Identify how interests relate to jobs.
    4. Describe ways the chosen job of interest relates to future personal goals.
80. *Identify Major Occupational Needs*
    1. Identify needs that can be met through one's occupation and rank them in order of personal preference.
    2. Identify personal-social needs met through work.
    3. Name status needs met through work.
    4. Identify factors that the student needs in a personal occupational environment.
    5. Identify the most personally satisfying aspects and the least satisfying aspects about a given job.
    6. Identify criteria one would use in selecting an occupation.

19. Exhibiting Appropriate Work Habits and Behaviors

81. *Follow Directions and Observe Regulations*
    1. Perform a series of tasks in response to verbal instructions.
    2. Perform a series of tasks in response to written instructions.
82. *Recognize Importance of Attendance and Punctuality*
    1. Identify reasons for good attendance and punctuality.
    2. Identify acceptable and unacceptable reasons for tardiness and absenteeism.
    3. Identify appropriate action to take if late or absent from work.

83. *Recognize Importance of Supervision*
    1. List roles and responsibility of supervision.
    2. Identify the appropriate response to a supervisory instruction.
    3. Complete a job following supervisor's instructions.
84. *Demonstrate Knowledge of Occupational Safety*
    1. Identify potential safety hazards on the job.
    2. Identify jobs that require safety equipment and identify the equipment.
    3. Identify main reasons for practicing safety on the job.
    4. Follow safety instructions on the job (e.g., wear rubber gloves, safety goggles).
85. *Work with Others*
    1. Identify reasons for working with others.
    2. Identify the importance of individual components of a cooperative effort.
    3. Complete a task working with other persons.
86. *Meet Demands for Quality Work*
    1. Identify minimum quality standards for various jobs.
    2. Identify reasons for quality standards.
    3. Perform simulated work tasks which have minimum quality standards.
87. *Work at a Satisfactory Rate*
    1. Identify the need for performing jobs at a satisfactory rate.
    2. Identify satisfactory rates required for specific jobs.
    3. List reasons why a job must be performed at a certain rate of speed.
    4. Perform a job at a satisfactory rate.

20. Seeking, Securing, and Maintaining Employment

88. *Search for a Job*
    1. Identify the steps involved in searching for a job.
    2. Identify a potential job through employment resources.
    3. Arrange a real or simulated job interview.
89. *Apply for a Job*
    1. Identify appropriate job application procedures.
    2. Collect a personal data sheet to be used for job application.
    3. Complete a real or simulated job application with spelling assistance.
    4. Apply for a real or simulated job in person or by telephone.
90. *Interview for a Job*
    1. Obtain an interview or carry out a mock interview.
    2. Identify interview behaviors.
    3. Complete a real or simulated job interview.
    4. Obtain transportation to and from the interview.
91. *Know How to Maintain Post-School Occupational Adjustment*
    1. Identify potential problems to be encountered on the job.
    2. For potential problems, identify potential solutions.
    3. Identify resources for assistance if problems cannot be personally resolved.
92. *Demonstrate Knowledge of Competitive Standards*
    1. Determine the minimum level of skill and performance requirements for a specific job.
    2. Identify potential remedial activities which might be required by an occupation.
    3. Determine the level of personal abilities required for a specific occupation.

93. *Know How to Adjust to Changes in Employment*
    1. Identify factors which determine successful employment adjustment.
    2. Identify factors which determine unsuccessful employment adjustment.
    3. Identify potential employment variations within a specific occupation.
    4. Identify factors which lead to termination of employment.
    5. Identify factors which lead to promotion at place of employment.

21. Exhibiting Sufficient Physical–Manual Skills

94. *Demonstrate Stamina and Endurance*
    1. Identify the need for stamina on the job.
    2. Perform at the 80% level of age-normed simulated work task.
    3. Identify jobs in which endurance and strength are critical.
95. *Demonstrate Satisfactory Balance and Coordination*
    1. Demonstrate satisfactory balance and coordination on nonwork tasks.
    2. Demonstrate satisfactory balance and coordination on simulated work tasks.
    3. Describe the relationship between balance and coordination and job performance.
96. *Demonstrate Manual Dexterity*
    1. State three different kinds of physical–manual dexterity.
    2. Demonstrate personal level of dexterity in both work and nonwork tasks.
    3. Demonstrate adequate dexterity on work tasks appropriate to an identified occupation.
    4. Identify reasons for dexterity.
    5. Name two occupations commensurate with determined dexterity.
97. *Demonstrate Sensory Discrimination*
    1. Describe five kinds of sensory discrimination.
    2. Demonstrate size and shape discrimination.
    3. Demonstrate color discrimination.
    4. State the need for sensory discrimination on an identified job.
    5. Demonstrate auditory discrimination.

SECTION IV—INTERPRETATION

Although it would be ultimately desirable for each student to achieve 100% mastery, it is difficult to predict whether this goal can be attained in any present educational setting. Each user will be faced with determining whether complete mastery of a specified percentage of the subcompetencies is preferable to a partial mastery of all the subcompetencies. At this time, the suggested method in interpretation involves the user's identification of student strengths and weaknesses. Such identification should prove useful for developing individualized education programs (IEPs), as well as evaluating IEP outcomes. Since the CRS items are actually the subcompetencies of the Life Centered Curriculum, low-rated items can be used to establish short-term objectives for individualized planning. Readministration of the CRS can then be used to evaluate the effectiveness of such planning by comparing pre- and postintervention ratings.

The CRS user can review student performance and behavior for any given rating period to determine deficient areas. Such a determination can assist both in general curriculum planning and in individualized planning. If a large percentage of students are deficient in particular areas (subcompetencies, competencies, or domains), emphasis on these areas could be incorporated into general curriculum planning. Individual weaknesses can be remedied through revised IEPs. The user should be aware that the rating key allows only three numerical ratings. The operational definition of the 1 rating ("at least one, but not all") makes student progress on a subcompetency possible without a change in numerical rating. A student might require several years to progress from a rating of 1 on an individual subcompetency to a rating of 2. Therefore, in the IEP evaluation, the user should look for short-term gains in the larger categories (competencies or domains). The present system will reflect short-term gains when used in this manner.

The CRS user can review student performance and behavior over several rating periods to determine progress as well as establish realistic expectancies for typical student growth and development. This interpretation not only provides the user with suggestions for immediate curriculum planning on a general and individual basis, but also provides suggestions for long-range curriculum sequencing. This type of data should prove particularly useful after systematic analysis, since there is little information available to predict typical developmental stages in the career education of these students.

Although the identified subcompetencies, competencies, and domains are felt to be generally comprehensive, there is no evidence at present that these divisions and their sequencing correlate strongly with student ability to master these objectives at any particular age or developmental stage. Thus, the CRS user has an opportunity to either formally or informally establish expectancies and sequencing in each particular setting. In summary, the CRS user can employ results to:

- Determine individual student strengths and weaknesses.
- Develop and evaluate IEPs for individual students.
- Determine group strengths and weaknesses.
- Plan immediate curriculum for groups of students.
- Monitor individual and group progress.
- Establish empirically derived expectancies for individuals and groups.
- Establish empirically derived developmental stages for these students in career education.
- Develop curriculum sequencing and modification to relate to expectancies and developmental stages.

Appendix B
Master Forms
for Duplication

The forms on the following pages are designed to be reproduced for use with the Life Centerned Career Education Curriculum. The following forms are given:

- Competency Rating Scale
    Daily Living Skills
    Personal–Social Skills
    Occupational Guidance and Preparation

- Individualized Education Program Form

LIFE CENTERED CAREER EDUCATION
Competency Rating Scale
Record Form

DAILY LIVING SKILLS

Student Name _____ Date of Birth _____ Sex _____

School _____ City _____ State _____

Directions: Please rate the student according to his/her mastery of each item using the rating key below. Indicate the ratings in the column below the date for the rating period. Use the NR rating for items which cannot be rated. For subcompetencies rated 0 or 1 at the time of the final rating, place a check (✔) in the appropriate space in the *yes* or *no* column to indicate his or her ability to perform the subcompetency with assistance from the community. Please refer to the CRS manual for explanation of the rating key, description of the behavioral criteria for each subcompetency, and explanation of the *yes* or *no* column.

Rating Key: 0 = Not Competent   1 = Partially Competent   2 = Competent   NR = Not Rated

To what extent has the student mastered the following subcompetencies?

Subcompetencies	Rater(s)							Yes	No
	Grade Level								
	Date(s)								
DAILY LIVING SKILLS									
1. Managing Personal Finances									
1. Identify Money and Make Correct Change	—	—	—	—	—	—	—	—	—
2. Make Responsible Expenditures	—	—	—	—	—	—	—	—	—
3. Keep Basic Financial Records	—	—	—	—	—	—	—	—	—
4. Calculate and Pay Taxes	—	—	—	—	—	—	—	—	—
5. Use Credit Responsibly	—	—	—	—	—	—	—	—	—
6. Use Banking Services	—	—	—	—	—	—	—	—	—
2. Selecting and Managing a Household									
7. Maintain Home Exterior/Interior	—	—	—	—	—	—	—	—	—
8. Use Basic Appliances and Tools	—	—	—	—	—	—	—	—	—
9. Select Adequate Housing	—	—	—	—	—	—	—	—	—
10. Set Up Household	—	—	—	—	—	—	—	—	—
11. Maintain Home Grounds	—	—	—	—	—	—	—	—	—
3. Caring for Personal Needs									
12. Demonstrate Knowledge of Physical Fitness, Nutrition, and Weight	—	—	—	—	—	—	—	—	—
13. Exhibit Proper Grooming and Hygiene	—	—	—	—	—	—	—	—	—
14. Dress Appropriately	—	—	—	—	—	—	—	—	—
15. Demonstrate Knowledge of Common Illness, Prevention, and Treatment	—	—	—	—	—	—	—	—	—
16. Practice Personal Safety	—	—	—	—	—	—	—	—	—

Subcompetencies	Rater(s)								
	Grade Level								
	Date(s)								
								Yes	No
4. *Raising Children and Meeting Marriage Responsibilities*									
17. Demonstrate Physical Care for Raising Children	—	—	—	—	—	—	—	—	—
18. Know Psychological Aspects of Raising Children	—	—	—	—	—	—	—	—	—
19. Demonstrate Marriage Responsibilities	—	—	—	—	—	—	—	—	—
5. *Buying, Preparing, and Consuming Food*									
20. Purchase Food	—	—	—	—	—	—	—	—	—
21. Clean Food Preparation Areas	—	—	—	—	—	—	—	—	—
22. Store Food	—	—	—	—	—	—	—	—	—
23. Prepare Meals	—	—	—	—	—	—	—	—	—
24. Demonstrate Appropriate Eating Habits	—	—	—	—	—	—	—	—	—
25. Plan and Eat Balanced Meals	—	—	—	—	—	—	—	—	—
6. *Buying and Caring for Clothing*									
26. Wash/Clean Clothing	—	—	—	—	—	—	—	—	—
27. Purchase Clothing	—	—	—	—	—	—	—	—	—
28. Iron, Mend, and Store Clothing	—	—	—	—	—	—	—	—	—
7. *Exhibiting Responsible Citizenship*									
29. Demonstrate Knowledge of Civil Rights and Responsibilities	—	—	—	—	—	—	—	—	—
30. Know Nature of Local, State, and Federal Governments	—	—	—	—	—	—	—	—	—
31. Demonstrate Knowledge of the Law and Ability to Follow the Law	—	—	—	—	—	—	—	—	—
32. Demonstrate Knowledge of Citizen Rights and Responsibilities	—	—	—	—	—	—	—	—	—
8. *Utilizing Recreational Facilities and Engaging in Leisure*									
33. Demonstrate Knowledge of Available Community Resources	—	—	—	—	—	—	—	—	—
34. Choose and Plan Activities	—	—	—	—	—	—	—	—	—
35. Demonstrate Knowledge of the Value of Recreation	—	—	—	—	—	—	—	—	—
36. Engage in Group and Individual Activities	—	—	—	—	—	—	—	—	—
37. Plan Vacation Time	—	—	—	—	—	—	—	—	—
9. *Getting Around the Community*									
38. Demonstrate Knowledge of Traffic Rules and Safety	—	—	—	—	—	—	—	—	—
39. Demonstrate Knowledge and Use of Various Means of Transportation	—	—	—	—	—	—	—	—	—
40. Find Way Around the Community	—	—	—	—	—	—	—	—	—
41. Drive a Car	—	—	—	—	—	—	—	—	—

Total Possible Score (TPS) = N x 2 _____

Total Actual Score (TAS) — — — — — — —

Average Score (AS) = TAS/N — — — — — — —

Comments: _____

_____

Use asterisk to denote skill areas of instruction noted in the student's IEP for the year.
Refer to the CRS manual for calculation and interpretation.

LIFE CENTERED CAREER EDUCATION
Competency Rating Scale
Record Form

PERSONAL-SOCIAL SKILLS

Student Name _____ Date of Birth _____ Sex _____

School _____ City _____ State _____

Directions: Please rate the student according to his/her mastery of each item using the rating key below. Indicate the ratings in the column below the date for the rating period. Use the NR rating for items which cannot be rated. For subcompetencies rated 0 or 1 at the time of the final rating, place a check (✔) in the appropriate space in the *yes* or *no* column to indicate his or her ability to perform the subcompetency with assistance from the community. Please refer to the CRS manual for explanation of the rating key, description of the behavioral criteria for each subcompetency, and explanation of the *yes* or *no* column.

Rating Key: 0 = Not Competent 1 = Partially Competent 2 = Competent NR = Not Rated

To what extent has the student mastered the following subcompetencies?

Subcompetencies	Rater(s)								Yes	No
	Grade Level									
	Date(s)									
PERSONAL-SOCIAL SKILLS										
10. Achieving Self-Awareness										
42. Identify Physical and Psychological Needs	—	—	—	—	—	—	—	—	—
43. Identify Interests and Abilities	—	—	—	—	—	—	—	—	—
44. Identify Emotions	—	—	—	—	—	—	—	—	—
45. Demonstrate Knowledge of Physical Self	—	—	—	—	—	—	—	—	—
11. Acquiring Self-Confidence										
46. Express Feelings of Self-Worth	—	—	—	—	—	—	—	—	—
47. Describe Others' Perception of Self	—	—	—	—	—	—	—	—	—
48. Accept and Give Praise	—	—	—	—	—	—	—	—	—
49. Accept and Give Criticism	—	—	—	—	—	—	—	—	—
50. Develop Confidence in Oneself	—	—	—	—	—	—	—	—	—
12. Achieving Socially Responsible Behavior										
51. Demonstrate Respect for the Rights and Properties of Others	—	—	—	—	—	—	—	—	—
52. Recognize Authority and Follow Instructions	—	—	—	—	—	—	—	—	—
53. Demonstrate Appropriate Behavior in Public Places	—	—	—	—	—	—	—	—	—
54. Know Important Character Traits	—	—	—	—	—	—	—	—	—
55. Recognize Personal Roles	—	—	—	—	—	—	—	—	—

Subcompetencies	Rater(s)								Yes	No
	Grade Level									
	Date(s)									
13. *Maintaining Good Interpersonal Skills*										
56. Demonstrate Listening and Responding Skills	—	—	—	—	—	—	—	—	—
57. Establish and Maintain Close Relationships	—	—	—	—	—	—	—	—	—
58. Make and Maintain Friendships	—	—	—	—	—	—	—	—	—
14. *Achieving Independence*										
59. Strive Toward Self-Actualization	—	—	—	—	—	—	—	—	—
60. Demonstrate Self-Organization	—	—	—	—	—	—	—	—	—
61. Demonstrate Awareness of How One's Behavior Affects Others	—	—	—	—	—	—	—	—	—
15. *Making Adequate Decisions*										
62. Locate and Utilize Sources of Assistance	—	—	—	—	—	—	—	—	—
63. Anticipate Consequences	—	—	—	—	—	—	—	—	—
64. Develop and Evaluate Alternatives	—	—	—	—	—	—	—	—	—
65. Recognize Nature of a Problem	—	—	—	—	—	—	—	—	—
66. Develop Goal-Seeking Behavior	—	—	—	—	—	—	—	—	—
16. *Communicating with Others*										
67. Recognize and Respond to Emergency Situations	—	—	—	—	—	—	—	—	—
68. Communicate with Understanding	—	—	—	—	—	—	—	—	—
69. Know Subtleties of Communication	—	—	—	—	—	—	—	—	—

Total Possible Score   Total Actual Score
    (TPS) = N x 2 _____   (TAS)   —   —   —   —   —   —   —

                              Average Score
                              (AS) = TAS/N   —   —   —   —   —   —   —

Comments: _____

_____

Use asterisk to denote skill areas of instruction noted in the student's IEP for the year.
Refer to the CRS manual for calculation and interpretation.

LIFE CENTERED CAREER EDUCATION
Competency Rating Scale
Record Form

OCCUPATIONAL GUIDANCE AND PREPARATION

Student Name _____ Date of Birth _____ Sex _____

School _____ City _____ State _____

Directions: Please rate the student according to his/her mastery of each item using the rating key below. Indicate the ratings in the column below the date for the rating period. Use the NR rating for items which cannot be rated. For subcompetencies rated 0 or 1 at the time of the final rating, place a check (✔) in the appropriate space in the *yes* or *no* column to indicate his or her ability to perform the subcompetency with assistance from the community. Please refer to the CRS manual for explanation of the rating key, description of the behavioral criteria for each subcompetency, and explanation of the *yes* or *no* column.

Rating Key: 0 = Not Competent   1 = Partially Competent   2 = Competent   NR = Not Rated

To what extent has the student mastered the following subcompetencies?

Subcompetencies	Rater(s)								
	Grade Level								
	Date(s)								
OCCUPATIONAL GUIDANCE AND PREPARATION								Yes	No
17. Knowing and Exploring Occupational Possibilities									
70. Identify Remunerative Aspects of Work	—	—	—	—	—	—	—	—	—
71. Locate Sources of Occupational and Training Information	—	—	—	—	—	—	—	—	—
72. Identify Personal Values Met Through Work	—	—	—	—	—	—	—	—	—
73. Identify Societal Values Met Through Work	—	—	—	—	—	—	—	—	—
74. Classify Jobs into Occupational Categories	—	—	—	—	—	—	—	—	—
75. Investigate Local Occupational and Training Opportunities	—	—	—	—	—	—	—	—	—
18. Selecting and Planning Occupational Choices									
76. Make Realistic Occupational Choices	—	—	—	—	—	—	—	—	—
77. Identify Requirements of Appropriate and Available Jobs	—	—	—	—	—	—	—	—	—
78. Identify Occupational Aptitudes	—	—	—	—	—	—	—	—	—
79. Identify Major Occupational Interests	—	—	—	—	—	—	—	—	—
80. Identify Major Occupational Needs	—	—	—	—	—	—	—	—	—
19. Exhibiting Appropriate Work Habits and Behaviors									
81. Follow Directions and Observe Regulations	—	—	—	—	—	—	—	—	—
82. Recognize Importance of Attendance and Punctuality	—	—	—	—	—	—	—	—	—
83. Recognize Importance of Supervision	—	—	—	—	—	—	—	—	—
84. Demonstrate Knowledge of Occupational Safety	—	—	—	—	—	—	—	—	—
85. Work with Others	—	—	—	—	—	—	—	—	—
86. Meet Demands for Quality Work	—	—	—	—	—	—	—	—	—
87. Work at a Satisfactory Rate	—	—	—	—	—	—	—	—	—

Subcompetencies	Rater(s)									
	Grade Level									
	Date(s)									
									Yes	No
20. *Seeking, Securing, and Maintaining Employment*										
88. Search for a Job		—	—	—	—	—	—	—	—	—
89. Apply for a Job		—	—	—	—	—	—	—	—	—
90. Interview for a Job		—	—	—	—	—	—	—	—	—
91. Know How to Maintain Post-School Occupational Adjustment		—	—	—	—	—	—	—	—	—
92. Demonstrate Knowledge of Competitive Standards		—	—	—	—	—	—	—	—	—
93. Know How to Adjust to Changes in Employment		—	—	—	—	—	—	—	—	—
21. *Exhibiting Sufficient Physical–Manual Skills*										
94. Demonstrate Stamina and Endurance		—	—	—	—	—	—	—	—	—
95. Demonstrate Satisfactory Balance and Coordination		—	—	—	—	—	—	—	—	—
96. Demonstrate Manual Dexterity		—	—	—	—	—	—	—	—	—
97. Demonstrate Sensory Discrimination		—	—	—	—	—	—	—	—	—
22. *Obtaining Specific Occupational Skills*										
a. _____		—	—	—	—	—	—	—	—	—
b. _____		—	—	—	—	—	—	—	—	—
c. _____		—	—	—	—	—	—	—	—	—
d. _____		—	—	—	—	—	—	—	—	—
e. _____		—	—	—	—	—	—	—	—	—

Total Possible Score (TPS) = N x 2 _____

Total Actual Score (TAS)	—	—	—	—	—	—	—
Average Score (AS) = TAS/N	—	—	—	—	—	—	—
Cumulative TAS	—	—	—	—	—	—	—
Cumulative AS	—	—	—	—	—	—	—

Cumulative TPS: 194

Comments: _____
_____

Use asterisk to denote skill areas of instruction noted in the student's IEP for the year.
Refer to the CRS manual for calculation and interpretation.

LIFE CENTERED CAREER EDUCATION
INDIVIDUALIZED EDUCATION PROGRAM FORM
(Use attachments as needed for each student)

Student Name: _____ School: _____ Grade: _____ Date: _____

SECTION I: Present Level of Educational Performance

SECTION II: Annual Goals
A. Academic Goals (see attachment)
B. LCCE Functional Skills for Transition Preparation (check those that apply)
This student will progress toward acquiring functional behaviors in the following competency areas. (Check the appropriate annual goals.)

____ 1. Managing Personal Finances
____ 2. Selecting and Managing a Household
____ 3. Caring for Personal Needs
____ 4. Raising Children and Meeting Marriage Responsibilities
____ 5. Buying, Preparing, and Consuming Food
____ 6. Buying and Caring for Clothing
____ 7. Exhibiting Responsible Citizenship
____ 8. Utilizing Recreational Facilities and Engaging in Leisure
____ 9. Getting Around the Community
____ 10. Achieving Self-Awareness
____ 11. Acquiring Self-Confidence

____ 12. Achieving Socially Responsible Behavior
____ 13. Maintaining Good Interpersonal Skills
____ 14. Achieving Independence
____ 15. Making Adequate Decisions
____ 16. Communicating with Others
____ 17. Knowing and Exploring Occupational Possibilities
____ 18. Selecting and Planning Occupational Choices
____ 19. Exhibiting Appropriate Work Habits and Behaviors
____ 20. Seeking, Securing, and Maintaining Employment
____ 21. Exhibiting Sufficient Physical–Manual Skills
____ 22. Obtaining Specific Occupational Skills

C. Other Transitional/Support Services Goals (check those that apply)

____ 1. Financial Assistance/Income Support
____ 2. Advocacy Legal Services
____ 3. Medical
____ 4. Insurance

____ 5. Transporation
____ 6. Other _____
____ 7. Other _____
____ 8. Other _____

SECTION III: Specific Educational Services Needed

Goal & Subcomp. Numbers	Special Services Needed	Special Media/Materials and Equipment	Individual Implementors

LIFE CENTERED CAREER EDUCATION
INDIVIDUALIZED EDUCATION PROGRAM FORM

SECTION IV: Short-Term Individual Objectives

A. Academic Goals (see attachment)

B. LCCE Functional Skills for Transition Preparation (check those that apply)

___ 1. Identify Money and Make Correct Change (1)
___ 2. Make Responsible Expenditures (1)
___ 3. Keep Basic Financial Records (1)
___ 4. Calculate and Pay Taxes (1)
___ 5. Use Credit Responsibly (1)
___ 6. Use Banking Services (1)
___ 7. Maintain Home Exterior/Interior (2)
___ 8. Use Basic Appliances and Tools (2)
___ 9. Select Adequate Housing (2)
___ 10. Set Up Household (2)
___ 11. Maintain Home Grounds (2)
___ 12. Demonstrate Knowledge of Physical Fitness, Nutrition, and Weight (3)
___ 13. Exhibit Proper Grooming and Hygiene (3)
___ 14. Dress Appropriately (3)
___ 15. Demonstrate Knowledge of Common Illness, Prevention, and Treatment (3)
___ 16. Practice Personal Safety (3)
___ 17. Demonstrate Physical Care for Raising Children (4)
___ 18. Know Psychological Aspects of Raising Children (4)
___ 19. Demonstrate Marriage Responsibilities (4)
___ 20. Purchase Food (5)
___ 21. Clean Food Preparation Areas (5)
___ 22. Store Food (5)
___ 23. Prepare Meals (5)
___ 24. Demonstrate Appropriate Eating Habits (5)
___ 25. Plan and Eat Balanced Meals (5)
___ 26. Wash/Clean Clothing (6)
___ 27. Purchase Clothing (6)
___ 28. Iron, Mend, and Store Clothing (6)
___ 29. Demonstrate Knowledge of Civil Rights and Responsibilities (7)
___ 30. Know Nature of Local, State, and Federal Governments (7)
___ 31. Demonstrate Knowledge of the Law and Ability to Follow the Law (7)
___ 32. Demonstrate Knowledge of Citizen Rights and Responsibilities (7)
___ 33. Demonstrate Knowledge of Available Community Resources (8)
___ 34. Choose and Plan Activities (8)
___ 35. Demonstrate Knowledge of the Value of Recreation (8)
___ 36. Engage in Group and Individual Activities (8)
___ 37. Plan Vacation Time (8)
___ 38. Demonstrate Knowledge of Traffic Rules and Safety (9)

___ 39. Demonstrate Knowledge and Use of Various Means of Transportation (9)
___ 40. Find Way Around the Community (9)
___ 41. Drive a Car (9)
___ 42. Identify Physical and Psychological Needs (10)
___ 43. Identify Interests and Abilities (10)
___ 44. Identify Emotions (10)
___ 45. Demonstrate Knowledge of Physical Self (10)
___ 46. Express Feelings of Self-Worth (11)
___ 47. Describe Others' Perception of Self (11)
___ 48. Accept and Give Praise (11)
___ 49. Accept and Give Criticism (11)
___ 50. Develop Confidence in Oneself (11)
___ 51. Demonstrate Respect for the Rights and Properties of Others (12)
___ 52. Recognize Authority and Follow Instructions (12)
___ 53. Demonstrate Appropriate Behavior in Public Places (12)
___ 54. Know Important Character Traits (12)
___ 55. Recognize Personal Roles (12)
___ 56. Demonstrate Listening and Responding Skills (13)
___ 57. Establish and Maintain Close Relationships (13)
___ 58. Make and Maintain Friendships (13)
___ 59. Strive Toward Self-Actualization (14)
___ 60. Demonstrate Self-Organization (14)
___ 61. Demonstrate Awareness of How One's Behavior Affects Others (14)
___ 62. Locate and Utilize Sources of Assistance (15)
___ 63. Anticipate Consequences (15)
___ 64. Develop and Evaluate Alternatives (15)
___ 65. Recognize Nature of a Problem (15)
___ 66. Develop Goal-Seeking Behavior (15)
___ 67. Recognize and Respond to Emergency Situations (16)
___ 68. Communicate with Understanding (16)
___ 69. Know Subtleties of Communication (16)
___ 70. Identify Remunerative Aspects of Work (17)
___ 71. Locate Sources of Occupational and Training Information (17)
___ 72. Identify Personal Values Met Through Work (17)
___ 73. Identify Societal Values Met Through Work (17)
___ 74. Classify Jobs into Occupational Categories (17)
___ 75. Investigate Local Occupational and Training Opportunities (17)
___ 76. Make Realistic Occupational Choices (18)
___ 77. Identify Requirements of Appropriate and Available Jobs (18)

LIFE CENTERED CAREER EDUCATION
INDIVIDUALIZED EDUCATION PROGRAM FORM

____ 78. Identify Occupational Aptitudes (18)	____ 89. Apply for a Job (20)
____ 79. Identify Major Occupational Interests (18)	____ 90. Interview for a Job (20)
____ 80. Identify Major Occupational Needs (18)	____ 91. Know How to Maintain Post-School Occupational Adjustment (20)
____ 81. Follow Directions and Observe Regulations (19)	
____ 82. Recognize Importance of Attendance and Punctuality (19)	____ 92. Demonstrate Knowledge of Competitive Standards (20)
____ 83. Recognize Importance of Supervision (19)	____ 93. Know How to Adjust to Changes in Employment (20)
____ 84. Demonstrate Knowledge of Occupational Safety (19)	____ 94. Demonstrate Stamina and Endurance (21)
____ 85. Work with Others (19)	____ 95. Demonstrate Satisfactory Balance and Coordination (21)
____ 86. Meet Demands for Quality Work (19)	
____ 87. Work at a Satisfactory Rate (19)	____ 96. Demonstrate Manual Dexterity (21)
____ 88. Search for a Job (20)	____ 97. Demonstrate Sensory Discrimination (21)

C. Other Transitional/Support Services Objectives (see attachment)

SECTION V: Date and Length of Time relative to specific educational services needed for this student

Goal Number	Beginning Date	Ending Date	Goal Number	Beginning Date	Ending Date

SECTION VI: Description of Extent to which this student will participate in the regular educational program

	Percentage of Time	Narrative Description/Reaction
Language arts	_____ %	
Math	_____ %	
Science	_____ %	
Social science	_____ %	
Vocational (Bus.) & Work Study	_____ %	
Physical education	_____ %	
(other) _____	_____ %	
(other) _____	_____ %	

LIFE CENTERED CAREER EDUCATION
INDIVIDUALIZED EDUCATION PROGRAM FORM

SECTION VII: Justification for type of educational placement of this student

Narrative Description/Reaction

SECTION VIII: Individual Responsible for implementing the individualized education program and transitional services

Name   *Role/Responsibility*

SECTION IX: Objective Criteria, Evaluation Procedures, and Schedule for assessing short-term objectives

Objective Criteria can be found in the LCCE Competency Rating Scale (CRS), the LCCE Knowledge Battery (KB), and the LCCE Performance Battery (PB). Criteria listed reflect the short-term individual objectives checked in Section IV, Part B, of this form.

Evaluation Procedures can be determined by the IEP Committee reviewing the manuals for the Competency Rating Scale, Knowledge Battery, and Performance Battery.

Schedule for Assessment should include time, date, frequency, place, etc.

SECTION X: Estimated Date, Location, and Time for next IEP Committee Review Conference

Appendix C
Correlation of Original Life Centered Career (LCCE) Curriculum with the Modified Curriculum (LCCE-M) Competencies

**Correlation of Original Life Centered Career Education Curriculum
with the Modified Curriculum (LCCE-M) Competencies**

LCCE-Original	LCCE-Modified

Daily Living Skills

1. Managing Personal Finances
   1. Count money and make correct change
   2. Make responsible expenditures
   3. Keep basic financial records
   4. Calculate and pay taxes
   5. Use credit responsibly
   6. Use banking services

2. Selecting and Managing a Household
   7. Maintain home exterior/interior
   8. Use basic appliances and tools
   9. Select adequate housing
   10. Set up a household
   11. Maintain home grounds

3. Caring for Personal Needs
   12. Demonstrate knowledge of physical fitness, nutrition, and weight
   13. Exhibit proper grooming and hygiene
   14. Dress appropriately
   15. Demonstrate knowledge of common illness prevention and treatment
   16. Practice personal safety

4. Raising Children and Meeting Marriage Responsibilities
   17. Demonstrate physical care for raising children
   18. Know psychological aspects of raising children
   19. Demonstrate marriage responsibilities

5. Buying, Preparing, and Consuming Food
   20. Purchase food
   21. Clean food preparation areas
   22. Store food
   23. Prepare meals
   24. Demonstrate appropriate eating habits
   25. Plan/eat balanced meals

6. Buying and Caring for Clothing
   26. Wash/clean clothing
   27. Purchase clothing
   28. Iron, mend, and store clothing

7. Exhibiting Responsible Citizenship
   29. Demonstrate knowledge of civil rights and responsibilities
   30. Know nature of local, state, and federal governments
   31. Demonstrate knowledge of the law and ability to follow the law
   32. Demonstrate knowledge of citizen rights and responsibilities

---

1. Managing Money
   1. Count money
   2. Make purchase
   4. Budget money

   5. Perform banking skills

2. Selecting and Maintaining Living Environments
   7. Maintain living environment
   8. Use basic appliances and tools
   6. Select appropriate community living environment
   9. Set up personal living space

3. Caring for Personal Health
   12. Maintain physical fitness

   10. Perform appropriate grooming and hygiene
   11. Dress appropriately
   13. Recognize and seek help for illness

   15. Practice personal safety

4. Developing and Maintaining Appropriate Intimate Relationships

   16. Demonstrate knowledge of basic human sexuality

5. Eating at Home and in the Community
   19. Purchase food
   22. Demonstrate meal clean-up and food storage
   22. (See above)
   20. Prepare meals
   21. Demonstrate appropriate eating habits
   18. Plan balanced meals

6. Cleaning and Purchasing Clothing
   24. Wash/dry clothes
   25. Buy clothes

   42. Demonstrate appropriate citizen rights and responsibilities

8. Utilizing Recreational Facilities and Engaging in Leisure
    33. Demonstrate knowledge of available community leisure/recreational activities
    34. Choose and plan activities
    35. Demonstrate knowledge of the value of recreation.
    36. Engage in group and individual activities
    37. Plan vacation time

9. Getting Around the Community
    38. Demonstrate knowledge of traffic and safety
    39. Demonstrate knowledge and use of various means of transportation
    40. Find way around the community
    41. Drive a car

7. Participate in Leisure/Recreational Activities
    26. Identify available community leisure/recreational resources
    27. Select and plan leisure/recreational activities
    28. Participate in individual and group leisure/recreational activities
    29. Select and participate in group travel

8. Getting Around in the Community
    30. Follow traffic rules and safety procedures
    32. Access available transportation
    31. Develop and follow community access routes

Personal-Social Skills

10. Achieving Self-Awareness
    42. Identify physical and psychological needs
    43. Identify interests and abilities
    44. Identify emotions
    45. Demonstrate knowledge of physical self

11. Acquiring Self-Confidence
    46. Express feelings of self-worth
    47. Describe others' perception of self
    48. Accept and give praise
    49. Accept and give criticism
    50. Develop confidence in oneself

12. Achieving Socially Responsible Behavior
    51. Develop respect for the rights and property of others
    52. Recognize authority and follow instructions
    53. Demonstrate appropriate behavior in public places
    54. Know important character traits
    55. Recognize personal roles

13. Maintaining Good Interpersonal Skills
    56. Demonstrate listening and responding skills
    57. Establish and maintain close relationships
    58. Make and maintain friendships

14. Achieving Independence
    59. Strive toward self-actualization
    60. Demonstrate self-organization
    61. Demonstrate awareness of how one's behavior affects others

15. Making Adequate Decisions
    62. Locate and utilize sources of assistance
    63. Anticipate consequences
    64. Develop and evaluate alternatives
    65. Recognize nature of problems
    66. Develop goal-seeking behavior

9. Acquiring Self-Identity
    33. Demonstrate knowledge of personal interests and abilities
    34. Demonstrate appropriate responses to emotions
    35. Display self-confidence and self-worth
    36. Demonstrate giving and accepting praise and criticism
    35. (See above)

10. Exhibiting Socially Responsible Behavior
    39. Demonstrate respect for others' rights and property
    40. Demonstrate respect for authority
    37. Demonstrate appropriate behavior
    38. Identify current and future personal roles

11. Developing and Maintaining Appropriate Social Relationships
    53. Demonstrate listening and responding skills
    44. Develop friendships; 45. Maintain friendships

12. Exhibiting Independent Behavior
    47. Demonstrate self-organization

13. Making Informed Decisions
    50. Use appropriate resources to assist in problem solving
    52. Demonstrate decision making
    51. Develop and select best solution to problems/conflicts
    49. Identify problems/conflicts
    46. Set and reach personal goals

16. Communicating with Others
    67. Recognize and respond to emergency situations
    68. Communicate with understanding
    69. Know subtleties of communication

14. Communicating with Others
    55. Communicate in emergency situations
    54. Demonstrate effective communication

Occupational Guidance and Preparation

17. Knowing and Exploring Occupational Possibilities

    70. Identify remunerative aspects of work
    71. Locate sources of occupational and training information
    72. Identify personal values met through work
    73. Identify societal values met through work
    74. Classify jobs into occupational categories
    75. Investigate local occupational and training opportunities

15. Exploring and Locating Occupational Training and Job Placement Opportunities
    56. Identify rewards of working
    57. Locate available occupational training and job placement possibilities
    56. (See above)
    56. (See above)

18. Selecting and Planning Occupational Choices
    76. Make realistic occupational choices

    77. Identify requirements of appropriate and available jobs

    78. Identify occupational aptitudes

    79. Identify major occupational interests

16. Making Occupational and Job Placement Choices
    61. Plan and make realistic occupational training and job placement decisions
    60. Identify possible and available jobs matching interests and strengths
    59. Demonstrate knowledge of occupational strengths and weaknesses
    58. Demonstrate knowledge of occupational interests

19. Exhibiting Appropriate Work Habits and Behavior

    80. Identify major occupational needs
    81. Follow directions and observe regulations
    82. Recognize importance of attendance and punctuality
    83. Recognize importance of supervision
    84. Demonstrate knowledge of occupational safety
    85. Work with others
    86. Meet demands of quality work
    87. Work at a satisfactory rate

18. Developing and Maintaining Appropriate Work Skills and Behavior

    66. Perform work directions and meet requirements
    67. Maintain good attendance and punctuality
    68. Respond appropriately to supervision
    69. Demonstrate job safety
    70. Work cooperatively with others
    71. Meet quality and quantity work standards
    71. (See above)

20. Seeking, Securing, and Maintaining Employment

    88. Search for a Job
    89. Apply for a job
    90. Interview for a job
    91. Know how to maintain postschool occupational adjustment
    92. Demonstrate knowledge of competitive standards
    93. Know how to adjust to change in employment

17. Applying for and Maintaining Occupational Training and Job Placements

    63. Apply for occupational training and job placements
    64. Interview for occupational training and job placements

    65. Make adjustments to changes in employment status

21. Exhibiting Sufficient Physical/Manual Skills

    94. Demonstrate stamina and endurance
    95. Demonstrate satisfactory balance and coordination
    96. Demonstrate manual dexterity

    97. Demonstrate sensory discrimination

19. Matching Physical/Manual Skills to Occupational Training and Employment
    75. Demonstrate stamina and endurance

    72. Demonstrate fine motor dexterity in occupational training and job placements
    74. Demonstrate sensory discrimination in occupational training and job placements

22. Obtaining Specific Occupational Skills
    There are no specific subcompetencies listed here since they depend upon the specific occupational training selected.

Appendix D
LCCE Resources
Available from
CEC

Life Centered Career Education:
A Competency Based Approach
Fifth Edition
Donn E. Brolin

The fifth edition of the basic LCCE text includes improvements that make it easier to use in conjunction with the LCCE Complete Curriculum Package. Pages have been tabbed for quick reference to the Daily Living, Personal-Social, and Occupational Guidance and Preparation domains. Objectives have been numbered to coincide with the lesson plans in the Complete Curriculum Package. The competencies have remained the same, and the 97 subcompetencies and over 400 objectives continue to provide the most comprehensive career education program available. The guide also contains the Competency Rating Scale (CRS), a subjective assessment instrument used to rate student achievement. This is a very useful screening device and is extremely helpful in selecting areas for instructional planning.

No. P180G. 1997. 175 pp. ISBN 0-86586-292-3. $30; CEC Members $21

Life Centered Career Education
Modified Curriculum for Individuals
with Moderate Disabilities
Robert J. Loyd and Donn E. Brolin

This modified version of the LCCE Curriculum provides practitioners with the same easy-to-use format of the original text. A correlation table allows teachers to identify corresponding competencies in each curriculum in the event that students are able to move from this more basic version to the more advanced objectives of the original work. The major difference between the original and the modified curriculum programs is that the modified curriculum focuses on the critical skills and outcomes that individuals with moderate disabilities need to perform to assist them in making a successful transition from school to work and community living. Another significant difference is that attention to both support needed and participation levels are embedded in the curriculum activities and individuals are encouraged to seek assistance when necessary. A modified Competency Rating Scale (CRS-M) is included in the text. This instrument is useful in determining appropriate objectives to be included in the IEP or other planning documents.

No. P5194. 1997. 111 pp. ISBN 0-86586-293-1. $30; CEC Members $21

LCCE Demonstration Video

This 55-minute video provides an explanation of the LCCE curriculum and demonstrates administration of the Knowledge and Performance Batteries as well as a number of instructional lessons. This product can be used to support inservice training or to model teaching and testing strategies to teachers who are new to the program. The video follows the content of LCCE Training Workshops.

No. M5189. Edited 1996. 55 min. VHS. $75

The IEP Planner for LCCE Transition Skills

Allows teachers to incorporate Life Centered Career Education (LCCE) skills into students' IEPs. Each competency from the LCCE Curriculum is listed along with up to 9 objectives for each of the 97 competencies—more than 400 objectives altogether. The program allows teachers to edit any objective or add special goals and objectives as needed. Easy to update for annual reviews and progress reports. You can even import your own district's curriculum. The package includes:

- Disks for both Macintosh and DOS-based computers containing LCCE objectives and an IEP form template.
- A spiral-bound book of codes for LCCE competencies and goals and the IEP form.
- A copy of Life Centered Career Education: A Competency Based Approach, the foundation text by Donn E. Brolin.

No. S5174. 1996. Price $220

Life Centered Career Education:
The Complete Curriculum and Assessment Package

Includes over 1,100 lesson plans covering Daily Living Skills, Personal-Social Skills, and Occupational Skills; Knowledge Batteries (10 copies of each of two alternative forms); Performance Batteries; Administration Manuals; and Technical Report. Descriptions of the individual components follow.

No. P371. 1992. $980

LCCE: Daily Living Skills
Donn E. Brolin

Includes 472 lesson plans covering personal finances, household management, personal needs, family responsibilities, food preparation, citizenship responsibilities, and leisure.

No. P367. 1992. 1,556 pp. 3 loose-leaf binders. ISBN 0-86586-224-9. $400

LCCE: Personal-Social Skills
Donn E. Brolin

Provides 370 lesson plans for developing self-awareness, self-confidence, socially responsible behavior, good interpersonal skills, independence, decision-making, and communication skills.
No. P368. 1992. 1,348 pp. 3 loose-leaf binders. ISBN 0-86586-225-7. $400

LCCE: Occupational Guidance and Preparation
Richard T. Roessler and Donn E. Brolin

Includes 286 lesson plans to help students explore occupational possibilities; make occupational choices; develop appropriate work habits; seek, secure, and maintain employment; exhibit sufficient physical/manual skills; and obtain specific occupational competencies.

No. P369. 1992. 670 pp. 2 loose-leaf binders. ISBN 0-86586-226-5. $300

LCCE: Competency Assessment Knowledge Batteries

Available in parallel forms, each Knowledge Battery consists of 200 multiple-choice questions that cover the first 20 competencies. Primarily a screening instrument, the Knowledge Batteries were designed to pinpoint specific competency deficiencies. Package includes an Administration Manual, a Technical Report, and samples of each form of the test. Also included are two introductory sets of 10 Knowledge Batteries, Forms A and B, to use with students.

No. P370K. 1992. 152 pp. ISBN 0-86586-239-7. $125

LCCE: Competency Assessment Performance Batteries

The Performance Batteries consist of two alternative forms for each of the 21 competency units. Items are primarily performance based and should be administered to students before and after instructional units have been taught. Performance Batteries are administered individually or with small groups of students. Test materials must be reproduced as needed. Performance Batteries are packaged in a loose-leaf binder along with an Administration Manual.

No. P370P. 1992. 675 pp. ISBN 0-86586-240-0. $225

Additional Sets of Knowledge Batteries

Packages of 10 tests may be ordered separately to be used by students. Students may answer questions directly in the test booklets by circling the correct choice or may use a standard machine-scorable form. Knowledge Batteries may not be reproduced.

LCCE: Knowledge Battery Form A (10 per package) No. P372. $20
LCCE: Knowledge Battery Form B (10 per package) No. P373. $20

Prices change without notice. Please call 1-800-CEC-READ (232-7323) to confirm prices and shipping charges.

LCCE on-site training is also available. For more information about LCCE workshops, regional events, and technical assistance, call 703-264-9443.

The Council for Exceptional Children
1920 Association Drive
Reston, VA 20191-1589
1-800-232-7323
Fax: 703-264-1637